Artistic Individuality:
A STUDY OF SELECTED
ARTIST NOVELS ca. 1910–2010

Artistic Individuality:
A STUDY OF SELECTED
ARTIST NOVELS ca. 1910–2010

Živilė Gimbutas

Library of Congress Control Number:		2012916235
ISBN:	Hardcover	978-1-4797-1111-6
	Softcover	978-1-4797-1110-9
	Ebook	978-1-4797-1112-3

Grateful acknowledgement is made to Unbridled Books, Publishers, for permission to reprint excerpts from *Lost Son* by M. Allen Cunningham, copyright © 2007 by M. Allen Cunningham. From *Seek My Face* by John Updike, copyright © 2002 by John Updike, used by permission of Alfred A. Knopf, a division of Random House, Inc. Scattered excerpts from *To the Lighthouse* by Virginia Woolf, copyright © 1927 by Harcourt, Inc. and renewed 1954 by Leonard Woolf, reprinted by permission of Houghton Mifflin Harcourt Publishing Company. All rights reserved.

This book was printed in the United States of America.

Cover illustration by Kaja

Rev. date: 05/13/2013

To order additional copies of this book, contact:
Xlibris Corporation
1-888-795-4274
www.Xlibris.com
Orders@Xlibris.com
116159

In Memory of

Alexander Martyn Gimbutas

Acknowledgements

For providing background and impetus for this study, I am grateful to my professors of nineteenth-century literature, especially Romanticism, in the Comparative Literature Program at Indiana University, Bloomington: Luis Beltrán, Matei Calinescu, and Henry H. H. Remak, as well as Faculty who mentored teaching assistants in "Major Themes in Western Literature." For a chance to explore artist novels, I extend thanks to the English Department at Vytautas Magnus University (Kaunas, Lithuania), which encouraged visiting Faculty to teach courses of our own choice and design in the early 1990's; to Milda Danys, erstwhile Chair, who scheduled "Representations of the Artist in Modern Literature" and "Interdisciplinary Approaches to Literature" in subsequent years.

I thank Mariagrazia Pelaia for taking interest in my essay "The Nature of the Artist" and arranging for its publication, Mary Cigan for recommending a few novels that enhance the subject matter of my chapters, particularly "Childhood"; Al Zolynas for reading my manuscript and commenting constructively on the text as well as the choice of title.

The cover illustration is by Karilė Baltrušaitis. The images prefacing Chapters 1, 2, 4, 8, 9, 10, 11, and 12 are from *Art Nouveau Designs in Color* by Alphonse Mucha, Maurice Verneuil, and Georges Auriol (New York: Dover, 1974); those heading Chapters 3, 5, 6, and 7 are provided by Xlibris Corporation. Many thanks.

Contents

Introduction

Artists have inspired life stories by their unique personalities as well as their achievements in literature, music, and the visual arts at least from the time of Giorgio Vasari's *Lives of the Artists* (late sixteenth century). Proverbially eccentric, individualistic, and so different from the norm, artists have been portrayed as being at odds with society (Hamerton, "Artists in Fiction" 1885), but they are also shown to be agents of society and humanity as they interpret the spectrum of human experience, elucidate universal values, and forge bonds with audiences through artwork and performances. Accordingly, their social status has alternated between center and periphery, and the stereotypes attributed to artists have ranged from prophet, model, and magician, to rebel, outsider, and parasite. This paradoxical combination of qualities and shifting social perspectives on artists gave rise to the literary genre "artist novel" (G. *Künstlerroman*), or "portrait-of-the-artist novel," an offshoot of the novel of character development (*Bildungsroman*), in an era that appreciated both the individuality and the artistic achievement: the Romantic era, *ca.* 1790-1830 (in Great Britain and Continental Europe). Known for its valuing of creativity and imagination over reason and intellect, as well as its cult of art and artist, this historical era is essentially a mindset that existed to some degree at all times and persisted into the nineteenth and twentieth centuries—as attested by the continuing vitality of the artist novel among other affirmations of Romantic values.

From the beginning of the nineteenth century we have, for example, Novalis' (Friedrich von Hardenberg's) *Henry of Ofterdingen*, the story of a young poet's striving for the ideals of love and imagination in the course of a real journey that is also an inner journey of growth and development as an artist; E.T.A. Hoffmann's *The Golden Pot,* featuring the student Anselmus' excursions from the kindly green sward of his bourgeois world to the dreamlike, magical realm of Archivarius Lindhorst with its fairy garden of glowing fire lilies, marble fountains, and marvelous trees tinkling with silver bells: departures from the ordinary and natural to the supernatural. The end of the nineteenth century gave us Romain Rolland's epic *Jean-Christophe,* the portrayal of a musical genius who is consummately human in his need for freedom, creativity, companionship, and love, and who is remarkable as a Romantic artist for his love of nature and the incorporation of impressions of nature and natural sounds in his musical compositions. Whereas the earlier German novels present the artist above or apart from the mainstream of humanity, the later French and English novels (for instance, Samuel Butler's *The Way of All Flesh*) tend to focus on the character of the artist within society, extraordinary though he or she might be by virtue of artistic talent or gift.

Maurice Beebe's study *Ivory Towers and Sacred Founts,* The Artist as Hero in Fiction from Goethe to Joyce (1964) indicates a proliferation of the genre "artist novel" in the nineteenth century. Beebe comments that numerous portraits offer not only insight into the artist's psyche and creative process but also the possibility of comparative study, making for a better understanding of the artist in general, or model artist. To be sure, we have documentary sources for research on artists: notebooks, diaries, letters, and memoirs. But fiction is apt to be more informative about the mind and soul of the artist than non-fiction, Beebe remarks: "The very fact that the artist novel is a product of the imagination, in which the experience it uses is distorted and transcended, makes it often more revealing than primary documents, for writers frequently tell more about their true selves and convictions under the guise of fiction than they will confess publicly" (Beebe 4-5).

In the works he considers, from Gustave Flaubert's *Sentimental Education* and Samuel Butler's *The Way of All Flesh* to Marcel Proust's *Remembrance of Things Past* and D.H. Lawrence's *Sons and Lovers,* Beebe finds a recurrent plot concerning the trials and loves of a sensitive youth that the artist novel shares with the novel of character development, and recurrent patterns in the artists' behavior and approach to creative endeavor. These patterns are the "Ivory Tower" (a term for the artist's private retreat), suggestive of reliance on one's inner resources for creativity and therefore an equation between art and religion more than experience; the "Sacred Fount" (derived from the name of a novel by Henry James), referring to experience as the main source of art and to the artist who nourishes his creative work by living more fully than most; and the "Divided Self," signifying a separation between the artistic self and the human being with a personal life, who is a vehicle for creative expression (supported by Carl G. Jung's theory of the artist as agent or instrument of the collective unconscious). With their numerous variations, especially combinations of "Ivory Tower" and "Sacred Fount," these patterns delineate the model, "archetypal," artist in Beebe's view.

Studies of portraits of women artists complement Maurice Beebe's focus on representations of male artists. Linda Huf's *A Portrait of the Artist as a Young Woman,* The Writer as Heroine in American Literature (1983) differentiates the woman's artist novel from the man's with regard to the main conflicts and problems encountered by the protagonists, especially the conflict between women's conventional social roles and the demands of art, and proceeds to examine a series of novels, from Fanny Fern's *Ruth Hall* (1855) to Sylvia Plath's *The Bell Jar* (1963), in terms of these distinctive problems, that is, from a feminist perspective. Huf concludes that the woman's artist novel exhibited considerable change in the latter part of the twentieth century, comparing its heroine to "a phoenix rising out of the ashes of her past" (Huf 159). Grace Stewart's *A New Mythos,* The Novel of the Artist as Heroine, 1877-1977 (1981) considers the predicament of women artists in terms of recurrent and often interlocking patriarchal myths, which tend to forestall or complicate women's artistic aspirations: those of Faust and the "Eternal Feminine," Demeter/Persephone, and the journey to the interior (relative to the heroic journey set forth by Joseph Campbell in *The Hero with a Thousand Faces,* 1949). Stewart concludes that the ground has been cultivated for the emergence of a new mythos: that of an integrated woman artist, who is both an artist, with the courage for doing, and a woman with feminine qualities of being (Stewart 13, 180). In *Aesthetics and Gender in American Literature,* Portraits of the Woman Artist, *ca.* 1850-1920 (2000), Deborah Barker employs cultural, sociological, and feminist perspectives to discuss women painters in works by writers also known as "literary domestics": Fanny Fern, E.D.E.N. Southworth, Elizabeth Stuart Phelps, Louisa May Alcott, Kate Chopin, Edith Wharton, and Jessie Fauset. Barker finds that portraits of women painters address issues of gender and social status while they assert women's creativity and aesthetic seriousness, reflecting the work of their authors. "[The lady novelists], through their praise of the qualities of the professional female painter . . . draw on the tradition of *ut pictura poesis* to construct an analogy between their own writing and the visual arts and to renegotiate the boundaries between high and low culture" (Barker 11).

These studies indicate wide-ranging scholarly interest in the artist novel as well as various dimensions of the genre. While addressing the basic challenge of comparative studies, which is the search for unifying factors in a diversity of literary material, the studies employ psychological, feminist, cultural, and sociological perspectives, appropriated to the contexts and emphases of the chosen literature. The exploration of cultural and social issues with regard to artists, particularly gender and social status, exemplifies the interrelation between literature and the social sciences as well as cultural history. The psychological perspective, especially the attempt to discover the "archetypal" artist, points to the relation of literature to depth psychology as it recalls studies in comparative mythology, such as those by Otto Rank and Joseph Campbell. The studies evince mutual illumination between literature and other fields of study while they suggest overall that the artist portrayed in literature since the Romantic era is increasingly more integrated in and accepted by society.

My study of several twentieth-century artist novels focuses on psychological issues, behavioral and depth, in the representation of male and female artists, which lead in turn to a consideration of aesthetics. It draws on psychological studies to illumine experiences that are referenced or intimated in the portraits. (The relation between the artist and society is of secondary importance in the selected novels, except perhaps in Virginia Woolf's *To the Lighthouse* and Dodie Smith's *I Capture the Castle.*) Although the initial project was a search for unifying factors, in the tradition of comparative studies, the outcome is an elucidation of the artists' individuality rather than a model, or archetypal, artist. In other words, the common denominators that I find—the importance of childhood and childlikeness, sensuality, an urge for self-expression, relation to nature, and creative work—are at the same time parameters of the artists' individuality, and they all influence creative achievement and signature styles, which are by definition original and unique. The artists represented in the novels, including Symbolists, Modernists, and Abstract Expressionists, harbor values associated with Romanticism, namely the expression of the inner "I," imagination, idealism, regard for nature, religiosity, and the individuality that is a requisite for creative work. Their genealogy harks back to the Romantics, historical and fictional. However, their particular traits and values are shared by many people; they are not exclusive to artists.

My interest in the artist novel began with a course I taught in Lithuania in the 1990's: "Representations of the Artist in Modern Literature," derived somewhat from "Major Themes in Western Literature," an undergraduate course in comparative literature at Indiana University, Bloomington, revolving on topics such as the outsider, the madman/woman, father, and family. Core reading material for the course, comprising Novalis' *Henry of Ofterdingen,* E.T.A. Hoffmann's *The Golden Pot,* James Joyce's *A Portrait of the Artist as a Young Man,* Vincas Mykolaitis' *In the Altars' Shadow,* and Virginia Woolf's *To the Lighthouse,* was prefaced by a survey of various myths of the artist and the changing social roles of artists since the Classical era. Literary interpretation was complemented by psychological perspectives, particularly studies by Sigmund Freud and Carl G. Jung. However, no consensus was reached concerning artistic character or personality.

A decade later, I included a few twentieth-century artist novels—Willa Cather's *The Song of the Lark* and Virginia Woolf's *To the Lighthouse*—in the literary component of English 1A at a local California community college. I chanced upon John Updike's *Seek My Face,* a fictional portrayal of the Abstract Expressionist painter Jackson Pollock, in a bookstore and essayed a study of the dominant traits or issues in four artist novels: the importance of childhood, sensuality, the urge for self-expression, and enjoyment of creative process, highlighted respectively in Cather's *The Song of the Lark,* Joyce's *A Portrait of the Artist as a Young Man,* Updike's *Seek My Face,* and Woolf's *To the Lighthouse* ("The Nature of the Artist" 2008). This collection of British and American artist novels was expanded by the retrieval of W. Somerset Maugham's *The Moon and Sixpence,* a fictional biography of Paul Gauguin, from a bookshelf; a friend's recommendation of Dodie Smith's *I Capture the Castle* as well as the Australian writer's Patrick White's *The Vivisector,* and last but not least, the receipt of M. Allen Cunningham's *Lost Son,* a fictional biography of Rainer M. Rilke, from Unbridled Books in 2008. *Lost Son,* published in 2007, renders my twentieth-century framework *ca.* 1910 to 2010.

The selection of novels includes fictional autobiography (Joyce), autobiographical fiction (Cather), semi-autobiographical fiction (Smith, Woolf, White), and fictional biography or portraiture (Cunningham, Maugham, Updike): on the one hand, imaginative reorganizations of personal experience and perspectives; on the other, interpretations and fictional renditions of documentary material about the artists chosen for literary representation. Whereas fictional autobiography is an imaginative rendition of the author's own life or part of it, featuring fictional characters closely related to real life acquaintances and family members, as well as one's real identity, autobiographical fiction is predominantly fictive narrative, with an invented story line that incorporates aspects of character and setting from the author's real life experience. In semi-autobiographical fiction, real life experience is transformed to such an extent that the similarities between elements of fiction and the author's real life experience appear to be incidental.

Fictional biography, based on the authors' research of an artist's life and work, might highlight particular traits, behaviors, or experiences, according to the authors' understanding and insight, offering a certain psychological interpretation—a stylized portrait if you will—with which the reader might agree or disagree with reference to non-fiction. For example, Somerset Maugham appears to exaggerate Paul Gauguin's "primitive" aspect in the character of Charles Strickland (*The Moon and Sixpence*); M. Allen Cunningham emphasizes the influence of childhood memories on Rainer M. Rilke, employing numerous flashbacks to the poet's early days in Prague and his years at military schools (*Lost Son*). The various interweavings of fiction and fact, personal and impersonal, are similar with respect to the authenticity of the life stories, the psychological credibility of the characters, and often the presence of a universal dimension in artistic character.

The novels exhibit innovative narrative techniques, which enhance the aforementioned aptitude of fiction to be more revealing of artists' mind and psyche than documentary material: interior monologue, stream-of-consciousness writing, and multiple narrative perspectives. "Stream-of-consciousness" and "interior monologue," initially associated with the work of James Joyce and Virginia Woolf, tend to present feelings, attitudes, and reflections more accurately than objective, third-person narration. "Interior monologue," occasionally overlapping with the former, might be limited to unspoken thoughts and feelings vis à vis persons and mental deliberations that exceed the train of spoken dialogue. "Stream-of-consciousness" writing, contrary to the literal meaning of the term, involves unconscious influences on the mind in the form of dreams, day-dreams, visions, reveries, and déjà vu impressions, as well as the flow of thought propelled by memories of previous events and stages of life (flashbacks). Stream-of-consciousness and interior monologue thus bring forth subjective time in the midst of linear time, by which episodic plot progresses. The subjective dimension complements objective narrative, making for representation that approaches the fullness of a life or personality within the story of a life. Multiple narrative perspectives, whether invented or based on real life reminiscences of the artist (interviews with acquaintances) and interpretation of diverse documentary sources, may serve both to complicate narrative plot and enrich an artist's portrait with various perceptions of his or her character.

Granted considerable variety in my selection of artist novels, puzzlement as to the unifying factors and bonds among fictional artists persisted. Why did artists inspire literary representations of their lives? What differentiated the artist from the norm? What were the artists' remarkable traits and characteristics? To answer such questions, I proceeded to investigate recurrences of the features I had explored earlier: childhood and childlikeness, sensuality and sensitivity, the urge for self-expression, creative process. The project was a study of the outstanding traits of artists represented in the novels. The procedure was inductive, beginning with no preconceived thesis concerning the artist, fictional or non-fictional. Investigation of the artists' individuality would have contradicted the search for unifying factors. But unbeknownst to me at the outset, the artists portrayed in my random selection of novels were similar with regard to their aesthetic orientation—their search for beauty or related ideal—as opposed to a socially or politically engaged mindset, which of course influenced the possibility of finding coherence among the literary works.

Chapters 1, 2, and 3 elicit some overlap between the influence of childhood and childlikeness, sensuality, and the urge for self-expression while addressing each issue separately. The most all-embracing topic, childhood, is limited by the number of novels that represent the artist's early life (Cather, Cunningham, Joyce, White). Sensuality and receptivity, discussed in Chapter 2, are various manifestations of artists' well known sensitivity, distinguished on the one hand by their relation to nature and on the other, by their access to the transcendent sphere. Chapter 3, "The Urge for Self-Expression," presents fictional renditions of various influences on creativity and creative drive, including a few digressions from the core novels to Franz Kafka's *The Metamorphosis* and Vincas Mykolaitis' *In the Altars' Shadow*. The topic benefits by reference to psychological theories of creativity and inspiration, particularly the psychoanalytical (Jungian) concepts of *"anima"* and "self." Creative work, the topic of Chapter 5, is a recurrent theme in the novels, as important for artistic achievement as the artist's growth, which is usually considered the main theme of artist novels. Creative work follows from the urge for self-expression while it anticipates the artwork that reveals artists' aims, ideals, or concepts of beauty (discussed in Part II).

The artist's relation to nature, or "kinship with nature," the topic of Chapter 4, appeared to attend all other recurrent issues and to figure prominently in the aesthetic concerns. Usually established in childhood, regard for nature is inextricable from sensuality, and it is a source of strength and inspiration for self-expression and creative work. Moreover, nature is often the milieu for episodes of awakening to artistic vocation, thus evident as an impetus for the latter. Ubiquitous but diffuse, the literary representation of artists' relation to nature might be taken for granted as a traditional feature, apparent in art history, the lyric genre from classical times, Romantic and other literature. But with the discovery that nature is the source of aesthetic aims and concepts of beauty in the selected novels—concepts such as radiance, integrity, vitality, vibrant stasis, and transformation—the artists' relation to nature asserted itself as the most consistent element in the portraits: the most common denominator or unifying factor, suggestive of a unifying theme for my study.

Was the artist a natural being, epitomized by Zack McCoy, who claims that he *is* Nature (Updike, *Seek My Face*)? If so, how does nature figure in Cassandra Mortmain's fairy tale vision of the castle (Smith, *I Capture the Castle*) or the transcendent dimension of Rainer M. Rilke's poetry (Cunningham, *Lost Son*)? This question may be answered by psychoanalytical theory, which posits nature as the realm of the unconscious and the archetypes; by the Romantic poets and Transcendentalists, who speak of nature as a bridge to the transcendent sphere or to God; or by traditional lore, which maintains spirits in nature from the beginnings of civilization. As stated eloquently by S. T. Coleridge, nature holds to the principle of unity in multiplicity, the unity pertaining to its universal dimension and the multiplicity to its infinite variety, offering a diversity of facets with which to identify and to adapt to self-expression. Consequently, in relating to nature, an artist is not necessarily identifying with trees, rocks, or flowers, but rather yearning to assert his or her individuality and longing for self-expression, which ideally pertains to universal experience. The most ubiquitous element in the portraits then proves to be the cornerstone of the artists' individuality.

Individuality, elicited by childhood behaviors, sensuality, receptivity, the urge for self-expression, and creative work, as well as kinship with nature, appears to be a mode of being driven by unconscious influences, therefore often sought or affirmed in relation to nature. Individuality is not exclusive to artists; the aforementioned traits, more pronounced in artists, are evidently characteristic of people in all walks of life. Contrariwise, the various traits and qualities, temperaments and dispositions, typical of humanity at large are shared by artists, who may be extraverted or introverted, sanguine or phlegmatic, altruistic or egoistic, generous or miserly, liberal or conservative, assertive or shy, and so on. The differentiating factors are the intensity of creative drive (urge for self-expression) and artists' dedication to creative work, which, in this series of novels, featuring aesthetically oriented artists, reflect their kinship with nature.

The colorful personalities in these twentieth-century artist novels are securely based in the Romantic tradition with regard to individuality and other remarkable values or traits (self-expression, idealism, imagination, religiosity, naiveté, primitivism). A few are explicitly Romantic: Thea Kronborg in Willa Cather's *The Song of the Lark*, outstanding for her idealism and love relationships in addition to her regard for nature; Cassandra Mortmain in Dodie Smith's *I Capture the Castle*, who assumes the project of romanticizing daily life in the castle while keeping her journal. Charles' story in Somerset Maugham's *The Moon and Sixpence* recalls Romantic exoticism in its progression from bohemian life in Paris to adventure in the South Seas. Nevertheless, the artists are more assimilated in society than the heroes of Romantic novels, who tend to come forth as superhuman, like the idealist Henry, elevated above the norm in Novalis' novel, or extraordinary verging on sinister, like Archivarius in Hoffmann's *The Golden Pot*, or generally as outsiders. Instead of a cult of art and artist, or differences between artists and other members of society, the novels reflect interest in the artist as a human being and member of society.

Literary portraits of artists offer insight into the psyche of artists while asking in some cases for explanation from the field of psychology, making for mutual illumination between literature and psychology. The "creative personality" that emerged in the Romantic era is contextualized and elucidated by Otto Rank's *Art and Artist* (1932). The importance of childhood, highlighted in several novels, is explained primarily as the child's access to the realm of archetypes by Eric Neumann in *Art and the*

Creative Unconscious (1959). The "self" that is the end of self-expression, intimated but vague in most literary representations, is also illuminated by psychoanalytical theory, particularly Carl G. Jung's *The Integration of Personality* (1940). Day-dreaming and reverie, recurrently displayed in the fiction, gain clarity by reference to Sigmund Freud's essay "The Relation of the Poet to Day-Dreaming" (1908) as well as James Hillman's lengthy study *Anima* (1985), which elaborates Jung's comments on *anima*. For explication of kinship with nature, I refer to ecological psychology, particularly James Swan's *Nature as Teacher and Healer* (1992), which considers the traditional lore that is basic to environmental studies. Indeed, the "primitivism" and naïveté perceptible in several novels (Cather, Maugham, Smith, Updike) call for retrospect as well as psychological theory that embraces the timeless yet mysterious transcendent sphere. However, I do not presume to be exhaustive in the area of psychological research pertinent to the selected literature, for instance, studies on sensitivity, sensuality, and receptivity. I appropriate psychological perspectives to topics and issues that elude interpretation to be gotten by close reading, for my study aims mainly to show what fiction tells us about artists.

PART I

Parameters of Individuality

-CHAPTER 1-

The Importance of Childhood and Childlikeness in the Artist

The formative influence of childhood is apparent in fictional autobiography, notably James Joyce's *A Portrait of the Artist as a Young Man,* beginning with the author's infancy in Blackrock (in the vicinity of Dublin, Ireland), as well as autobiographical fiction, for example, Willa Cather's *The Song of the Lark,* which transposes her childhood in Red Cloud, Nebraska, to the fictive heroine's provenance in Moonstone, Colorado. The importance of childhood in an artist's career might also be perceived on the basis of research and reading, as demonstrated in M. Allen Cunningham's *Lost Son,* a fictional biography of Rainer M. Rilke, harking back to Rilke's early days in Prague. These novels highlight childhood as basic ground for artistic development and a persistent influence in the artist's adult career.

A time of increasing sense awareness and creativity, childhood elicits both sensuality and an urge for self-expression in the artist. But these traits, distinct in adulthood, tend to be subsumed in the totality of the child's experience, with body and mind, conscious and unconscious, operating in unison, previous to the disassociation of faculties in adulthood (according to Eric Neumann). The child is exceptionally receptive to impressions from the surrounding environment and inclined to impart experiences forthwith in words, colors, shapes, or musical sounds. As shown in Joyce's, Cather's, and Cunningham's novels, childhood not only features the budding artist but also provides a storehouse of memories to nourish creativity in adulthood. On the other hand, the deprivation or foreshortening of a normal childhood, illustrated in Cunningham's *Lost Son,* is continually lamented and, by implication, compensated for by extraordinary receptivity and openness to experience in adulthood. The incomplete childhood is nevertheless a source and impetus for the poet's creative work.

Artist novels which represent childhood and emphasize its importance in artists' lives inevitably support psychological studies that maintain the importance of childhood as a formative period for everyone, not only artists, for example, Jerome Kagan's *The Nature of the Child* (1994). Kagan points to the connectedness between stages of development, including the relevance of the distant past for the present, as a premise for theories of human development, consistent with the "Aristotelian idea that each natural state contains within it the seeds of the next higher state" (Kagan 80, 82). With regard to psychological studies focusing on artists or creativity (which involve some controversy concerning the importance of childhood, for instance, Otto Rank's questioning of the value and importance to be ascribed to childhood influences, *Art and Artist* 421), the fictional portraits considered here concur with Eric Neumann's perspective on childhood as a wellspring of creativity. Neumann explains that the unitary experience of reality, which he sees as fundamental to the artistic personality, is taken for granted in childhood and informs creativity in adulthood. (The unitary experience of reality is described as the "one" reality, or the wholeness of being, previous to the experience of the duality of conscious and unconscious, personal and transpersonal, inner and outer worlds, *Art and the Creative Unconscious,* 173, 177, 179-182.) Neumann observes that the receptivity essential for a creative personality is most typical of childhood; thus he speaks of "the fateful persons and places of childhood," especially for the creative personality: "But here [creative man's childhood] even more than in other childhoods, the personal is always intermingled with the suprapersonal, the personal locality with an invisible world. And this world is not merely a 'childlike' world, it is the true, the real, or, as Rilke called it, the "open" world" (Neumann 182).

The second topic in this section, "childlikeness," is a corollary of the influence of childhood in the life and work of an artist as well as a manifestation of the archetypal "eternal child," "something that is always becoming, is never completed . . . the part of the human personality that wishes to develop and to complete itself" (Jung 1940, 284). Dodie Smith's *I Capture the Castle* illustrates childlikeness in an artist-writer, in addition to the connection between childhood and creativity in adulthood, because her childlike narrator, also the main character in the novel, represents the author, who was approaching fifty when she wrote the novel. Smith's work contains autobiographical elements from her childhood in Kingston House, near Manchester, England, transposed to a castle setting, much as Cather's *The Song of the Lark* draws from the author's childhood in rural Nebraska. In Smith's narrator, Cassandra, traits we readily associate with children but apparently still vital in the author—imaginativeness, playfulness, affection, receptivity—nourish a maturing talent for storytelling.

We may find childlike traits and behaviors in artists' portraits that do not represent childhood, for example, those of Lily Briscoe in Virginia Woolf's *To the Lighthouse* and Zack McCoy in John Updike's *Seek My Face*. Lily relates affectionately to Mrs. Ramsay as might a young daughter, and it is her effervescent love for the whole family and their summer home on Skye that motivates her painting. She immerses herself in the *process* of painting, regardless of the outcome of the finished artwork. In Updike's novel, Hope McCoy, reminiscing about her former husband Zack, likens the painter's absorption in his work to childish bouts of creativity ("childish absorption in the *doing*," 103). She also remembers his temper tantrums, his need for immediate gratification of desires, and excellent rapport with children at beach gatherings and lawn parties. These behaviors, if not incidental, are relevant to the artists' urge for self-expression and so linked with the latter topic (Ch. 3); in Lily's case, they also pertain to feminism, briefly discussed in connection with Lily's aesthetic aims (Ch. 9).

One might also glean childlikeness or childishness in the sense of irresponsibility and aversion to conventional adult roles in the artist novels. For instance, Rainer is reluctant to take the position of bank clerk in Prague, thereby to provide more financial stability for his family (Cunningham's *Lost Son*). Charles Strickland leaves his stockbroker's position and family in London in order to pursue painting in Paris, with no provision for his wife and children (Maugham's *The Moon and Sixpence*). These facets of childishness are evidently a consequence of the poet's and painter's affirmation of artistic vocation or their inclination to give priority to creative endeavor and the realization of their talents (also tied with the urge for self-expression in Ch. 3). Psychologically, from the artist's point of view, such irresponsibility is inextricable from the influence of the "eternal child" on the adult artist.

In Maugham's fictive portrait of Paul Gauguin (*The Moon and Sixpence*), instead of overt childlikeness, we find "primitive" elements in the painter's aspect and manner, interrelated with his drive to paint and aesthetic sensibility. They are suggestive of the "pre-conscious" state, or childhood, of the human species—the macro-childlikeness that is the source of micro-, or individual, childlikeness. In psychological perspectives as well as anthropological studies of primitive ritual, this pre-conscious state is characterized by a lack of differentiation between consciousness and unconsciousness—"a chronic twilight state of consciousness" (Jung, *Psyche & Symbol* 116)—and an openness to the transcendent realm of archetypes, similar to the unitary experience of the child described by Neumann. Thus the artist-hero in Maugham's novel, a huge hunk of a man known as "the Red One" among the natives of Tahiti, indicates the root condition of childlikeness, or prototypical childlikeness.

1.A.1. WILLA CATHER, *THE SONG OF THE LARK*

Willa Cather's *The Song of the Lark* (first published in 1915) was inspired by her friendship with Olive Fremstad, a singer at the Metropolitan Opera *ca.* 1903-1914, with whom she shared the experience of growing up in a rural town as well as artistic talent and a taste for opera, particularly an interest in Richard Wagner's works. However, this novel is considered one of Cather's most autobiographical ventures: a conflation of the author's experiences— her childhood, her travels in the southwestern United States, her years in New York—and her perspectives on art with those of the model singer (as remarked by Sherrill Harbison, Editor of the 1999 Penguin Edition, and Edith Lewis, author of *Willa Cather, Living,* 1953). The change of locale from Red Cloud, Nebraska, to the fictive Moonstone, Colorado; of canyons in New Mexico to those in Arizona, and the shift in medium of expression from writing to singing, give the author free rein to elaborate on the process of an artist's growth, reflecting her own path within the framework of a vocal artist's, the fictive Thea Kronborg's, career.

The influence of childhood experiences on later career is explicit in Cather's story of Thea's growth as a singer from her early years in Moonstone to her stardom at the Metropolitan Opera in New York. Thea's childhood is in fact presented as a measure of her achievement, an indication and a standard. The Moonstone scale of values keeps Thea on track and well grounded. Memories of childhood events and sense impressions inspire her interpretations of songs and opera scores and sustain her in the competitive world of opera. The colorful personality of the singer perceived by audiences at the Met is a florescence of the child Thea. Nonetheless, when Thea remarks, "The stream has reached the level of its source. That's our measure," in conversation with her friend Dr. Archie toward the end of the novel, she refers to a yet unattained goal (Cather 382). Like a child, the artist is continuously becoming and growing, exploring self and world.

At about age seven, little Thea wanders off barefoot to the Mexican quarter of Moonstone, lured by the sound of a guitar. She listens on a doorstep for a while, then asks Spanish Johnny to sing and repeats the air beautifully without the words. When Thea's father comes looking for her, Johnny remarks, "She gotta some music in her, that child. Where she get?" (Cather 193)—from the grandfather who played oboe in Sweden, Mr. Kronborg conjectures. Thea is thereafter friendly with the Mexicans on account of their musicality and love of song.

Eventually, Thea takes piano lessons from Professor A. Wunsch, who lives with Fritz and Paulina Kohler on the outskirts of Moonstone. Once a week in winter and twice in summer, she treks more than a mile beyond the depot and the adobe houses of the Mexicans, over a deep ravine toward the sand hills en route to the Kohlers' home. She often finds her teacher tending the garden with Mrs. Kohler as she enters the gate through a profusion of pink tamarisk blossoms. After lessons Thea might sing for Mrs. Kohler from her repertoire of church hymns, then enjoy this garden, fragrant with honey-colored linden, filled with cherry trees, peaches, golden plums, grapevines, and a balm of Gilead. There are sunflowers, tiger-lilies, phlox, zinnias, lady's slippers, and giant holly hocks surrounding a turreted dove-house and in the background, a windmill reminiscent of villages in the Rhine Valley. On her birthday one Saturday in July, Thea is invited to see a cuckoo clock inside the house and Fritz Kohler's handiwork in the drawing room. This is a piece-painting, sewn of pieces of wool fabric, representing Napoleon's retreat from Moscow, with the emperor and his men crossing a bridge, leaving behind a conflagration of domes and minarets.

Leisure time in the Kohlers' verdant garden is especially well suited to the "nature voice" with which Thea is endowed. When Professor Wunsch teaches her Heinrich Heine's song *"Im leuchtenden Sommermorgen"* ("In the soft-shining summer morning") amidst flower beds and lindens, he notices that she reads verse with a range of feeling and sensitivity to the lyrics, reflecting, "It was a nature voice . . . breathed from the creature and apart from the language, like the sound of the wind in the trees or the murmur of water" (69-70). This is the voice Thea later discovers for herself as she basks in the rock cliffs of Panther Canyon in Arizona and melodies rise in her of their own accord, stimulated by sensations of fragrance, color, and sound in the surrounding elements.

Thea's musical training, in contrast to the romantic interludes, is classical and strict. Mr. Wunsch takes Thea on as a pupil and teaches her at his home because he is interested in her power of application and stubborn will. Mrs. Kohler is accustomed to hearing the sound of effort, "the cheerful sound of effort, of vigorous striving" (Cather 27), as Wunsch commands the various chords and scales and conducts his student through movements in Clementi's sonatas. When the Professor informs Mrs. Kronborg that her daughter has talent, she is promptly set to four hours of practice a day rather than dressed for public performances. Thea dutifully participates in the choir at her father's church, playing accompaniments and the organ when called on. At a Christmas concert sponsored by the churches of Moonstone, she is obliged to play her teacher's selection, Reinecke's "Ballade," yielding the spotlight to her rival, Lily Fisher, who is allowed to sing "The Rock of Ages" and "Home Sweet Home." On occasion, Thea is given a taste of opera by Professor Wunsch, such as a sample of arias from Glück's "Orpheus," or her teacher reminisces about musicians and singers he had heard, expressing his appreciation of authenticity and excellence in musical performance.

After piano practice at home, Thea is encouraged to pursue excursions outside, pulling her baby brother Thor in an express wagon. She explores the sand hills for gems and rocks, or heads for streets on the poorer side of town, with native plants sprawling wildly about. She makes numerous friends on her rounds: matrons who treat her to sweets; Dr. Archie, who lends her books and takes her along on a home call; Ray Kennedy, a railroad engineer, who arranges for longer expeditions in his caboose. Ray takes the Kronborg brood and Spanish Johnny to the Turquoise Hills beyond Moonstone, where Thea finds brilliant stones—crystals, agates, and onyx—and over lunch, listens happily to Johnny's guitar or Ray's tales of adventure in the Grand Canyon and Death Valley. Thea has occasion to attend dances and festivities in the Mexican quarter. Her early musical experiences are thus complemented by various other adventures, making for a rich, romantic childhood. She is given a chance to satisfy her *wanderlust*, her attraction to nature, and curiosity about people, and so nourish the musical vehicle that is her personality.

The combination of grinding piano lessons and enjoyable leisure activities in Moonstone prepares Thea for musical training in Chicago, which, however, proves to shift the balance between work and leisure. Her application and effort as a child prefigure the ambition and drive that bring her to the stage of the Metropolitan Opera. In Chicago, Thea studies with the renowned concert pianist Andor Harsanyi until her voice is rediscovered and recommended to a specialist in voice, Madison Bowers. Thereafter, she applies herself to the routine of playing accompaniments in Bowers' studio in order to pay for the voice lessons, all the while singing in the choir at a local Swedish church and performing solo at funeral services to earn her room and board. She attends symphony concerts and savors yet unknown musical scores, like Dvořák's "From the New World," which fuel her imagination and resolve to dedicate herself to art. She finds respite at the Chicago Art Institute on Michigan Avenue, where she is drawn particularly to an equestrian statue of a general and to pictures that tell stories, for example, Gérôme's "The Pasha's Grief." (Later, we hear about her decade of study in Germany, behind the scenes of the novel, from her accompanist at the Metropolitan Opera in New York.)

Thea's personality, the vessel of her voice, expands proportionately. Compared early on with a sunflower or yellow prickly-pear blossom that opens up in the desert ("her broad eager face, so fair in color, with its high cheek bones, yellow eyebrows and greenish hazel eyes . . . a face full of light and energy," Cather 86), Thea is likened to Swedish summer when she sings in Chicago society, and later, in the role of Fricka, goddess of love and beauty in Wagner's "Rheingold," to "the light of sunset on distant sails" and the "look of immortal loveliness, the youth of the golden apples" (371). Her shining beauty, radiating in the atmosphere about her, is adequate to her voice. When Thea attains star status at the Metropolitan, audiences marvel at the personality of this singer and the power of her voice to carry ideas. "She simply *was* the idea of the Rhine music . . . the Rhine voice," one viewer comments (330), recalling for the reader the ideas, more like sensations, that rose like melodies in her in Panther Canyon and much earlier, the melodies she repeated for Spanish Johnny without knowing the words. This colorful voice, inseparable from mind and heart, is born in a singer, they say; it is the musical gift suggested by *Thea,* meaning "a gift of the gods." The personality is essentially the child Thea, as her beau, Fred Ottenburg, observes when speaking of her aura:

> The enveloping air about her head and shoulders was subsidized— was more moving than she herself, for in it lived the awakenings, all the first sweetness that life kills in people. One felt in her such a wealth of *Jugendzeit* [youth], all those flowers of the mind and the blood that bloom and perish by the myriad in the few exhaustless years when the imagination first kindles (Cather 310).

Observing Thea in the role of Sieglinde, her former piano teacher in Chicago, Andor Harsanyi, remarks, "At last, somebody with enough!" (394), implying perfection in her rendering of the musical score and attunement of her expressive style to Wagner's opera. These are results of her musical training, beginning with Professor Wunsch's demanding lessons and his conversations with Thea about artistry and good taste, as well as an adequate nurturing of the personality that is a vessel for her voice.

Thea confides in her old friend Dr. Archie, who visits from Colorado, that it is the old things that save her in the competitive world of opera and grueling routine of rehearsals. Memories of Moonstone—the Kohlers' garden, the sand hills, expeditions in Ray's caboose, singing with the Mexicans; the ideas and books she treasured in her attic room at home—bring back her childlike attitudes, which are an artist's attitudes. "A child's attitude toward everything is an artist's attitude. I am more or less of an artist now, but then I was nothing else," she says (381). The old things are basic to all that she does now, she reflects, turning to the piano to play a song, an old Scottish air they both remember from the Moonstone days.

1. A. 2. JAMES JOYCE,
A PORTRAIT OF THE ARTIST AS A YOUNG MAN

Joyce's portrait of Stephen Dedalus brings him to an affirmation of artistic vocation and threshold of his writing career, the composition of a poem dedicated to Emma Clery and discussion of aesthetic theory with his friend Lynch being milestones in this direction. We can only infer the influence of Stephen's childhood on his later career, but infer confidently, on the basis of an evident connection between Stephen's early behaviors that demonstrate artistic traits and the turning points just noted. We may also refer to the widely held view that Joyce's childhood in Ireland is the wellspring of his later works—*The Dubliners, Ullysses, Finnegan's Wake*—or to one of the author's remarks concerning *A Portrait*, cited by his biographer Richard Ellman: "the book's pattern, as he explained to Stanislaus [James Joyce's brother], is that we are what we were; our maturity is an extension of our childhood" (Ellman 115), which accords with the psychological principle of the connection between stages of development.

Certain components of Stephen's childhood experiences and behaviors may be seen as conducive to and culminating in his awakening to artistic vocation, for they surface clearly in the epiphanies on the strand, the narrative transition to his artistic career as well as his days at the University. These are the allure of the feminine for the child Stephen; his responsiveness to environment, which includes his interest in the relation between time and space; and his imaginative capacity, manifest in his early "mental adventures"—apt to be day dreaming and reverie, which enhances both his attraction to the feminine and his relation to environment.

The allure of the feminine is expressed in brief but deeply impressive episodes that linger in Stephen's mind for days, even years, suggesting soulful experiences of girls and women as aspects of the archetypal *anima* (lit. "psyche" or "soul"), variously defined as the image of the feminine in a male, the archetype of psyche, the archetype of life, and mediatrix to the unconscious (*see* the discussion of anima in Ch. 3, "The Urge for Self-Expression," pp. 69-71). The women and girls to whom Stephen relates—his mother, Eileen Vance, Mercedes, Emma Clery—take on additional attributes and various shapes in his mind as a result of an interweaving of sense impressions and mental associations, fantasies and reflections. The earliest impressions pertain inevitably to Stephen's mother, Mrs. Dedalus. At the very beginning of Joyce's novel, Stephen finds the fragrance and rosy flesh of his mother's body more attractive and pleasant than his father's hairy face. He dances to tunes played on the piano by his mother, "tralala." In the course of his elementary education at Clongowes Wood College, a boarding school, Stephen is sustained by thoughts of his mother: memories of her farewell, when she lifted her veil to kiss him goodbye, memories of her goodnight kisses, or the larger memory of hearth and home with mother at the center. When Stephen is sick with fever in the infirmary, he thinks of lying on the hearthrug by the fire at home and his mother sitting with legs stretched to the fender, her jeweled slippers emitting a warm fragrance (Joyce 16). He looks forward to Christmas vacation when she would preside at the festive table by the fireplace, radiating warmth and comfort.

One of Stephen's playmates in Blackrock (in the environs of Dublin, where the Dedaluses live) is Eileen Vance, a Protestant girl. Feeling her hands on his forehead in a game of tig, Stephen is impressed by their softness. Her hands are also long and white and cold, like ivory, he reflects, and so assimilated in his mind with the "Tower of Ivory," a traditional epithet for the Virgin Mary. Eileen's blonde hair resembles golden rays of sunlight flowing in the air, therefore like the "House of Gold," another epithet for the Blessed Virgin. However, Stephen often preferred reading and entertaining himself to playing with children in his neighborhood. Reading Alexander Dumas' *The Count of Monte Christo* sparks his imagination with regard to dark island caves and sparkling Marseilles, the brave character of Count Edmond, and especially his beautiful, beloved Mercedes. Stephen would carry images from the novel on his walks outside Blackrock and identify Mercedes' fictional home on the Mediterranean with a white house and rose garden en route to the mountains, whence further adventures and encounters evolved. He could see himself in a moonlit garden with Mercedes, gallantly offering his courtesy or refusing her love. The fictive

Mercedes is as real to Stephen as a real playmate and perhaps more vital in that she stimulates his experience of the hitherto subliminal *anima*. Mercedes' character resonates with his inner image of the feminine, or feminine soul image, and nourishes his ideal of woman in-the-making, as suggested by the fact that brooding on Mercedes brought on fever, a restless heart, and a longing for the real counterpart of his soul image. "He wanted to meet in the real world the unsubstantial image which his soul so constantly beheld" (Joyce 65). So deeply lodged in the recesses of Stephen's mind, Mercedes enters Stephen's consciousness again and again. Amid the confusion and rebellion of his adolescent years, "The image of Mercedes traversed the background of his memory" (99), the backdrop of white house and rose trellises on the path to the mountains providing balm for his agitated state.

The Dedaluses' move to Dublin prolongs Stephen's holiday from boarding school, allowing for occasions to visit with relatives and attend children's parties, which involve girls and women. Mention is made of an aunt and her daughter, of a girl named Ellen, but the most important experience by far is Stephen's meeting with Emma Clery at a children's party at Harold's Cross. Although cheered by the merriment of the party, Stephen retreats to a corner of the hall and revels in the excitement he feels from the glance of a girl within the circle of dancers—Emma—"flattering, taunting, searching" (69). After the party, Stephen escorts Emma to the tram, enjoying every whiff of her breath and tap of her shoes on the pavement. On the ride home, he experiences this rendezvous as a déjà vu event, perhaps a recurrence of his imagined encounters with Mercedes or the soul image that had animated his visions of Mercedes. "His heart danced upon her movements like a cork upon a tide. He heard what her eyes said to him from beneath their cowl and knew that in some dim past, whether in life or in revery, he had heard their tale before" (69). The influence of anima, of stirrings of the unconscious along with Emma's presence, is further indicated by Stephen's subsequent day-dreaming about Emma and attempts at writing verses dedicated to her. These verses told "of the night and the balmy breeze and the maiden luster of the moon" (Joyce 70), images associated with the archetypal feminine (night and moon) and the anima (breeze, which is a breath of life).

Two years after the party at Harold's Cross, in the event of Stephen's performance in a Whitsuntide play at Belvedere College, his school in Dublin, he is consumed by the tender emotions he had felt at first meeting Emma as he anticipates her glance from a seat in the auditorium. "All day he had thought of nothing but their leave taking on the steps of the tram at Harold's Cross . . . The old restless moodiness had again filled his breast as it had done on the night of the party" (77), as if their togetherness two years ago were prolonged in the present, partaking of an eternity immune to the passage of time and the bustle surrounding him the night of the play. The touch of Emma's fingers on the palm of his hand is still vivid, warming Stephen's entire person. Whether Emma is in the audience we do not know, but Stephen is inspired and strengthened in his resolve to play a farcical pedagogue by the mere expectation of her presence: "He saw her serious alluring eyes watching him from among the audience and their image at once swept away his scruples [the humiliation he felt at the thought of his part and the taunts of his friends] leaving his will compact" (85).

Stephen's fascination with Mercedes and Emma is presented as definitely a part of Stephen's boyhood, with one episode in the background of children's play in Blackrock, the other in the contexts of a children's party and school play in Dublin. Nonetheless, Stephen's experience of feminine allure, fictive and real, by way of day-dreaming and reverie differentiates him from his playmates and schoolfellows. He is in turn a loner, a watchful observer, and play-actor, directed by inner voices rather than the camaraderie and opinions of his fellow students as he embraces the influence of anima and the imaginative life that it nurtures. Stephen's early encounters with anima images illustrate Eric Neumann's observation that "infantile experiences on the bodily plane . . . always contain both archetypal and worldly factors," that is, they contain "symbolically significant elements" amid the real factors (Neumann 188, in agreement with C.G. Jung's reference to the polyvalent disposition of the child).

* * *

Stephen's responsiveness to environment indicates relation to milieu, natural and cultural, as well as rootedness in the earth and its elements. Rather than taken for granted by Stephen, environment is explored, investigated, and elaborated by mental adventures, as is his relation to girls. His first neighborhood in Blackrock was made familiar by routine activity— walks with his father and granduncle Charles, running in the park with his trainer Mike Flynn, rounds with the milkman, and adventures with his ally Aubrey Mills—so that Stephen's particular relation to his surroundings is more noticeable at every move away from home: at Clongowes College, in Dublin, during the journey to Cork with his father, and, we may infer, his move to the Continent, anticipated toward the end of *A Portrait*, whereby the relation to Ireland, established in childhood and adolescence, is appreciated from a distance and the workings of memory.

Upon arrival at Clongowes Wood College, Stephen finds himself in a game of scrimmage, running, kicking, and stamping the ground of the playing field beneath a cold grey sky. With the walls of the study hall and castle nearby, lights in the turrets to left and right, it is a kind of square universe, abounding in the elements (earth, air, fire, water) and their mixtures and combinations. Stephen pays heed to every aspect of his new environment while he experiences pleasant and unpleasant variations in each. The air in the corridors would be humid and chilling, but warm when the gas was lit; the atmosphere in the chapel alternately light and dark. The water in the lavatory was cold or hot, depending on the cock he turned. And what difference he felt between the cold and slimy ditch into which he was shouldered one day and the warmth of hearth rug and fire back home!

Stephen demonstrates a keen awareness of relativity as he makes comparisons between sensations and impressions of milieu. These are especially vivid when he is ill with fever (a state in which sensations are typically acute) as a result of the episode in a cold ditch. Observing the fire in the infirmary, he compares it with waves ("the fire rose and fell on the wall. It was like waves," Joyce 27) and with the sound of human voices breaking the silence in the room, he likens the fire to the sound of waves. This effect ushers in a mental image of a sea of waves at night, a larger vision of time and space. Later, when Stephen anticipates Christmas vacation and counts the number of days in between, he compares the interval to a train ride involving passages through tunnels and makes associations with every in and out of the tunnel, until his drowsiness brings his reverie to an abrupt close: "Term, vacation; tunnel, out; noise and stop" (Joyce 17).

Stephen's imaginative responses to environment tell of his attempts to make sense of the awesome complexity within him and without, as well as his incipient aesthetic sensibility, whereby the surrounding world becomes metamorphic and metaphorical (to be discussed in Ch. 2, Sensuality). Yet Stephen is primarily exploring his relation to milieu: his position vis à vis home or school and the universe that begins to expand during his years at Clongowes. Joyce makes a point of Stephen's interest in a picture of the earth in his geography book, "a big ball in the middle of clouds" (15), and his learning that the earth contains countries and continents and revolves around the sun. Stephen can now position himself in the broader sphere, recording on the flyleaf of his notebook:

> Stephen Dedalus
> Class of Elements
> Clongowes Wood College
> Sallins
> County Kildare
> Ireland
> Europe
> The World
> The Universe (15).

This kind of positioning would recur in the scene on the strand, strengthened by his awakening to vocation and new sense of identity.

However, Dublin does not seem to fit into the universal scheme, accosting Stephen with crowds of people, bustling trade activity, and gloom.

Whereas Blackrock spelled comfort and quaintness, Dublin was vast and strange. On the road outside Blackrock, Stephen had seen rose trellises and likenesses of Mercedes' whitewashed house in sunny Marseilles. On his treks to the docks and quays on the waterfront in Dublin, he finds muddy water with corks bobbing on the surface "in a thick yellow scum" (Joyce 66). The forebodings he had felt upon arrival in the city prove real: the yellow scum in the docks is emblematic of the squalor and lesser standard of life his family experiences in the city.

As the change of circumstances brings bitterness and disquiet, Stephen detaches himself from his environment or attempts to ameliorate it. Returning to school, Belvedere College, he immerses himself in curricular and extracurricular activities. His participation in the Whitsuntide play indicates his interest in drama. Stephen also focuses his attention on essay writing, seeking the company of other writers in his leisure. He shines among his schoolmates on account of his literary interests and writing ability. When he is awarded a monetary prize of thirty-three pounds for an essay, he sets out to improve his circumstances, creating a temporary aura of luxury at home and exploring the cultural life of Dublin.

Stephen treats family and friends to gourmet dinners, abundant groceries and delicacies. He lavishes presents on all and leads daily excursions to the theatre, his pockets filled with Viennese chocolates. He organizes a mini-commonwealth for his household, relegating duties and responsibilities to his siblings; he initiates a loan bank for their benefit. He renovates his room—until the paint and his funds run out. In his enthusiastic attempt "To build a breakwater of order and elegance against the sordid tide of life without him and to dam up, by rules of conduct and active interests and new filial relations, the powerful recurrence of the tides within him" (98) there is a considerable element of childish play: the magic circle with its illusion of boundless possibilities. Returning to the norm of his Dublin life is all the more painful and disillusioning.

On the threshold of adolescence, at about age fourteen or fifteen, Stephen feels alone, torn between idealism ("fierce longings of the heart," 98) and his rebellious flesh ("wasting fires of lust," 99). On his perambulations of the grey streets of Dublin, images of Mercedes and her idyllic abode come to mind and recede to the borders, yielding to new adventures and trials on the path to maturity.

* * *

The vitality of Stephen's imagination is apparent in his responsiveness to milieu as well as his reveries about girls. Nevertheless, one of its manifestations calls for further comment, namely Stephen's fascination with words, which often provokes reflection and an effort at comprehension. We have noted the association of Eileen's white hands with the "Tower of Ivory"; her fair hair with sunlight and the "House of Gold," attesting to Stephen's habit of connotation. We may find numerous examples of Stephen's remarkable appreciation of words, especially at the early stage of his education at home in Blackrock and at Clongowes College. This verbal interest is undoubtedly stimulated by his school texts, the church liturgy, the conversations he hears at home and school, and the songs and stories he was taught as a child.

At Clongowes College, Stephen is often seen pondering the meanings of words and their ambiguities. One of these words is *suck,* ugly in the context of name calling, but also indicative of the sound of water going down a drain in a basin when the stopper is pulled. Another is *kiss,* a little noise lips made on a cheek, as when his mother kissed him goodnight. Yet Stephen asks himself what the word *means*; as a result of being teased by his schoolmates, he even wonders whether it was right to kiss his mother goodnight. Amid thoughts of the universe and its grandeur, *God* occurs to him. He knew that there were different names for God, for the French said *Dieu* when they prayed although theirs was the same God (16). During a writing lesson Stephen hears that a few boys had taken a monstrance and some altar wine from the sacristy and were caught as a result of the smell of wine lingering on them. He is awed by the sinfulness of the deed as he visualizes the scene of the crime and their drinking of the altar wine. But soon his thoughts shift to the day of his first holy communion and traces of wine on the rector's breath upon receiving the bread of communion. Then he reflects on the sound of *wine* and relevant images: "The word was beautiful: *wine.* It made you think of dark purple because the grapes were dark purple that grew in Greece outside houses like white temples" (Joyce 46-7).

Lying in the infirmary at Clongowes, imagining the possibility of his own death and funeral, Stephen hears bells tolling and recalls one of the songs he had learned at home:

> Dingdong! The castle bell!
> Farewell, my mother!
> Bury me in the old churchyard
> Beside my eldest brother.
> My coffin shall be black,
> Six angels at my back,
> Two to sing and two to pray
> And two to carry my soul away (24).

He is taken with the beauty of these lyrics, particularly *Bury me in the old churchyard,* and their sadness, which brings him to the brink of tears. From the effect this song has on Stephen, it is clear that he responds to the aural and visual qualities of words, their tones and imagery, as well as their literal meanings.

At home in Blackrock during Christmas vacation and a holiday from school previous to his family's move to Dublin, Stephen listens to conversations about politics and religion; he hears songs from his father's and Uncle Charles' abundant repertoire. He realizes that words are important in relating to people and the world at large; in fact, they might influence one's particular world view and comprehension of events and people. Therefore, Stephen exerts himself in the effort to understand words, in preparation for the day when he would assume a role in society. "Words which he did not understand he said over and over to himself till he had learned them by heart: and through them he had glimpses of the real world about him" (62). Though he intuited a "great part" for himself in the future, he was not yet aware of the literary calling that would begin to assert itself at Belvedere College and flourish in subsequent years at the University.

* * *

Proceeding to Stephen's long walk on the strand on the day of his entrance into the University, we find him musing on a lyrical phrase, "A day of dappled seaborne clouds" (Joyce 166), as he steps from a bridge to the sandy beach, ushering in the richly colored, feeling-toned scene that follows. When he hears his schoolmates splashing in the water and calling to him, playing on his name, "Hello Stephanos! Here comes the Dedalus! . . . Stephanos Dedalos!" (167-8), Stephen is still musing, with eyes raised skyward to the dappled clouds, so that their voices merge with voices within him ("a confused music within him as of memories and names," 167) that conjure a winged form in the clouds: the master craftsman Daedalus or his son Icarus, along with Stephen's inner "I". The sound of his name has quite a profound effect in his reflective mood: his heartbeat quickens, his soul soars in ecstasy, and his throat can hardly stifle a cry of greeting to the world. Stephen's entire person is animated and radiant. In this moment of "epiphany," a revelation or coming to light of his essential self, the image of the winged form in the air with which Stephen identifies is prophetic of his artistic path, specifically his forthcoming flight from Ireland to the Continent, while it is also a culmination of his tendencies in childhood.

These tendencies—Stephen's responsiveness to environment and to feminine allure as well as the influence of *anima*—are intensified during his walk on the strand, suggesting that they are decisive factors in his awakening to vocation. They are basic to the worldly orientation Stephen affirms at the close of the scene, contrasting with his earlier experience of an ascetic phase, when he considered the religious path and joining the Jesuit Order: the sense of feet on the ground, of earthiness, even though his soul might be soaring. "He felt above him the vast indifferent dome . . . and the earth beneath him, the earth that had borne him, had taken him to her breast" (172).

Stephen feels entirely in his element in the physical world of earth, air, and water about him while borne aloft to the extra-sensible world by his fiery imagination. As he strides along an embankment of rocks toward the mouth of the river and looks back through hazy sunlight to the outlines of Dublin, he perceives "the seventh city of Christendom" ("like a scene on some vague arras," Joyce 167), also referred to as an ancient Danish kingdom. Looking upward, he sees the clouds metamorphosed into "a host of nomads on the march, voyaging high over Ireland, westward bound" (*ibid.*) from the distant Continent, imbued with layers of history. In this progression of spatial images to the imminent appearance of the hawk-like form of Daedalus in the clouds, it seems that the past is condensed in the present and time is at a standstill. "So timeless seemed the grey warm air, so fluid and impersonal his own mood, that all ages were as one to him" (168). Stephen is totally immersed in the spatial scene of earth, sky and the elements, poised in the present or in eternity. (We may recall that he had perceived time spatially, as a ride in and out of tunnels, at Clongowes College when he anticipated Christmas vacation.)

With lightness in his step, Stephen walks onward toward a rivulet in the tide-swept sand. Reveling in warm air, the touch of sand and water on his bare feet, he observes moving seaweed and drifting clouds reflected in the dark water of a stream: again an image linking earth and sky, suggestive of the merging of conscious and unconscious in Stephen's mind, as did gazing at the clouds while listening to music within. When in front of him Stephen sees a girl wading in the water, looking out to sea, she appears to him like "a strange and beautiful seabird" (171). There are indications of a bird's form in her real features—her long slender legs like a crane's, the white fringes of her drawers at the hips "like featherings of soft white down"; her blue skirt, gathered about the waist, trailing like a tail; her soft bosom like "the breast of some dark-plumaged dove" (*ibid.*)—but his affective perception takes in the image instantaneously, holistically, rather than analytically. The girl's appearance merges with a feminine image inherent in Stephen's unconscious mind (a "soul image" in Stephen's words, voiced amid reveries of Mercedes) as did the sound of his name, Stephanos Dedalos, with the image of the archetypal Daedalus. Stephen is fascinated as the girl's eyes meet his prolonged, adoring gaze, as "her image . . . passed into his soul forever" (Joyce 172). This encounter literally ignites Stephen—"His cheeks were aflame; his body was aglow"—and inspires him with creativity, suggested by his singing to the sea as he walks on.

The bird is one of the inhuman forms that traditionally personify *anima* in dreams, tales, and myths (Hillman 145), so that the girl's impression on Stephen may be understood as an encounter with anima in train of his previous experiences of anima in connection with Emma and Mercedes. The present image might be an archetype, or image, of life—not merely a feminine soul image or archetype of psyche—for at the moment preceding Stephen's perception of the girl, he is described as being "near to the wild heart of life" (171) and in the afterglow of the encounter, lying on the sand in a languorous state, Stephen envisions a blossoming flower like an exquisite rose pervading the atmosphere, surely symbolic of life or creativity: "it spread in endless succession to itself, breaking in full crimson and unfolding and fading to palest rose, leaf by leaf and wave of light by wave of light, flooding all the heavens with its soft flushes, every flush deeper than the other" (172).

Stephen's reverie of the luxuriant flower prefigures the "roselike glow" in his mind when he writes the villanelle dedicated to Emma Clery while it refers to reveries stimulated by Emma and Mercedes in his childhood, particularly his association of Mercedes with a rose garden. Stephen's relation to milieu during his walk on the strand, intensely physical and imaginative, involving the experience of wholeness, harmony, and radiance, is a wellspring of his theory of beauty, which he later discusses with his friend Lynch. These aesthetic experiences are essentially progressive stages of Stephen's responsiveness to environment and feminine allure in childhood: his metaphorical perceptions of time and space at Clongowes College, his day dreams of Mercedes and Emma, and his attempt "to build a breakwater of elegance and order" in Dublin. Thus the scene on the strand, comprising epiphanies of self and life, is a turning point from Stephen's childhood and adolescence to maturity, indicative of the persistent influence of childhood experiences on the artist's growth and later orientation.

1.A.3. M. ALLEN CUNNINGHAM, *LOST SON*

In M. Allen Cunningham's fictional biography of Rainer M. Rilke, the poet's memories of his childhood are shrouded in colorless shades of grey and black. His mother's, Phia Rilke's, black sleeves enfolded little René as she dressed him in skirts and ribbons, a surrogate for his deceased sister, Ismene. The photographer's camera for which he posed was draped in black. Mother's dark shadow loomed over him when she came to pray at his bed, crucifix in hand, and Mama herself is remembered as "an outlandish pile of black" (Cunningham 37). The umbrageous labyrinth of streets in Prague that led to school or church is overlaid in his memory by the ashen dormitory and grey halls of the military academy at Saint Pölten and the desolate cemetery nearby. In fact, Prague and Saint Pölten are referred to as the "darknesses" of his past (184, 202, 425) and forms of "the old nightmare" (16, 37, 45-6, 202).

The days René enjoyed in his family's apartment, exploring books and exquisite things—pictures with gilt frames, figurines, china, napkin rings—or memorizing poems and writing his own verses, were forestalled by some gender confusion and then curtailed by his entrance into the military academy at age ten. (On the one hand, a state resembling chaos; on the other, rigidity, both prime obstacles to creativity in Eric Neumann's view.) Consequently, Rilke bemoans his "incomplete," "unfinished," "unachieved," or "unaccomplished" childhood (44, 178, 185, 201), and Cunningham recurrently juxtaposes the poet's adult experiences and his extraordinary vulnerability with flashbacks to childhood as if to indicate a certain influence of the early years on his personal life and creative work, as well as a continual filtering of childhood memories by the poet's conscious mind and thus a gradual correction of or compensation for the lack in his childhood.

While attentive to Rilke's character and creative work, the plot of Cunningham's novel is too vigorous to admit psychological commentary, but from the course of the life represented, with the poet's inner, subjective world of memory and reflection inundating chronological events, the reader might glean and consider several effects of the poet's incomplete childhood.

First and most evident are the "seams" and "cracks" in Rilke's constitution, by which "everything gets fast inside him" (24): an aggravation of his receptivity, which we treat separately as a remarkable artistic trait in Chapter 2. Second, there is Rilke's aversion to conventional adult roles, particularly his resistance to taking the job of bank clerk in Prague, offered by his father when Rilke starts a family. However, this resistance attaches to artistic vocation and the condition of *puer aeternus,* as we may find in other artists' novels, notably Maugham's *The Moon and Sixpence.* Third and most important, for decisive in both his personal life and poetry, is Rilke's incessant yearning and search for wholeness, shown by his discoveries of "home" in various persons and places (déjà vu experiences) and his fascination with the invisible world that complements the visible one, including his way of seeing phenomena as symbolic of a larger whole, his interest in death, and the relation between transience and eternity.

The yearning for wholeness may be considered a consequence of Rilke's incomplete childhood or an aspect of poetic sensibility intensified by an unachieved childhood if the latter is understood not only as a chronologically shortened childhood but also a disruption of the experience of wholeness during childhood, which seems to be the case in Rilke's childhood. As explained by Eric Neumann, who, incidentally, refers to Rilke in his discussion of the creative personality, the child's experience is unitary or whole, contrary to the duality of inner and outer worlds, body and mind, subconscious and conscious, experienced by the adult. A child's experiences on the bodily plane (his term "bodily plane" replacing Jung's and Freud's "infantile sexuality") involve mental and spiritual impressions. A child's interaction with things, people, and places comprises both conscious (real) and unconscious (archetypal) factors, making for numinous attributes and symbolical significances in the real factors. Thus the child, the kernel and model of creative man for Neumann, is open and receptive to the transpersonal, or eternal realm, as well as the personal and transitory.

Rilke's childhood involved disjunction between experiences on the bodily plane and his mind and psyche, at home in Prague and the military academy at St. Pölten. As a toddler, René resisted being dressed, coiffed, and coddled like a girl, a substitute for his deceased sister, by his pious mother, Phia Rilke. He insisted on bringing along a little riding whip, a "buggy crop" (Cunningham 10), when asked to pose for a photographer in girls' clothing. But he enjoyed his mother's attentions while pursuing his interest in books and writing verses. Phia Rilke read Schiller's poetry to him and praised his verses, calling him "little poet" (*Bubi Dichter,* 41), and she walked him to school each day. This ambiguity was replaced by sharper contrasts between the child's identity and physical circumstances when René was enrolled in a military academy at age ten. While subjected to shrill morning whistles, announcing routine and physical discipline, alien to his poetic sensibility, René also suffered from a lack of appropriate stimulation, therefore frequent bouts of illness and insomnia. Deprived of both his mother and the creative freedom he had at home, René sought refuge at a nearby cemetery, where he would read Mama's letters and intuit a transcendent realm. In retrospect, his experience at the military school is described as "the daily despair of a ten, a twelve, a fourteen-year-old boy" and "a singularly foreign, most unrecognizable life" (from Rilke's letters, quoted in Cunningham 44).

The yearning for wholeness turns out to be the main theme of *Lost Son,* as well as an important thread interweaving layers of memory, reflection, and events in Rilke's life. This yearning oscillates between a longing for home and a need for isolation in order to cope with impressions and experiences. On the one hand, we find relationships and travel; on the other, escapes into solitude—until the ideal of home is equated with the domain of creative process, his psyche, that would eventually find shelter at Duino Castle on the Adriatic Sea, the Hôtel Biron in Paris, and the Castle at Muzot, Switzerland. Here the poet would feel at home in the mere wholeness of his experience of a unitary world (characteristic of the creative personality as well as the child) and his dedication to the creative endeavor of expressing the multifaceted dimensions of his experience in poetry.

The course of Rilke's life journey is greatly influenced by his meeting with Lou Andreas-Salomé, in whom he finds a mother figure, thus a "home," and a strong *anima* influence for his creative work in the guise of a friend, lover, and companion. In fact, the title of Cunningham's novel,

Lost Son, stems from Rilke's relation with Lou, expressed in a letter quoted in the Preface of the book: "I however, Lou, your somehow lost son, not for a long time yet can I become a sayer, one who foretells his own way, nor a describer of my former fates . . . what you hear is the noise of my footsteps" (Rilke, November 9, 1903). This self-description echoes Rilke's comparison of himself to a "lost thing" in the diary he kept in Paris (Rilke, November 19, 1902; Cunningham 200, 477). The chapters concerning Rilke's adolescence after his years in military academies (a senior academy at Mährish-Weisskirchen having followed his years at St. Pölten), previous to his departure from Prague to Műnich, to be a poet, are titled "Toward Lou: 1890-1897," suggesting their meeting and relationship as predestined or fateful.

Amid the clatter of cups and conversations at an evening tea gathering in Műnich (1897), René recognizes Lou as someone he knows although he'd never seen her before—déjà vu. René had read one of Lou's published essays; he now sends her his "Visions of Christ," and they would discover numerous common interests concerning art, poetry, philosophy, and travel. Lou reads his poems from the collection *Dream Crowned* and responds frankly, urging him to strive for simplicity, to write in a way readers might understand. She invites him to her summer cottage in the Bavarian Alps, where they enjoy nature, the company of other writers, and each other in spirit, body, and mind. She soothes him in bouts of nightmares and talking in his sleep, again the child in Prague and St. Pölten. While René feels a falling off of his former self in the presence of Lou, an awakening to a new beginning, she finds a new name for him: Rainer, more befitting the man and poet.

Twice over the span of two years, Lou and Rainer travel to Russia, which proves to offer another déjà vu experience and a home. Sailing along the Volga River past villages with exotic names, sweeping plains with huge burial mounds (kurgans) sculpted in their midst, and grassy steppes, Rainer has the sense of returning to a place he knew. "The vast outer landscape seemed to mirror the vast one in you [Rainer], which Lou had helped you discover. It didn't matter that you had never before been in Russia—it was *home* to you . . . And how Russia reverberates in you" (Cunningham 27). The months in Russia yield the "Russian Prayers," basic to Rilke's *The Book of Hours,* so memorable for the image of the great tree "in myriad beings ramifying," symbolic of wholeness and, like the circle whose center is everywhere and circumference nowhere, an image of God.

Déjà vu moments attest to the vitality of Rilke's unconscious mind or the connection between his psyche and the transcendent dimension, which is tantamount to unitary experience. Another facet of the experience of wholeness is shown by Rainer's perception and description of things as numinous or symbolic of universal experience, especially the rose that is a book of life and the all-encompassing tree. The symbolization process begins with the poet's experience of these phenomena as animate beings, illustrated by Cunningham's representation of Rainer's encounter with a huge acacia on his treks with Lou in the Alpine forest: "The presence of this tree struck you [Rainer] like a fist. On that morning the path had lain sun-dappled, hypnotic" (186). Rainer clutches Lou's arm and instinctively verbalizes his impressions instead of letting them settle and gestate in his mind. Confronting the tree a few days later, he knows to keep silence and acquiesce to the demands of the tree.

> And now the acacia stands before you once more. The acacia remembers . . . . The acacia remembers, for already it is changing, changing, transmogrifying in the injury you have done to it and it will not forget oh no it will go on changing and it wants to get inside and grow, grow to something black and clotted—yes a bundle of murky phlegm in your brain . . . . And who were you to think you could capture this power so casually? (*ibid.*).

Surely the tree has mysterious power, invisible to normal eyes, that calls for respect along with an effort at comprehension and symbolization.

On a smaller scale we have Rilke's way of seeing and describing things to include their "inscape," or essence, along with their outer physical form. Cunningham tells of Rilke's perambulations of the streets of Paris, the Zoo, and the Luxembourg Gardens, where he finds subject matter for his poems, or rather the people, animals, and flowers impress themselves upon him and get inside of him so that he empathizes and relates to their inner selves. For instance, the panther pacing in its cage, intent on freedom but locked behind bars, stirs extreme inner tension as the poet observes the animal, its "blind brain muzzled and reeling in its muscled skull ah fantasy of the night-thick hunt in the city's magnesium glare and nevermore the wild murdering chase in the crazed light of the moon" (Cunningham 96). Rainer would return to the zoo to watch the panther and again empathize with its plight before writing "The Panther":

> His gaze, from the passing bars,
> Has grown so weary that it can hold nothing else.
> To him there are a thousand bars
> And beyond the thousand bars no world at all.
>
> The soft drop of the dread sleek steps,
> Conscribed to a tight circle,
> Is like a dance of stamina around a center
> In which a greater will stands stunned.
>
> Yet sometimes the curtain of the pupil stirs,
> Opens itself soundlessly—then an image gets inside,
> Passes through the silent tension of the limbs and—
> Snared in the heart, ceases to be (199, tr. Cunningham).

Rainer's interest in the invisible world that permeates the visible is apparent even in his most visually-oriented phase of developing a "sculptural" style while working as secretary to Auguste Rodin. Rainer is fascinated by the statue of the Buddha on the grounds of Rodin's estate, no doubt for the spiritual state suggested by its features. He interprets classical myths—Apollo, Artemis, Leda—and numerous Biblical personages and prophets in his poems of this period. On an excursion to Chartres with his master, Rainer fixes his attention on a Romanesque angel sculpted in relief, holding a sundial to heaven, which he would address as the "Laughing angel, sympathetic stone" in "The Angel of the Sundial" (*New Poems* II). Try as he might, Rainer cannot fully identify with the angel, a supernatural creature at home in the invisible world. But he can re-evaluate its symbolic meaning in terms of his own experience, and he associates the angel particularly with transformations and new beginnings, the leitmotifs of his life, instanced by his encounter with Lou, his move to Paris, his meeting with Rodin, and his writing of the *New Poems,* in addition to the thresholds he crosses in solitary reflection in the process of writing.

As *Lost Son* focuses on the human side of Rilke ("to give readers an entirely human rendition of Rainer Maria Rilke the man and artist," Author's Note, 469), Cunningham understates the poet's dialogue with angels, prioritizing human relationships, especially those with his wife, Clara Westhoff, his daughter, Ruth, their mutual friend Paula Modersohn-Becker, and of course Lou Andreas-Salomé, who graciously fill in for angels on various occasions. The plot of Cunningham's fictional biography brings Rilke's poetic career to the composition of the *Duino Elegies,* in the course of which Rilke parts ways with angels and resigns himself to saying things, *"But to* say . . . / *oh to say these things / in such a way / that the* things *themselves would never / have thought to exist so earnestly"* (from the Ninth Duino Elegy, tr. Cunningham, 335). "Things" recall the beautiful objects that surrounded Rainer in his family's apartment in Prague—"The potpourri dish with its thread-thin scallops of blue paint. The china doll. The pear-shaped perfume bottle. The miniature gilt-framed pictures" (38)—which he had found animate, alongside the books he enjoyed during the bright days of his childhood. With the darknesses of his childhood gradually dispersed along his path, Rainer comes full circle to an affirmation of his childhood as the proper measure of his achievement. Thus the "unachieved childhood" that he had mourned appears to have directed his path, with its incessant search for wholeness and links with the unconscious realm of archetypes, for ways of seeing things in the light of eternity, until, full to the brim with images, his inner life could hold no more, and he elegizes the human condition instead of his own childhood experiences. Lou had said that his work "would come from all that [the darknesses of the past]," that his work awaited him in all that (425, *cf.* 184-5), and Rainer had acknowledged that all of his childhood, the incomplete past as well as the things that he helped create with words, needed him. All of his experiences were necessary for his poetry, and in this sense all were beneficial.

It is interesting to note that the writing of the *Elegies,* begun at Duino Castle in 1912, is interrupted by World War I and Rilke's mandatory service in the Austro-Hungarian Army. The final chapters of *Lost Son* represent Rilke's conscription to basic training, followed by frightful days in the infantry, from which he is soon removed to the Vienna Imperial War Archives, thanks to the intercession of friends. Effecting not only a disruption of his creative work but also a deprivation of home (as a result of the bombing of Duino Castle), Rilke's experience of this war presents a parallel in adulthood to his subjection to the rigors of a military academy in childhood: a full-blown version of the old nightmare. The darkness of his childhood might then be taken as a pre-figuration, unforeseen but destined, of his military experience in adulthood, thus a preparation for the latter. Both this military experience and his years at St. Pölten and Mährisch-Weisskirchen precipitate new beginnings in his life story.

1.B. CHILDLIKENESS: DODIE SMITH, *I CAPTURE THE CASTLE*

Dodie Smith's *I Capture the Castle* presents a few years in the life of an artistic family from the perspective of a childlike narrator, Cassandra, who is the author's persona and at the same time the main character in the story she narrates. As the author's persona, Cassandra expresses the child persisting in and remembered by the adult writer; as the main character in the novel, she exemplifies the creative child. The two roles of the child narrator are bridged by her representation as an adolescent, one who looks younger but feels older than her seventeen years (Smith 4). By Smith's legerdemain, she is credible as both an observant, precocious narrator and the most childlike member of the Mortmain family—a child relative to her older sister, Rose, as well as the adults in the family, and a child in the eyes of the community. She proves to be "a wonderful child" (146) and an "astonishing child" (221). In J. K. Rowling's words featured on the cover of a recent edition, "This book has one of the most charismatic narrators I've ever met." Indeed, Cassandra exudes the charisma of a child.

Smith's novel unfolds as Cassandra fills one notebook after another— "The Sixpenny Book," "The Shilling Book," and "The Two-Guinea Book"— with entries on her family's daily life in an old castle in the countryside near London. At the outset Cassandra describes her journal keeping as an "apprenticeship," a way of teaching herself how to write. She practices this skill while her sister, Rose, and her stepmother, Topaz, occupy themselves with sewing, housework, or playing musical instruments. Her dad, James Mortmain, reads detective novels in the gatehouse; her brother, Thomas, attends school, and Stephen, an orphan who lives with the Mortmains, performs all kinds of chores in the castle and grounds. Her journal is enriched by her relationships with family and community and her participation in the immediate life she records. On the fictional level, Cassandra's roles of narrator (journal keeper) and Mortmain sibling are thoroughly intertwined, as are the author's persona and main character from a literary perspective.

At the beginning of her journal Cassandra relates the family's search for a new home after her father's initial success as a writer: a house-hunting expedition that ended felicitously with the discovery of Godsend Castle. She remarks on her first impression of the castle—like "one in a fairy tale" (Smith 29)—as it stood glistening in afternoon sunshine. She remembers her family's tour of the interior and her father's dismay at various Victorian "improvements"—fake ceilings, fake fireplaces, partitions and such—on authentic seventeenth-century and medieval architecture. With the aid of research, she provides a brief history of the castle: it was a house built in the time of Charles II, grafted onto a fourteenth-century castle, with a wall holding two towers, proximate to the remains of a yet older castle, Belmotte Tower on a mound (4, 13). Its name, "Godsend," also attributed to a village in the vicinity, is an abbreviation of "Godys End," from Etienne de Godys, the Norman knight who built Belmotte Castle, and later de Godys.

Cassandra reflects on the spring day when her family moved into a freshly restored castle with shining wood paneling and handsome antique furniture, when she enjoyed the view of flowerbeds in the garden and swans gliding in the moat outside the mullioned windows. Although these memories contrast with the current state of the castle, with its faded chintz curtains, junk shop furniture, and leaky roof, Cassandra never ceases to see the castle in the light of the past, of her first impressions and the romance of spring. A fairy tale ambience infuses the spacious rooms, hovering over the day to day activities she records while positioned on her four-poster bed or the window seat beneath latticed windows, or the kitchen, the attic, the barn, or the mound. As a matter of course, the castle she captures contains princesses—herself and Rose—and princes—Neil and Simon Cotton, heirs to the castle, who return from America when old Mr. Cotton of Scoatney Hall passes on. Her story features a stepmother in the beautiful Topaz, of pallid face and deep voice; a fairy godmother in the person of Mrs. Cotton (widow of the deceased owner of the castle), who arranges for Rose's trousseau and otherwise flutters her wand generously; and a witch, or temptress, in the person of Leda Fox-Cotton, one of the guests at Scoatney, described as "greasy" and perceived as shady in her negotiations. A benevolent father figure inheres in James Mortmain, and an old wise man in the Vicar of Godsend Village, who provides moral support for the Mortmains and is always open to conversations about art and religion. Miss Marcy, the librarian and schoolmistress in Godsend Village, personifies a helper figure as she provides books, biscuits, and other assistance to the Mortmains on a variety of issues. Last but not least, Stephen Colly, who has lived with the Mortmains since his mother, formerly the maid, passed on, is the country lad of low estate but noble bearing ("very fair and noble-looking," 9), very solicitous of Cassandra and referred to as her swain.

The overlap of fantasy and reality in this castle befits a narrator on the threshold between childhood and maturity and attests to the persistence of her childlikeness. Cassandra is imaginative and open to manifestations of the marvelous in everyday reality; on the other hand, she is observant and discerning of moral valences in the behavior she describes, including her own. She is thus perfectly suited to don the rose-colored glasses that convey Dodie Smith's perspectives in this novel, and so to fulfill the role of author's persona.

"Persona" is sometimes termed an author's "mask" and understood as a means to differentiate the creative work from its author or to feature a particular facet of the author's personality. In Smith's novel, the persona highlights the author's childlikeness, representing the author in her youth as well as the child in the mature author; masking is achieved by the fictive setting, characters, and plot. *I Capture the Castle* is based on Smith's childhood with her mother's side of the family, the theater-loving Furbers, in Kingston House near Manchester (England) and the production, in her thirties, of an autobiographical journal of her adolescent years (Grove 3-17; Smith, *Look Back With Love*). Both the author and her persona are "consciously naïve," as Cassandra is described at one point by Simon Cotton. Therefore, when we consider Cassandra an imaginative, playful, affectionate, and observant narrator, we are also implicitly referring to childlike traits in the mature author, Dodie Smith.

Cassandra's imaginative disposition is often shown in contrast to her sister's more realistic and practical views. While Rose feels shut up in crumbling, "mouldering" ruins on rainy March days with no prospects ahead of her, Cassandra finds cozy corners in the castle to immerse herself in the activity of journal keeping. She pads the draining board above the kitchen sink with a doggie blanket and enjoys a bird's-eye view of the goings-on below; on the four-poster in her bedroom, she profits by imaginary dialogues with Miss Blossom, a dressmaker's dummy acquired in a junk shop. A dripping ceiling and stretches of grey cloudy sky outside do not dampen her enthusiasm for capturing her family's life in the castle. Cassandra never tires of the castle, never ceases to wonder at the past history of its rooms and towers. She never gets used to it to the point of taking it for granted, etched as it is in her mind as a fairy tale setting. Unlike Rose, Cassandra is naturally close to the other imaginative or artistic characters in the novel. She is very fond of her stepmother, Topaz, delighted with her theatrical gowns and lute-playing, whether "artsy pose" or art, and sympathetic to her habit of communing with nature on the mound. Cassandra shares bookishness and writing talent with her father, James Mortmain, and is alert to signs of his emergence from writer's block. She strikes up a friendship with Simon, the music-loving, poetry-reciting, scholarly Cotton, whereas Rose relates more easily to Neil Cotton, the athletic rancher who grew up in California.

Cassandra is playful: she concocts games and adventures other than "capturing the castle." In quick response to Rose's jest that she would sell her soul for relief of boredom if there were a Devil's Dyke or Devil's Well somewhere, Cassandra instigates her sister's tête à tête with the gargoyle above the kitchen fireplace. Stephen and Thomas are forthwith testing the ropes to haul Rose up to the carved stone head. When the Mortmains host a dinner for the Cottons at Godsend Castle, Cassandra improvises a few scenarios to give the incipient romance between Rose and Simon a chance to flourish. She has her brother light a lantern for a castle tour in an attempt to seclude the couple on Belmotte Tower. This failing, she invites Neil for a swim in the moat surrounding the castle walls, leaving Rose and her beau on the window seat in the bedroom. With the time spent in finding bathing suits, conversing with Neil to delay the agony of descent into cold water, making a complete circuit of the moat, then procuring towels and dressing, she has provided opportunity for her sister's engagement with Simon!

Cassandra still practices the Midsummer Eve rites, including dancing round a votive fire, which she has done together with her sister since age nine. (Rose lost interest when she reached Cassandra's age.) Initially inspired by a book on folklore, the preparations are now customary. She gathers mallow, campion, and blue bells for a garland, foxgloves to carry, and wild roses for her hair (Smith 206); she collects twigs for the fire; then fills a basket with cakes, port for libations, herbs (a charm against witchcraft), and salt to ward off bad luck. At sundown she dresses in her green linen frock, adorns herself with garland and wild roses, and sets off for the mound, "consciously naïve," as Simon once described her, and full of vigor for the festivity which she fears might be her last, a memorial to her childhood with Rose.

At the onset of the evening, we see Cassandra fused with the colors of twilight—watery yellow with a streak of bright green, wrapped in the peaceful blue of moonlight spreading over the fields: a creature at one with nature. After the rites, on her descent from the mound, she nearly faints as she looks toward the rolling, creeping mist, as though confronting the shape she once saw with Rose, believing it was an "elemental" they conjured with a spell. Both the natural imagery surrounding the Midsummer Eve rites and Cassandra's wholehearted participation suggest the unitary experience in which conscious and unconscious, as well as body and mind, work in harmony, that is attributed to childhood and to creative personalities.

Another prominent characteristic that endears Cassandra to family and other characters is her affectionate nature, typical of most if not all children and more typical of children than adults. Her expression for affection is "fondness," as in feeling "so very very fond" (6) and "extra fond" (169). She has such affection for Topaz on account of her stepmother's genuine kindness, motherliness, and cooking, aside from the artsy pose she admires and the communing with nature she imitates. Cassandra shares Topaz's loving concern for James Mortmain's extended writer's block. She is unconditionally accepting of Rose and confides in her sister regularly, letting memories of all their good times together strengthen her love and loyalty. Cassandra demonstrates fondness for Stephen on a daily basis, keeping cocoa for him when he's late for tea, delayed by chores; asking him to drop the "Miss" from his address; not being brisk with him as advised by her father. The affection she shows for the Cotton brothers, Neil and Simon, on numerous occasions results in reciprocation in the form of presents—chocolates, a new notebook, a wireless—and contributes to their prolonged perception of her as an entertaining child, a girl rather than a young woman.

Cassandra's affectionate nature influences the playfulness we have noted, in addition to her friendliness toward family and friends, the librarian and the Vicar. She has affection even for the gargoyle above the kitchen fireplace, advising Rose to pat him on the back: "It must be hundreds of years since anyone showed him any affection" (Smith 146). We may come to see her affection for the family circle and community as a motive for attempting to capture each character in her journal, along with the castle. Thus Cassandra's loving attitude toward her subject matter compares with that of Lily Briscoe (in Virginia Woolf's *To the Lighthouse*), whose painting is motivated by her "love for this all"—the Ramsays and their summer home on the isle of Skye—and whose portrait also represents the author, Virginia Woolf.

As Dodie Smith's persona and narrator in *I Capture the Castle,* Cassandra must be observant. Like most children, she is competent in assessing her parents and siblings, alert to changes in their moods and behaviors. She easily evaluates positive and negative traits, occasionally yielding clear contrasts, such as those between an arrogant James Mortmain and a humble one, or the benevolent Mrs. Cotton and the deceptive Leda Fox-Cotton. But the narrator's perceptions inevitably merge with the adult authoress' powers of observation, and it is difficult to separate one from the other at every turn, that is, to distinguish childish observations from mature observation. For instance, toward the end of the novel, we may wonder whether Cassandra turns down Simon's invitation to travel with him to the United States because she recognizes herself as the child she is perceived to be and understands that she will have to wait (according to the author's wish to maintain perception of Cassandra as a child) or because the author wants to stop short of involving her persona in a fairy tale ending and so maintain her narrator's credibility.

Suffice it to say that the childlike perspective contributes to the clarity of the characters and plot in Smith's novel. Cassandra's association of the setting with fairy tales enhances the romance of the story, and story-telling by way of practicing writing in her journal makes for a lightness and playfulness that differentiate Smith's work from the usually more serious artist novel. Cassandra's values and aspirations are simple, relative to the complexity and mercenary concerns of the adults. She values creativity, learning, fun, and personal happiness for all members of her family. She aspires to be a writer, but for the time being, her main concern is capturing the castle in a story with a happy ending, consistent with her childlike vision of the castle.

As noted earlier, *I Capture the Castle* is based partly on Smith's childhood in England. Like Smith's former home in Kingston House, the fictive castle is replete with fine fittings, a kitchen fireplace and fireside bath, candle light, and a grand piano (Smith, *Look Back with Love* 6; Grove 5, 164). Upon closer examination of Smith's memoirs, one may find analogies between members of her family and characters in the novel, but this line of research is discouraged by the initial discrepancy between Smith's close relation to her deceased mother, Nell Furber-Smith, and Cassandra's forgetfulness about her deceased mother in the novel: the models of her characters appear to be masked. Primarily, *I Capture the Castle* reveals the author's mindset, especially its childlike components of imagination, playfulness, receptivity, and affection, along with corresponding attitudes and perspectives on the life surrounding her. In this respect Smith's novel compares with Willa Cather's fictional portrait of the singer Thea Kronborg in *The Song of the Lark*, clearly influenced by the author's perspectives, values, and beliefs, as well as autobiographical elements from her childhood in Red Cloud, Nebraska. Cather features a bond between the adult singer and the child Thea, which reflects her own association of childhood memories with creativity. Similarly, Smith draws from a wealth of childhood memories as she captures the castle and, via the childlike narrator, Cassandra, expresses the vitality of the child in her.

-CHAPTER 2-

Sensuality and Receptivity

The spectrum of sensuous temperaments represented in the artist novels confirms the traditional view of artists as being "sensitive" (readily affected by the senses or susceptible to physical and psychological sensations) while illustrating variations in this sensitivity, or sensuality, as I call it, at least as diverse as the range of meanings of the words. Take the variations in meaning of the adjectives *sensual* and *sensuous* offered by Random House. *Sensual*: inclined to the gratification of the senses or appetites; carnal; voluptuous; lewd or unchaste; worldly, materialistic; pertaining to the senses or physical sensations. *Sensuous*: perceived by or affecting the senses; readily affected through the senses (e.g., a sensuous temperament). *Voluptuous,* given as a synonym for *sensual* and *sensuous,* implies a luxurious gratification of sensual desires (e.g., voluptuous joys, voluptuous beauty) as well as indulgence in luxury. Add to these definitions the mental or psychological dimensions of *sensibility*: quickness and acuteness of apprehension; keen consciousness or appreciation; delicacy of emotional or intellectual perception; the property of being readily affected by external influences as well as the capacity for sensation or feeling, responsiveness or susceptibility to sensory stimuli. The latter definitions imply the receptive component in sensuality and sensitivity, both physical and psychological. A receptive condition might be associated with vulnerability and introversion or with psychological depth in the artist's responsiveness to sensory stimuli and with the accumulation of sense impressions over time, whereby the artist has inner resources for creativity in the absence of stimulation in the immediate environment.

Sensuality in the artist is remarkable mainly for its manifestation in the art work—the poem, the picture, or the musical performance—that tells of the artist's responsiveness to sense impressions by way of the individual style that emerges in the course of creative activity. Thus sensuality is linked with aesthetic sensibility, involving consciousness as well as the vitality of the senses: mental susceptibility and apprehension, motivating reflection, musing, or day-dreaming. Such workings of the mind are expressed in the interior monologues intermittently attributed to characters by James Joyce, Virginia Woolf, Willa Cather, and M. Allen Cunningham, but these ruminations tend to be vague or fragmentary. A connection between sensuality and aesthetic sensibility is also revealed in moments of an artist's awakening to vocation, for example, Stephen Dedalus' epiphanies on the strand in Joyce's *A Portrait of the Artist as a Young Man* and Thea Kronborg's definitive awakening to the vocation of singer amid the rock cliffs of Arizona in Cather's *The Song of the Lark.* These moments are likewise rarely explicit, for they are inner, subjective experiences; however, they are prime clues to the importance of sensuality as motivation for creative activity. Scenes of awakening to artistic vocation refer to tendencies in childhood and prefigure subsequent creative endeavors, indicating a continual influence of sensuality on creativity.

We proceed then from a brief survey of the artists' portraits with regard to sensuous temperaments to more extensive commentary on portraits that feature an artist's awakening to vocation, namely Thea's and Stephen's. M. Allen Cunningham's fictional biography of Rainer M. Rilke, *Lost Son,* is discussed separately under the term "receptivity," for it offers an example of sensitivity, sensuality, and sensibility in the extreme, distinguished by the psychological depth of the poet's responsiveness to sensory stimuli. "Receptivity" was indicated at the outset by Cunningham's references to the poet's "receptive eyes" and to his "porousness" and "vulnerability," representing extraordinary sensitivity. However, there is no clear boundary between Rainer's receptivity and other artists', say Stephen Dedalus', sensitivity and sensuality; in fact, "receptivity" is an alternate term for the latter, perhaps more suggestive of the interrelation of sensuality and aesthetic sensibility.

*   *   *

Lily Briscoe, the painter who visits with the Ramsays at their summer home on Skye (off the coast of Great Britain) in Virginia Woolf's *To the Lighthouse,* is chaste like a flower image evoked by her name, not at all carnal or voluptuous, but with senses alert, especially her "Chinese" eyes. She delights in the colors of flowers and hedge on the edge of the lawn, the shimmering blue bay beyond, the ocean breeze. The elements of earth, water, and air rouse her senses to keen appreciation of the environment; the physical beauty and kindly, nurturing disposition of Mrs. Ramsay inspire admiration and love for the hostess at this summer retreat. Henceforth Lily's sensuality manifests itself in her effort to grapple with mounds of paint on her palette in order to convey her particular vision, suffused with feeling, of the colors, forms, and textures of the natural milieu, as well as the person of Mrs. Ramsay.

By contrast, Charles Strickland in W. Somerset Maugham's *The Moon and Sixpence,* a fictive portrayal of Paul Gauguin, is possessed of a rude and coarse visage, with a remarkably sensuous mouth. He is prone to carnal indulgence, demonstrated by his hearty appetite for delicious food and his attraction to women (Blanche Stroeve in Paris and Ata in Tahiti), but he is more inclined to forego the gratification of his appetites and channel his sensual instincts into artistic expression—painting. He lives on bread and milk for months in Paris while producing numerous paintings. He forswears his relationship with Blanche upon completion of her voluptuous portrait in the nude. He is totally oblivious to his surroundings until he reaches Tahiti, the isle of his dreams, where the luxuriance of the terrain corresponds with his inner vision, providing stimulation for his art to the end of his days. Clearly, Charles' portrait illustrates selectivity in his sensual tastes, subject to his particular aesthetic sensibility.

Hurtle Duffield, in Patrick White's *The Vivisector,* exhibits voluptuousness as well as eager appreciation of his natural surroundings with his sight, smell, and "tactile mind" (White 221). When a child, he is immediately impressed by the chandeliers, soft carpets, and fragrances in the rooms at Sunningdale, a wealthy residence where his mother worked as a laundress and brought him along occasionally; he occupies himself in drawing those chandeliers, which he associates with beauty and light. He could "feel each drop of crystal light trickle through him from the chandelier" (112) as though "he had inside him his own chandelier" (53). At Sunningdale, which becomes his home, he could also climb tall trees or descend moss-covered steps to luxuriate in the colors and scents of a verdant garden and apple orchard. On journeys to ranch country at Mumbelong, where his adoptive father raised cattle and sheep, Hurtle rode horses, felt sheep's soft tangled wool, and absorbed himself in a "world of light" (105). He observed distant hills glistening like sapphires or interweaving skeins of pastel textures on the horizon at sunrise and sundown; at night, the moon's silver light flickering in trees, turning massive rocks liquid.

Soon after his return to Sydney after service in the military during World War I, Hurtle builds a shack for himself in the outskirts of the city, on the edge of a gorge in a landscape of eucalyptus and ironstone, asserting his attachment to nature. Henceforth, he dedicates himself to painting, attempting visual abstractions of natural forms, expressive of the "endlessly changing coloured slides in his magic-lantern of a mind" (209): translations of the object in his own terms. But curiously there is no sequel to his endeavors in adolescence to paint light as he saw it in nature; "he couldn't manage the light: it remained as solid as human flesh" (158). Hurtle's prevailing approach to painting is the practice of "vivisection," piercing the object of the painting with eyes like knives or daggers, which obscures the world of light he had treasured in childhood. There is a disjunction between expressions of Hurtle's sensuality, especially his attraction to light, and his aesthetic as a mature painter (a disjunction unique among the artists' portraits).

Zack McCoy, remembered by his widow, Hope, in John Updike's *Seek My Face,* a fictional portrait of Jackson Pollock, has the sensuous nature of a child beneath the strong muscular build and graceful movements seen in photos of his "performance art." Like a child, Zack insisted on immediate gratification of his needs and impulses, whether to punch someone at a party or build sand castles on the beach with his nieces and nephews. When spring came, he burrowed in the yard for hours. "He dug and planted a big garden for vegetables and melons, the way his father had done years ago" (Updike 80). He would ride off on his bicycle to see what farmers and fishermen were doing or how the ocean mellowed in warmer weather. However, Zack was most childlike and most sensual in the process of painting: in mixing paints, dripping, spattering, pouring paint onto the canvas as he moved about, working with his whole body. Zack's art, compared briefly to Indian sand painting, involved the sense of touch more than most. Describing his paintings, Hope remarks on their various textures—dense, clotted, or smooth—as well as their composition and color arrangements.

Cassandra Mortmain, the adolescent narrator in Dodie Smith's *I Capture the Castle,* is well-rounded in sensuous temperament: she is responsive to the sound of music, the taste of food, the texture of a new linen frock, the smell of dye on clothing, as well as the fragrance of spring in the English countryside. She is mainly reliant on sight and hearing in gauging characters and keeping her journal of daily life in the castle. In fact, her journal was inspired by her first view of the castle, compared to one in fairy tales she had heard. Like her stepmother, Topaz, Cassandra communes with nature, for instance, in celebrating Midsummer Eve on the mound by dancing round a bonfire, performing libations, and other customary rites, decked in garlands of wildflowers.

The aspiring writer and seminarian in Vincas Mykolaitis' semi-autobiographical novel *In the Altars' Shadow* (Lith. *Altorių šešėly*), Liudas Vasaris, enjoys leave from the seminary at his family's homestead amid fields and forests, especially walks to his favorite hill with its breathtaking views. His wholehearted, sensual embrace of nature is apparent even on the ride homeward for summer vacation:

> The city remained far behind, the towers of seminary and
> cathedral obscured by forest—and the farther those towers

descended into summer's verdure, the more the sun's rays heated him through his black sutane, the lighter Vasaris' heart and the clearer his eyes. He thought of nothing and pondered nothing, as if his whole body had become mere sensation and his spiritual life, mere feeling. He was directly intoxicated, and he could barely contain the force of this sensation and feeling.

Slender pines, branching fir trees and white-vested birches glided slowly by . . . . But the passing landscape and its distinct features hardly attracted Vasaris' gaze. He now felt Nature itself, her entirety and wholeness expressed in woods, lakes, hillocks, sun's rays, the chirping of grasshoppers, the twitter of birds and the abundance of every other kind of natural phenomenon (Mykolaitis 23).

Later, immersed in the duties of priesthood, Vasaris frequents the woods beyond his parish in leisure hours, and on occasion, the splendid gardens of a baronial estate adjacent to these woods.

*   *   *

Thea Kronborg's sensual vitality, apparent from childhood to adulthood, is highlighted in the scene of her awakening to the vocation of singer, which indicates the influence of sensuality on creativity. Throughout *The Song of the Lark* Willa Cather emphasizes the nurturing of Thea's personality by way of sense impressions and the refinement of her aesthetic sensibility. She maintains personality as, metaphorically, the vessel of Thea's voice, complementing Thea's portrait with a sensual image of art. The image of a vessel arises during Thea's summer in Arizona when she explores rock chambers for relics of the ancient cliff dwellers' ceramic art and finds numerous samples. One morning Thea reflects, "What was any art but an effort to make a sheath, a mould in which to imprison for a moment the shining, elusive element which is life itself" (Cather 254), thinking of Indian pottery as well as her own bodily vessel for the voice.

In childhood, the vessel was nourished by the Kohlers' luxuriant garden, Paulina Kohler's cuckoo clock, and Fritz Kohler's piece-painting of Napoleon's retreat from Moscow, which Thea enjoyed after her piano lessons with Prof. Wunsch; her explorations of the sand hills beyond Moonstone for rocks and gems; and her friendship with the Mexicans, who impressed her with the sensuous qualities of their music and dancing. During Thea's years of musical training in Chicago, the diversions of her childhood are supplanted by similar, yet magnified, attractions in the city and beyond. Thea attends symphony concerts and participates in musical evenings hosted by Chicago society. She explores the halls of the Art Institute on Michigan Avenue, where she is especially attracted by a grand sculpture of an army general and a painting by Jules Breton titled "The Song of the Lark" (1885), representing a peasant girl in the midst of wheat fields at sunrise. Instead of leisure time in the sand hills and Turquoise Hills, Thea has the good fortune to vacation on a ranch in Arizona after a few years of voice lessons and playing accompaniments in her teacher's studio.

The specific location in Arizona is Panther Canyon, an array of rock cliffs adjacent to the Ottenburg ranch that is studded with desert brush, yuccas, and cactus and surrounded by pine forest. Thea's routine here consists of an early morning trek to the canyon, lunch basket in hand; bathing in a stream below the cliffs, shielded by cottonwoods; then climbing up to her niche in the rocks to bask in the sun. In the afternoons, she investigates other rock chambers in the canyon, looking for fragments of pottery and sundry utensils, surmising the way of life of the ancient people who once inhabited these cliffs, particularly the uses of pottery to carry and store precious water and grains. She visualizes the ancient women wearing down trails as they carried jars of water daily. She handles pottery shards, admiring their color combinations and intricate patterns crafted in overlay or relief—all supererogatory to the uses of jars for storing food or water but infinitely pleasing to the touch and sight.

Thea languishes for days and weeks, imbibing fresh air, sunlight, and the natural sounds of the canyon. Piano and voice scores are far from her mind, but eventually melodies rise in her spontaneously amid sensations of fragrance, color, and sound. "A song would go through her head all morning, as a spring keeps welling up, and it was like a pleasant sensation indefinitely prolonged" (Cather 251). Her habit of thinking yields to a surrendering to sense impressions: "She could become a mere receptacle for heat, or become a color, like the bright lizards that darted about on the hot stones . . . or she could become a continuous repetition of sound, like the cicadas" (*ibid.*). Contrary to her former view of voice training as academic routine, struggle, and drudgery, she now reflects that voice is essentially vitality. "She had begun to understand that—with her, at least—voice was, first of all, vitality; a lightness in the body and a driving power in the blood" (257).

Thea's voice had been discovered by Spanish Johnny in Moonstone, by her piano teachers, Professor Wunsch and Andor Harsanyi, and by her friend Fred Ottenburg, but her definitive awakening to the vocation of singer occurs amid the rock cliffs of Panther Canyon. In the context of nature and the elements, she experiences an integration of body and mind, thought and sensation. Like Stephen Dedalus in the scene on the strand (Joyce's *A Portrait*), Thea experiences a sense of wholeness and being an integral part of nature, as well as a part of the human endeavor at large, represented by traces of the ancient cliff dwellers in the air and the rock chambers. Like Stephen, she is revived by this experience to the point of radiance. In Panther Canyon Thea decides to pursue vocal training in Germany and to attempt opera. Later it becomes clear that the "power of sustained sensation" (251) which she acquires in Arizona distinguishes her performances at the Metropolitan Opera. She has the ability to convey a Swedish sunset, the northern lights, or the heat of battle by her presence: her personality, the vessel of her voice, infuses an array of color into the roles she performs.

*   *   *

James Joyce's *A Portrait of the Artist as a Young Man* begins with Stephen's infancy at home and the education of his five senses by way of stories and songs as well as physical sense impressions. Stephen takes pleasure in touching his mother's rosy flesh and inhaling the fragrance of her body, lesser pleasure in exploring his father's hairy face. He handles Aunt Dante's soft velvet brushes, maroon and green, and tastes delicious cachous [sic]. For lack of exposure to the outer world, Stephen acquires impressions of flora and fauna from stories told by his father and the lyrics of songs. He identifies with "baby tuckoo," a boy who meets a cow coming down the road in one of the stories. When he hears of wild roses blossoming in "the little green place" (Joyce 7) that was his country, Ireland, he conjures a green rose and attaches a new line to the song, "O, the green wothe botheth." Perhaps it was Joyce's intention to establish the link between sense impressions and aesthetic capacity at the outset, by representing Stephen's ability to imagine the moocow and the roses while hearing about them and to retain them in memory, for the story beginning "Once upon a time" and verses of song—works of art—dominate the feast of the senses that introduces Joyce's novel. Stephen's sensuality is linked with aesthetic sensibility throughout his childhood and adolescence, as shown by his musings on sense impressions and eventually his interest in a theory of beauty that resonates with his sensual experience of its components (wholeness, harmony, and radiance). Apropos, one may note the old philosophers' observation that "The principle of conscious life is: *nihil est in intellectu, quod non antea fuerit in sensu*: 'There is nothing in the mind that was not first in sensation'" (Jung 1940, 153; *cf.* Coleridge 1907, 187).

The education of Stephen's five senses involves numerous trials, proceeding from elementary experiences of pleasure and pain to positive and negative sense impressions, to the extremes of sensuality and asceticism, in a kind of dialectical procedure toward his affirmation of the mundane world of sense experience. In this framework of contrasting sense impressions, it seems that the painful or negative are usually suffered or avoided while the pleasant or positive provoke aesthetic responses. Stephen does not dwell on the sensation of falling into a cold and slimy ditch at Clongowes Wood College but recurrently turns to the sights of castle lights, fireplace, and playground fixtures. In Dublin, he is repulsed by corks floating in the filthy water of quays at the waterfront but drawn to order, elegance, and theater lanterns. Nonetheless, unpleasant sensations enhance Stephen's appreciation of their opposites: the principle of relativity undoubtedly influences his sensibility.

At Clongowes Wood College Stephen associates the pleasant with the earthy and concrete as opposed to the abstract. In an arithmetic competition between teams designated by red and white roses on silk badges, Stephen's focus on sums is distracted by the rich color of a red rose on a boy's blue sailor shirt, and so he reflects on the colors of roses, red and white, "pink and cream and lavender" (Joyce 12) that resemble the colors of cards given to winners. Preferring geography over arithmetic, he enjoys a picture of earth, like "a big ball in the middle of clouds" (15), which his friend Fleming colors green and maroon. He likes a book with pictures of Holland and imagines vineyards in Greece in his effort to comprehend *wine*. He explores his immediate environment, discovering variations in atmosphere inside and out of school hall and castle, relating to the elements of earth, air, water, and fire—especially when propelled from a cold wet ditch to a bed by the fireplace in the infirmary. Observing crackling flames, he compares them with waves, wandering in his reverie to a tumultuous sea at night, or he reminisces about the hearth fire back home, with his mother's jeweled slippers sparkling on a warm fender. His sensual experiences are thus consistently mediated by his imagination, yielding new images or revisions of previous impressions.

In the playground, the sound of cricketbats amid bouncing balls, "pick, pack, pock, puck," seem "like drops of water in a fountain slowly falling in the brimming bowl" (41). And we hear them again, tinged with the fragrance of country fields in mild grey air, on Stephen's last day at Clongowes: "like drops of water in a fountain falling softly in the brimming bowl" (59). More likely Joyce's retrospective observation than Stephen's other synaesthetic impressions, this lyrical comparison resounds with symbolical significance. Drops of water, representative of all elements or the sensory stimulation afforded by the environment at Clongowes, provide sustenance, nourishment, and inspiration for creativity in Stephen, symbolized by the fountain.

In the interim between Stephen's formal education at Clongowes Wood College and Belvedere College in Dublin, the child artist flourishes at home in Blackrock. Stephen has books, friends, and adventures on foot and on wheels. One of these pastimes, riding with the milkman on his rounds as far as the countryside at Carrickmines, is particularly revealing of Stephen's aesthetic sensibility, especially his attraction to light. Stephen enjoys views of cattle grazing at pasture on sunny days in the country, as well as mounting a mare on the field. Come autumn, he is disgusted by the same pasture, bare of cows, spotted with greenish puddles, dung, and brantroughs. On evening rounds, when the milk car stops before a house, Stephen seeks "a glimpse of a well scrubbed kitchen or a softly lit hall" (64), instinctively moving away from darkness and cold toward warmth, light, and order. His family's forthcoming move to foggy Dublin would therefore prove to be a trial for his sensitive nature and an acute experience of relativity.

While Stephen's first home in Blackrock is apt to be remembered in festive Christmas décor, with garlands adorning the chandelier above a richly laid table and a splendid fire warming family and guests, there is no comparable picture of the Dedaluses' home in Dublin. The lights are far from home: downtown, at relatives' homes, at a children's party at Harold's Cross. Later we glimpse a sticky kitchen table laden with glass jars and jam pots used for tea and scattered "crusts and lumps of sugared bread, turned brown by the tea" (163) after Stephen's numerous siblings take their afternoon repast. This scene betrays his family's lesser standard of life in Dublin, referred to as "squalor" and "the sordid tide of life" (98), which Stephen tries to ignore or ameliorate.

Disquieted by the change in circumstances, Stephen immerses himself in school work and extracurricular activities at Belvedere College. He participates in plays and essay contests. When he is awarded a monetary prize of thirty-three pounds for one of his essays, he sets out to replenish his immediate environment, creating a temporary aura of elegance and luxury. He treats his family to abundant groceries, dried fruits, and chocolates. He leads daily excursions to restaurants or theaters in Dublin. He endeavors to repaint his room in a shade of pink, until funds run out and he reverts to wandering through the grey city streets.

Poised between boyhood and adolescence, with reveries of Mercedes (from Alexander Dumas' *The Count of Monte Christo*) and Emma (from the children's party at Harold's Cross) sustaining traces of childhood and his rebellious body leaping toward sexual initiation, Stephen is bound for the successive extremes of debauchery and asceticism. Aesthetic sensibility is temporarily extinguished when Stephen appears in turn a "baffled prowling beast" (Joyce 99), succumbing to lust and gluttony, and a repentant revenant, mortifying each of his five senses. But an interlude between the two phases is worth noting: the retreat in honor of St. Francis Xavier, patron of Belvedere College, featuring Father Arnall's eloquent sermon about the last things, death, judgment, heaven and hell. This sermon abounds in sensual imagery pertaining to hell—its foul air, darkness, the stench of brimstone, the sound of howling, and the intensity of its furious everlasting fire—that repels Stephen and, together with the intellectual content of the priest's peroration, moves him to remorse. Moreover, the ambiance of the chapel he frequents during the retreat, with muted scarlet sunlight filtering through blinds, illuminating the brass candlesticks on the altar "that gleamed like the battleworn mail armor of angels" (116), comforts Stephen, facilitating his reconciliation with the Church. Also comforting are the beautiful white flowers adorning the altar in church.

Stephen's ensuing piety, marked by prayers, devotions, rosaries, and rigorous discipline of each of his senses proves to be a *via negativa* toward worldliness instead of preparation for the religious path, as viewed by his Jesuit teachers. Not for lack of zeal or sincerity in his devotion, but rather the vitality of his instincts and the resurfacing of imperfections in his behavior related to pride in his individuality. "To merge his life in the common tide of other lives was harder for him than any fasting or prayer and it was his constant failure to do this . . . which caused in his soul at last a sensation of spiritual dryness together with a growth of doubts and scruples" (151-2). Inherent in this individuality is Stephen's aesthetic sensibility, which obviously interferes with the religious path under consideration. Envisioning a future life among Jesuits, Stephen is repelled by its "chill and order" (161) as well as the faded color of the faces surrounding him. Taking leave of the director of the school, who had summoned him to discuss the matter of vocation for priesthood, Stephen sees in the priest's face "a mirthless mask reflecting a sunken day" (160). At home, he is irritated by his mother's sneezing but cheered by the chorus of his siblings singing melodies late into the night.

Stephen's readiness for a breakthrough of individual sensibility and an epiphany of his identity is suggested by the restlessness and excitement he exhibits by pacing up and down the street while his father meets with a tutor at the University one fine day. His restlessness soon manifests itself in subliminal promptings, described in turn as an "elfin prelude, endless and formless . . . he seemed to hear from under the boughs and grasses" (165), as "fitful music" and "flames leaping fitfully . . . out of a midnight wood" (*ibid.*): a prelude arising simultaneously from within him and from the outer world, or perhaps the world soul (*anima mundi*), in urgent need of harmony. As Stephen walks seaward and passes over a bridge to the strand, delighting in fresh air, blue skies, and sand under his feet, he murmurs "A day of dappled seaborne clouds" (166), enunciating the harmony he feels vis à vis nature. ("The phrase and the day and scene harmonized in a chord.") He also intuits inner harmony, more precisely integrity, or wholeness, as he looks back to the outlines of Dublin, the locus of his tempestuous adolescence, and looks up to the clouds, drifting westward from the Continent like a "host of nomads on the march" (167) as if they were messengers hearkening to him or omens of his imminent flight from Ireland.

Immersed as he is in his thoughts and his musing while gazing at the clouds, Stephen confuses the greetings of his schoolmates on the beach, "Hello Stephanos! Here comes the Dedalus!," with voices from beyond, for they merge with receding voices within ("a confused music within him as of memories and names which he was almost conscious of but could not capture," 167) as well as the sound of waves in the sea. The sound of his name out of the blue has the effect of a prophecy or revelation about his identity, with which he is so earnestly concerned on this day, and is forthwith envisioned as the winged form of Daedalus, "the fabulous artificer" (169), amid the clouds. This moment of identification with the archetypal artist, which comes like a bolt of lightning though anticipated for years, is felt in the quickening of his heartbeat and trembling of his limbs. For the first time in his life Stephen has a definite sense of his unique individuality (or the purpose of his being, "the end he had been born to serve and had been following through the mists of childhood and boyhood," Joyce 169). The epiphany is totally affirmative, for cleared of incertitude and error with regard to his path and of the despair, fear, and shame that had beset him recently. In his awakening to vocation and new joy of life, Stephen is radiant: "An ecstasy of flight made radiant his eyes and wild his breath and tremulous and wild and radiant his windswept limbs" (*ibid.*).

Strolling happily onward, Stephen is awestruck by a beautiful girl wading in a rivulet, appearing to him like a wonderful seabird and bringing a rush of blood in his veins. "His cheeks were aflame; his body was aglow" (172). The languorous swoon to which Stephen subsequently succumbs suggests that, while figuratively ignited, he was inspired with creativity at the sight of the girl. In other words, the encounter with the bird-girl was an *anima* influence, for the bird is one of the non-human forms by which anima is personified and the anima is an image or archetype of life with reference to clues in Joyce's text, especially Stephen's approach to "the wild heart of life" (171) in this scene. Moreover, the seabird is compatible with the throng of wild creatures pattering over Stephen's mind like fitful music or fitful flames in the "elfin prelude" that precedes his adventure on the strand and might be understood as a subliminal image of the wholeness that Stephen wishes to realize in the real world. The girl in the rivulet provides a sense impression conducive to the projection of an integral part of the image of wholeness in Stephen's soul (as, similarly, the sound of his name voiced by schoolmates facilitated his projection of an image of Daedalus in the clouds, and the sense impressions afforded by fresh air and blue skies were conducive to his verbal utterance of the feeling of harmony). Thus this last epiphany on the strand, a revelation of the source of art in the multifaceted beauty of life, complementing the revelation of Stephen's identity, definitely yields the sense of wholeness that was introduced at the beginning of the scene and was subsequently shown to subsume experiences of harmony and radiance.

In sum, the episode on the strand presents Stephen as a living, breathing, sensual microcosm vis à vis macrocosm of the world and its natural forces—a microcosm prefigured in the "brimming bowl," receiving and storing sense impressions "like drops of water in a fountain" (Joyce 59) at the close of Stephen's early education at Clongowes Wood College. The phrase "A day of dappled seaborne clouds" is drawn "from his treasure," analogous to the wealth of the horizon. The inner tumult that subsides with his awakening to artistic vocation and coalesces in a sensation of soaring in ecstasy is reflected without in veiled sunlight, voyaging clouds, and suddenly, the winged form of Daedalus in the clouds. The renewed vigor Stephen feels is complemented by the bird-girl and the breath of life she symbolizes. Lest this anima image be inadequate to its psychological effect of inspiration for creativity, we are given the luxuriant images of an unfolding crimson flower and breaking light, both real, corresponding to the world, and imagined by Stephen in a languorous swoon.

In following Stephen's adventure on the strand, we see that the awakening of his aesthetic sensibility is coincidental with or preliminary to his recognition of artistic vocation. The revelatory moments are essentially Stephen's aesthetic responses to sense impressions—of a bright horizon, the sound of his name in the air, the sight of the girl in a rivulet—yielding facets of beauty ingrained in his memory and subconscious mind by his lifelong practice of musing over vivid sensations. Stephen's experience of wholeness, harmony, and radiance (which he would later find as components of beauty in St. Thomas Aquinas' aesthetic theory and adapt to his own) envelops the discovery of his identity, which is also a culmination of his yearnings and tendencies in childhood and adolescence. Later, the series of experiences of facets of beauty on the strand are referred to as stages of aesthetic apprehension, and their coincidence with the call to an artistic path is basic to Stephen's eventual equation between art and beauty.

* * *

Surveying the portraits, it seems that sensuality is most consistently elicited by the artists' relation to and appreciation of nature. In other words, nature is the artists' primary source of sensory stimulation and in turn responsiveness. We see Stephen Dedalus glowing amid the elements on the strand, Lily Briscoe intently observing colors on the Isle of Skye, Charles Strickland luxuriating in the verdure of Tahiti, Liudas Vasaris breathing lightly in the woods, Cassandra Mortmain delighting in the English country-side, and Thea Kronborg exploring sand hills or desert canyons. Rather than communing with nature, Zack McCoy is portrayed as being a part of nature as he works in his barn in outer Long Island; he is quoted as saying "I am Nature" (Updike 159). In a few instances we may notice an interest in art that represents aspects of nature, like Stephen Dedalus' predilection for the Romantic poets or Thea's attraction to Jules Breton's painting "The Song of the Lark," as well as pottery fragments with decorative motifs modeled on natural forms. So these fictional artists concur with the universal preoccupation with nature and, being artists, continue the long tradition of expressing their relation to nature in poetry, painting, and music.

The artists' responsiveness to nature and expressiveness vis à vis natural phenomena appear to be primarily sensual, as it were a celebration of the vitality of the senses or a paean to nature. In his poem "Lamarck Elaborated" (subtitled "The environment creates the organ"), Richard Wilbur proposes that:

> It was the sun that bored these two blue holes [our eyes].
>
> . . .
>
> It was the song of doves begot the ear
> And not the ear that first conceived of sound:
> That organ bloomed in vibrant atmosphere . . .
>
> The yielding water, the repugnant stone,
> The poisoned berry and flaring rose
> Attired in sense the tactless finger-bone
> And set the taste-buds and inspired the nose.
>
> Out of our vivid ambiance came unsought

All sense but that most formidably dim (Richard Wilbur, *New and Collected Poems* 243).

By prioritizing his or her relation to nature, the artist instinctively affirms the fundamental bond implied in Wilbur's poem, seeking further refinement of the senses along with inspiration for creative work.

Receptivity: Rainer M. Rilke in M. Allen Cunningham's *Lost Son*

One of the most sympathetic and memorable characters in Cunningham's novel is Paula Modersohn-Becker, a close friend of Rainer M. Rilke and his wife, the sculptress Clara Westhoff, from the days of their meeting at an artists' colony near Bremen. Paula is a prodigy who demonstrates consummate artistry in her twenties and departs prematurely. She leaves behind an unfinished portrait of Rainer that startles viewers by the faithfulness and accuracy of its portrayal, particularly the "receptive eyes swallowing everything" (Cunningham 419), initiating the creative process of poetry. "His eyes, as she has seen them, receive and receive, while his mouth, like a dark low-slung nerve, wants to give back all that it has tasted and breathed. To return it all unalloyed, newly complete" (418). This visual portrait is revealing of the character that unfolds in Cunningham's larger, literary portrait by way of his representation of the poet's inner life of heart and mind: a wealth of impressions, memories, and reflections, which increases in the course of the chronological events of his life.

Receptive eyes are keys to the inner life; however, in Cunningham's portrait the poet appears to be totally porous, open to experience head to toe and vulnerable on this account. He is described as having seams and cracks in his constitution, whereby impressions of the surrounding world easily permeate him. Rainer has been this way since childhood, when he lay awake in the dormitory of the military academy at Saint Pölten, soaking in his fellows' nightmares and coping with the residue of daily terrors in this chill place: "He is root, for some part of him, somewhere deep, still has its pores wide open to a powerful intoxicant" (46). Whenever possible, he retreats to a nearby cemetery to pray and read Mama's letters, but these comforts are intercepted by teasing and bullying on the part of other cadets. Suffering from physical and mental exhaustion in the infirmary, with fever and doctors' hands constantly prodding him, little René is like "a palimpsest of strange imprints" (55). Indeed, the experience of the military academy proved traumatic to his extraordinary sensitivity and foreign to his poetic sensibility while it curtailed his childhood in Prague; moreover, this experience might have aggravated his receptive condition in adulthood, as Cunningham suggests by juxtaposing Rilke's adult experiences, especially his years in Paris, with flashbacks to Prague and St. Pölten.

In 1902, Rainer arrives in Paris fashionably dressed with stiff collar, broad hat, and cloth-trimmed shoes, yet "he looks a damaged vessel, as when he was a child. Something about him cleft bare and never closed" (11). The plight of rag pickers amid piles of trash, of sallow people, beggars and bedraggled children becomes his own; "every need becomes his conclusively, sits upon his heart like a stone" (82-3). On a walk along the Boulevard Saint Michel, Rainer sees a spastic man, whose limping and hopping accelerate to wild leaping in view of jeering bystanders—whom Rainer follows to Pont Saint Michel, commiserating and sharing the shudders of the spastic body as it finally collapses on the bridge. In the Luxembourg Gardens his eyes set on a homeless woman who is pried from a bench and taken beyond the gates by park attendants, whose predicament he revisions in a dream at night. Impressions of people in Paris evoke imprints of his early surroundings in Prague and Saint Pölten. Thoughts of invalids in pale shifts at the Hôtel Dieu, a hospital for the poor, overlap with memories of drifting in an oversized gown in the infirmary at the military school. The oppression of the grey city is associated with early images of his mother in black sleeves, with echoes of her grave voice, and his touch of the silver crucifix on her neck, evocative of the five wounds of Christ.

The misery of Paris is all the more wrenching in its contrast with the splendor of the city's architecture and gardens, as well as the aesthetic stimulation Rainer receives in Auguste Rodin's atelier and estate at Meudon. The metropolis nearly overwhelms him by the range of its spectacles of grandeur and decrepitude, the spectrum of humanity from the destitute to the privileged, while it stirs memories of his childhood in a similarly diverse city. In Paris, Rainer learns to cope with impressions and direct them into creative work. "The world's pain, the world's beauty, will get inside him. Daily, impressions almost lay him flat. No alternative but to reckon with all this in his art" (Cunningham107). He practices ways of seeing with the intention of transforming his observations to poetry, thus distilling deep impressions into simple verbal expression. Taking Rodin's sculptural work as an example, Rainer teaches "his eyes to shape and hew" (94) by focusing on the surface of things, the formal contours, then gleaning their essences. He describes classical statues, commenting on their mythical significance (Archaic Torso of Apollo, Cretan Artemis, Leda); he takes up Biblical subject matter alongside the beggar, the lunatic, and the blind man. He memorializes flowers, like the blue hydrangea and the multifaceted rose.

Rainer tempers his receptivity by developing a rhythm of in-gathering and withdrawal in order to settle impressions or transfer them forthwith to expression in verses, letters, or notes. Initially he protects himself in the solitude of his musty room at 11 Rue Toullier, writing letters to Clara, letting images gestate and ramify as poems. Later he finds oases in the National Library, where he reads Flaubert and savors the Symbolists—Verlaine, Baudelaire, Mallarmé; in the Gardens, abounding with flowers and fountains; and the Zoo at the Jardin des Plantes, where he gazes at the gazelle and flamingo as well as ferocious animals. He also spends endless days in Rodin's atelier and estate, researching the master's life and work for the purpose of writing a commissioned monograph, the reason for his move to Paris. When Clara joins him in October, at different quarters (3 Rue de L'Abbé de L'Eppée), Rainer works steadily on the Rodin book while Clara resumes sculpting in a neighboring studio.

The pattern of absorption and withdrawal to solitude assumes broader dimensions in time and space in proportion to the increasing assertiveness of the poet's inner life. Time and patience are needed for both writing and the reception of occasional spurtings of the fountain within, or the unconscious mind; changes of scene are required to recuperate from creative effort and find new strength. So Rainer determines to leave Paris for the warmer climate of Italy to benefit his health and the agglomeration of Parisian impressions lingering within him. In the spring of 1903 he sets off on a train journey that brings him beyond Torino, Genoa, and Santa Margerita to the village of Viareggio on the Ligurian Sea. Here, in the course of bathing, reading in his straw-thatched beach hut, and writing in his balcony room at the hotel, he completes *The Book of Hours* and lays the foundation for *The Book of Images*. Next year he avails himself of an extended stay at an artists' colony in Rome, the Villa Strohl-Fern, together with Clara.

During the productive phase in his cottage on the Roman *campagna,* the month of February, Rainer conceives of his fictive alter ego, Malte: an aspiring poet, a pilgrim in pursuit of knowledge and experience in a state of perpetual becoming, who has been knocking on the door to Rainer's consciousness for months in Paris. Malte occupies a shabby room at 11 Rue Toullier, as did Rainer. He frequents the National Library, wanders the city streets, and harbors a treasure trove of reminiscences and reveries about his relatives and ancestry. He is a mirror image of the poet, with the difference that Malte subsists almost entirely in the microcosm of his subjective life whereas Rainer is somewhat more securely grounded in reality. By transferring parcels of his inner and outer life to fiction (eventually published as *The Notebooks of Malte Laurids Brigge,* 1910), Rainer reckons with the receptacle that he is and objectifies it in his art, perhaps alleviating the burden of his excessively receptive condition.

In the Author's Note, Cunningham informs us that *"Lost Son* takes up a kind of direct discourse with Rilke's novel, *The Notebooks of Malte Laurids Brigge"* (470). In its formal aspect, the discourse consists in Cunningham's second person "you" address to Rainer throughout the novel, the same form of address that Malte uses to converse with the people and predicaments he observes with utmost empathy, and with himself in his diary entries. In view of the parallel forms of address, we may surmise that Rainer, the "you" in *Lost Son,* resembles the world perceived by and permeating Malte; that the poet is (essentially, inwardly) a microcosm similar to Malte's world.

Moreover, several story elements in *Lost Son* are inspired by or modeled on events in Rilke's novel, for example, Rainer's interest in his family's ancestry and his experiences in Sweden (events at Borgeby-gärd and Furuborg, to be discussed shortly), in addition to numerous incidents in Paris. Between the discourse and analogous episodes, Cunningham refers to Malte at numerous turns in his plot, from the poet's early intuitions of his fictive alter ego in the cauldron of Paris to his proper conception in Rome; from his obsession about Malte in Scandinavia, where he is given Danish provenance, to his escorting Paula Becker to Malte's fictive residence at the cul de sac of Rue Toullier in 1906, when Rainer begins to tackle the *Notebooks* in earnest. Recurrent mention of Malte suggests the personal importance of his novel to Rilke and the intimate bond between the poet and his fictive alter ego. (It might be noted that Cunningham's fictional biography can easily be read without awareness of the author's discourse with Rilke's novel, but the discourse is particularly relevant to a discussion of receptivity.)

The most obvious point of comparison between Rainer in *Lost Son* and Malte in Rilke's *Notebooks* is the effort made by each character to *see,* involving the inner eye as well as the outer, mental processes as well as the physical sense of sight. Malte says, "I am learning to see . . . everything penetrates more deeply into me . . . I am learning to see," (*The Notebooks of Malte Laurids Brigge* 14-15); in *Lost Son*, Rainer remarks, "All I can do is look around me. Look and be changed by my looking," and further, "But to *look* at all this first: to see it and know it and one day perhaps, to *say* it" (Cunningham 71, 122). The ability to see is linked with their receptivity to surrounding world and their awareness of the challenges offered by sight. With regard to the idea of the poet as microcosm, a subjective, inner world corresponding to the universe, or macrocosm, seeing is a recognition or identification of outer phenomena with inner resources as well as the subconscious mind. Wandering about Paris, Malte comments, "I recognize everything here, and that is why it goes right into me: it is at home in me" (Rilke, *The Notebooks* 48). In *Lost Son,* when Rainer and Clara ascend the steps of the church of Sacre Coeur to see the vast city below them, Rainer becomes dizzy from the view, "His head aswirl in a shock of recognition"

(Cunningham 107), for he recognizes it as the source of the weight and oppression he has felt in the few months since his arrival in Paris. Similarly, on his travels with Lou, Rainer had recognized Russia as home, for the spirit of the land reverberated in him: "The vast outer landscape seemed to mirror the vast one in you" (27).

Rainer's journeys northward to Sweden, soon after the months in Rome, bring him to new thresholds of perception and insight, which he would impart to Malte. In the summer of 1904 he is a guest at Borgeby-gärd, an estate belonging to friends of the writer Ellen Key: a country manor surrounded by green pastures, grazing cattle, gabled farm buildings, fragrant earth, and verdant trees. It is like a sanatorium, Rainer writes to Clara, so abundant in healthy food, fresh air, and quiet, so recuperative that "it must . . . become creative" (275). There is a family library on this estate, holding documents that motivate the poet's venture to an old chapel in a far corner of the grounds. Here, amid crumbling walls and caving roof, in the company of a giant stork roosting in moss-covered eaves, Rainer examines an old wooden altar and family insignia in an arch of stained glass, then rests his eyes on a triptych of portraits from the sixteenth century, faded images of an old Lord Chamberlain (Hans Spegel, vassal to Friedrich the Second) and his wives. Observing the weather-beaten portrait, Rainer discerns the Chamberlain's excellent character and his honor in battle. Then he descends to an old crypt containing a decayed coffin with skulls, bones, and bare joints; in this rain-soaked chamber he conjures the Chamberlain's unique death, corresponding to his exemplary life. That evening in his cottage, inspired by the day's discoveries in the chapel, Rainer resumes a story sparked by a paragraph in his uncle Jaroslav's family documents: "The Cornet," about Christophe Rilke, who fell in a Hungarian battle with the Turks in 1664.

Glad to prolong his time in Sweden, Rainer accepts an invitation to Ellen Key's country home in Jonsered in November 1904. A long train journey, followed by a sleigh ride through snow-covered fields, bring him to Furuborg, a new manor in the style of an old farmhouse, and to the landlady's warm welcome. What fascinates Rainer most at this arrival is an empty space adjacent to Key's home, with rows of stones marking the foundation of a previous mansion, for this space appears to him filled with the shapes of interior rooms and staircase of the former building—a presence of the invisible. His penetrating vision is ascribed to his restful months at Borgeby-gärd, allowing for cultivation and inner growth, refreshing his vigor and receptive power. "His eyes so enlivened and nothing to keep him from inhaling the world through them, tasting the world in all the chambers of his heart, breathing the world forth again" (281).

As demonstrated by the scenes at Borgeby-gärd and Furuborg, Rainer was prone to reach to the "other side" of nature in his vision and imagination, to see the invisible world of the deceased as part of an indivisible whole of life and death in our experience. Accordingly, Cunningham highlights Rainer's personal encounters with death: his uncle Jaroslav's and his father's, Josef Rilke's, passing, both involving a ceremonial piercing of the heart to ascertain death; later, the premature death of his soul mate, the painter Paula Modersohn-Becker. These dear people remain alive for the poet, at least in spirit. On one of his lecture tours, while speaking of Rodin in Berlin, Rainer sees his deceased father—his ghost, one might say—entering the auditorium and tipping his bowler hat with pride. Unable to attend Rainer's previous lecture in Prague due to illness, Josef Rilke comes posthumously. About a year after Paula's death, while writing the "Requiem" for her, Rainer finds himself in dialogue with Paula's apparition, enunciating his grievances for her untimely loss and for the unfulfilled creative capacity in her. (Incidentally, when Rainer was in Paula's atelier the previous year, viewing a self-portrait of the artist lying on a sofa with an infant in her arms, he had felt a shudder in his body, a "low unsettling shiver," which was, then unknown to him, a subliminal premonition of Paula's death shortly after the birth of her daughter the following year.)

> Yes, for every moment is a layer of eternity. Nothing that has happened ceases to happen; none of it goes away; we are but leached through one and another translucency as through planes of thinnest glass till at last we come out on a different side. It's merely a process of long transference, nothing more, and all along the way we bleed off our temporality (Cunningham 365).

These thoughts pass through Rainer's mind while he stands with Paula at 11 Rue Toullier (April 1906), pointing out Malte's room, reflecting on his own arrival at this address in 1902, which seems like yesterday. They are thoughts of a poet who must hold the past and the future within him if he is to perceive the present in terms of eternity and every phenomenon of his experience as a part of the whole. This poet would soon retreat in total solitude to devote himself to creative work, accepting as his most natural duty the imparting of all that he has received and sifted in the mills of his interior life by way of poetry. From the Hôtel Biron in Paris, where Rainer completes *The Notebooks of Malte Laurids Brigge,* he would go to Duino Castle on the Adriatic Sea and eventually to the castle at Muzot, Switzerland, where he completes the *Duino Elegies.*

It seems that in the years of writing *The Notebooks of Malte Laurids Brigge* (1906-1910), by imagining himself as the initiate Malte and objectifying his inner life in Malte's fictive experiences, Rainer comes to terms with his incomplete childhood or in fact achieves his childhood and reaches the threshold to maturity. In the course of recording Malte's observations, meditations, reveries, fears, and illnesses, Rainer attains mastery of his own inner life and proceeds to acknowledge his proper strengths and weaknesses, as if *The Notebooks* were a case study of himself. We may notice that while Cunningham takes up a discourse with Rilke's novel as an avenue to the expression of the poet's inner life and growth, he does not quote from this work as he does intermittently from Rilke's poems and letters, as if *The Notebooks* were superfluous to the poet's oeuvre but important for his personal life. Like a self-portrait by Paula Becker, which Rainer admires as a thing unto itself, inviting no communication or judgment from the viewer (described as a "transformative mirror, reflecting no one but the painter," meeting "no viewer's eyes but her own," Cunningham 374), his novel about Malte is self-contained and obscure to most readers. Malte is a perfect receptacle in comparison with his author, for whom impressions find closure in poetry and prose, thus gliding into eternity and making room for other murmurs from the accumulated treasure within.

-CHAPTER 3-

The Urge for Self-Expression

If *"imagination* may be the word for that all-important no man's land between the end of the receptive process and the start of the expressive one" (Gerard 237), the urge for self-expression may be understood as the use of one's imagination for creative ends. Like other noticeable traits—childlikeness, sensuality, or receptivity—the urge for self-expression is characteristic of people in other walks of life, but in the artist it is more pronounced and nurtured, to the extent of shaping a mode of life wherein self-expression takes priority and is the near equivalent of living and breathing. This mode of life appears to be an extension of the responsiveness and creativity associated with childhood, enhanced by application and will power (as suggested by Thea Kronborg's memories of childhood, when she was nothing other than an artist, or Rainer M. Rilke's concern with the "achievement" of his childhood). The *urge* for self-expression, an instinctive drive or need, stimulated by talent, motivates the identity of painter, writer, poet, or singer; the pursuit of *self-expression* reflects the artist's individual experience, aspirations and longings, as well as cultural influences on his or her identity and artwork.

Post-Romantic, twentieth-century artist novels are apt to support and exemplify Otto Rank's notion of the "creative personality," or "productive personality," that stems from the Renaissance and differentiates the modern artist from the artist serving a collective ideology in previous eras, such as the

European Middle Ages, yet is relative to the primitive artist who depicted his exploits on cave walls and luxuriated in bodily ornamentation (Rank, *Art and Artist* 1932, Chapter 1, "Creative Urge and Personality"). The artist portrayed in twentieth-century fiction is prone to be an "expressionistic" artist, R. P. Blackmur observes, as a result of the prevalence, at least in the first half of the century, of "expressionism," which is broadly the belief in the free expression of one's individuality or one's inner or subjective emotions and sensations ("The Artist as Hero" 1956). However, we find a variety of orientations in the artist novels—Romantic, Symbolist, Modernist, Abstract Expressionist, Feminist—as well as a variety of concepts of "self." Only in John Updike's *Seek My Face* is a concept of self explicitly discussed, and this in connection with the aims and aesthetics of Abstract Expressionism, the mid-twentieth-century art movement in which Zack McCoy participated. So we begin with the *urge* for self-expression, taking the "self" for granted, or the self as the "inner I" in Romantic tradition, and eventually resume the topic of self with reference to psychoanalytical theory, particularly C.G. Jung's concept of self as one of the archetypes of the collective unconscious. This theory is especially relevant in its elucidation of the universal dimension of "self," thus the expression of universal experience by way of self-expression, which is usually sought and attained by artists represented in the selected fiction.

The *urge,* the creative impulse that drives the cart of self or personality, is a multifaceted phenomenon, perceptible in various behaviors in the literary portraits. In its incipient stage, the urge manifests itself as vague unrest and attraction to beauty, for example, the glimmers of aesthetic sensibility, particularly an attraction to light, shown in Stephen Dedalus' and Hurtle Duffield's childhoods. "He loved the pepper tree breaking into light, and the white hens rustling by moonlight in the black branches . . . . He could do nothing about it, though. Not yet. He could only carry all of it in his head" (Patrick White, *The Vivisector,* 18). The urge for self-expression might inhere in moodiness, reflection, or preoccupation, especially in connection with day-dreaming, as in Stephen's detachment from the real scene at a children's party to savor Emma's glance, or the youthful seminarian's Vasaris' reflections on the sight of a veiled woman in the cathedral. On the other hand, the urge is equated with incessant need, as in Charles Strickland's need to paint or René M. Rilke's need to write. "The poet wrestles with the need inside him. Need that incessantly makes itself felt but cowers when he gives it leave to come forth as work" (M. Allen Cunningham, *Lost Son,* 34). The urge is also correlated with drive: in Hope McCoy's reminiscences, Zack was possessed of a "desperate creative drive" (John Updike, *Seek My Face,* 41). It might amount to a desire to make one's mark in the world, at least in a contemporary artistic or literary movement, as with Zack's involvement in Abstract Expressionism or Vasaris' in the European literary currents of the 1930's.

Reasons for the restlessness, moodiness, need, and drive are likewise diverse. Cather posits talent as well as "divine gift," which is the meaning of *Thea.* Maugham voices "genius" in the conversations of Charles Strickland's friends in Paris. Joyce indicates subconscious influences, analogous to mysterious or divine sources, in Stephen's childish day-dreams and the inner "fitful music" and "fitful flames" that attend the scene of his awakening to artistic vocation. Similarly, Cunningham envelops the budding poet with mystery: "They [words] trickle through his limbs from some indeterminate source. He looks behind the words for a source and finds only darkness" (*Lost Son* 41); later, Rainer hearkens to the murmurs of voices within, nourished by impressions of nature, people, and cultural phenomena. In *To the Lighthouse,* Virginia Woolf symbolizes creativity as the spurting of a fountain and water rippling, thereby attributing the creative impulse to an elemental force (though Lily Briscoe, the author's persona in the novel, is evidently motivated to paint by her love for everyone and everything on the Isle of Skye and by her desire to express her feelings of relatedness). Most of these answers call for reference to psychological concepts pertaining to creativity and inspiration, even in a discussion of the urge for self-expression in childhood, which is theoretically a state of unified experience, when the unconscious is undifferentiated from the conscious mind.

The Urge for Self-Expression in Childhood

Early creative effort appears to be instinctive and sensual, sparked by stimulation in the environment, especially by sights and sounds. Attracted by the sound of Spanish Johnny's guitar, seven-year-old Thea Kronborg wanders off to the Mexican quarter of Moonstone to listen at close range and repeats the melodies without the words. Impressed by the old castle that becomes her home as one in fairy tales she had heard, Cassandra Mortmain ventures to write her own story about living in a castle. Stephen Dedalus responds to the stories and songs he hears at home, chiming, "O, the green wothe botheth" to his father's "O, the wild rose blossoms / On the little green place" (Joyce 7). Stephen's habit of forming images in his mind and associating the various images of his experience increases in the course of his elementary education at Clongowes Wood College, resplendent with castle lights outside and fireplaces within. While exploring the things and books in his family's apartment in Prague, the child René finds poems by Schiller to memorize and proceeds to rhyme his own words, forming verses by age nine. Hurtle Duffield expresses what he sees and knows, like the chandeliers at Sunningdale estate, by drawing, for this is his particular way of relating to environment and world.

Though alert and open to the surrounding world, the child is not yet conscious of itself as the individual or self that it so fervently tries to express. A child's mind is said to be connected with the unconscious wellsprings of creativity, the transcendent realm of archetypes, and so described as being in a state of "waking sleep" in its experience of a "whole and undivided world" or "unitary reality" (Neumann 180, 173). The flourishing of self-expression in the receptacle that is a child will then initially depend on felicitous circumstances and adults in its environment. In artist novels that include childhood (Cather, Cunningham, Joyce, Smith, White), nourishment and nurture are shown to be helpful if not indispensible.

The liberal, laissez-faire attitude of the Dedalus family serves Stephen well, as does the provision of a good education for their eldest son. Mr. Dedalus, Sr., a would-be singer and poet, is supportive of Stephen's verbal talent and aesthetic sensibility; he is tolerant of Stephen's moodiness and wandering phases. Thea Kronborg is blessed with a mother who appreciates her musical gift as well as her need for freedom to seek mental and physical diversion to her heart's content. Mrs. Kronborg keeps Thea at the piano four hours a day but also encourages her excursions in Moonstone and the sand hills beyond town. In Dodie Smith's novel, the writer father and kindly, artistic stepmother appear perfectly tailored to Cassandra's apprenticeship in writing. Likewise Godsend Castle that is their home and the people of Godsend village nearby: there is room for the imagination in this castle, with window seats from which to observe people and a four-poster bed for retreat day or night; there are possibilities for entertainment and adventure in the village. In Patrick White's *The Vivisector,* set in the vicinity of Sydney, Australia, Hurtle is adopted at age six by the wealthy Courtneys of Sunningdale estate, where his mother is laundress for a time. A childhood of poverty in a family of nine is exchanged for one of luxury, privilege, and every possible attention.

Beneficial circumstances might be expected in the childhood of artists who write of their own experiences or inspire fiction, but we find exceptions. Hurtle foregoes the privileges of his childhood when he voluntarily enlists in the military at age sixteen, serves the Allies in World War I, and returns to a life of poverty and struggle in Sydney. (After his adoptive father's passing, Alfreda Courtney remarries and moves to England with her daughter, Rhoda. Eventually, we hear that Alfreda dies in poverty, her second husband having squandered the family's fortune.) However, destitution appears to have no adverse effect on Hurtle's pursuit of drawing and painting. He finds odd jobs, including a night shift as janitor in a department store, which allow time for painting during the day. He becomes totally absorbed in his art, all relationships being incidental and subservient to his need to paint, all living arrangements suited to his art. He becomes a famous, prosperous painter. The reader is left to decide whether his childhood in Sunningdale made any difference to his career, granted the considerable advantages it offered, of beauty and quiet, better education, travel, and perhaps a wider perceptive field than his first home.

Although White does not interpret the effects of successive changes of circumstance in Hurtle's childhood and youth, his portrait highlights Hurtle's childlikeness: his openness, responsiveness, and adjustment to whatever fortune brings, as well as the total absorption in his art and his indifference to social norms and expectations. Hurtle's childlike qualities appear to protect him from dwelling on misfortune, self-pity, and resignation. He hurtles onward, again Hurtle Duffield (versus Courtney), guided by the genius apparent in his precociousness at age five. Childhood is retrieved toward the end of the novel when Hurtle, about sixty, re-connects with his sister Rhoda Courtney, whom he finds feeding stray cats in the neighborhood, and invites her to share his home, presumably as a moral defense in his late years. In a conversation revealing of Hurtle's insight and perceptiveness, usually reserved for artistic expression, Rhoda says, "You were a child, weren't you? I think, perhaps, in many ways, you are still; otherwise you wouldn't see the truth as you do: too large, and too hectic" (White 470).

Another, contrasting exception is found in Rainer M. Rilke's childhood (Cunningham's *Lost Son*) when the child René is sent off to military school at age ten in keeping with tradition on the father's side, regardless of the boy's poetic inclinations. Rilke's foreshortened childhood, referred to as an "unachieved" or "unfinished" childhood, is recurrently lamented in adulthood. According to one of Rilke's letters quoted in the novel, the poet had to suppress and disown memories of his five years of military training at the academy in Saint Pölten in order to proceed with his life. In this portrait, the memories persist and the darkness of his childhood comes to be understood as propitious, indeed necessary, for his art, particularly the prose and poetry expressive of mankind's fears. As explained in conversation with Lou Andreas-Salomé, all of his experiences—Saint Pölten and, later, the shadow side of Paris—needed Rainer, to be transformed in his vast inner microcosm to the words and images of his poetry.

—Without me, Lou, it couldn't have . . . been real.
—It needed you. And I think . . . those things of your past, Rainer. That darkness. I think your work awaits you in all that . . . .

—Yes, because . . . because *everything* needs me, Lou. That unfinished past and everything else (Cunningham 184-5).

Rainer prolongs his childhood in his adult years ostensibly on account of the suppressed memories which erupt in days of fever and sleepless nights: "Memories swarm you in these suspended hours—memories, from childhood days, of the many rooms in which this fever came. These memories reduce you to that child again—still that child despite your striving, still mired in the long labor of finishing the unfinished boyhood behind you" (201). But in the attempt to complete his childhood, he is also compensating for the integrity and contentment of those early days in the family apartment when he first discovered his poetic identity.

As an adult, Rainer does not cease to yearn for wholeness and home, which he finds initially in the company of Lou in Műnich and in his travels to Russia. He is extremely receptive to all impressions and surroundings, driven to channel them into letters and poems. His openness to the world brings him to extraordinary, transpersonal experiences, such as his apprehension of the Beyond and communion with the deceased while exploring the crypt of a chapel in Sweden. Rilke's glimpses into a sphere beyond normal reality—experiences of transpersonal wholeness, involving the unconscious as well as the conscious mind—no doubt influenced his ability to represent the great tree as God's universe in *The Book of Hours,* the rose as a book of life, and to speak of numerous things as being much more than they normally appear to be. Eric Neumann explains that the creative artist, like the child, perceives phenomena of reality as symbolic, or numinous, of the archetypal realm that is "unitary reality"; this he likens to our sense of things or works of art becoming transparent, revealing something other, new, and different from their real identities, thus expanding in our view.

From childhood onward the creative individual is captivated by his experience of the unitary reality of childhood; he returns over and over again to the great hieroglyphic images of archetypal existence. They were mirrored for the first time in the well of childhood and there they remain until, recollecting, we bend over the rim of the well and rediscover them, forever unchanged (Neumann 181).

Both Hurtle's and Rainer's portraits, different as they are, offer support for James Hillman's "acorn theory," which maintains that children, more specifically, their geniuses or soul images, choose their parents, and that circumstances and experiences, favorable or not, even disastrous events, are essentially purposive and beneficial for the child in the long run. The acorn, i.e., the soul image or genius, makes use of experiences according to its requirements as it proceeds to grow into the oak tree (Hillman, *The Soul's Code* 1997, Chapter I, "In a Nutshell").

The Urge for Self-Expression in Adolescence and Adulthood

In the adult and already the adolescent, the urge for self-expression is sparked by conscious choice and pursuit of writing, painting, or musical performance, often prioritizing artistic endeavor over conventional roles and social expectations. Stephen Dedalus chooses entry into the University instead of the Jesuit Order and soon leaves Ireland for France in order to be free of the "nets" of family, nationality, and religion that constrain his self-expression. René M. Rilke neglects the study of law or business recommended by his family as alternatives to a military career and departs for Műnich to devote himself to poetry. Most strikingly, Charles Strickland (the fictive Paul Gauguin in Maugham's *The Moon and Sixpence*) terminates his position as stockbroker in a firm in London and leaves his social circle to pursue painting in the bohemian quarter of Paris. Otto Rank speaks of this kind of self-determination as "the self-making of the personality into the artist" and "appointing oneself as an artist" (*Art and Artist* 27-28); of the artistic endeavor as a "will to form," in accord with the importance of will in his psychology of creativity. Willfulness is certainly evident in the literary portraits, but it appears to be the result and affirmation of an urge for self-expression rather than its cause. (Thus willfulness pertains more directly to the productive work of artists, the topic of Chapter 5.) The urge for self-expression is usually associated with emotions and the promptings of unconscious influences or inspiration.

A brief survey of psychological theories pertaining to unconscious influences on creativity serves to elucidate some implications in the literary representations. We have noted Eric Neumann's concept of the creative individual's access to the transpersonal realm of archetypes; this is otherwise stated as access to the unconscious, which is at the root of the creative principle that transforms consciousness (Neumann 168-9). Similarly, Carl G. Jung found the creative urge to be irrational, influenced either by the personal unconscious or the collective unconscious (the objective psyche), productive respectively of "psychological" and "visionary" works of art ("Psychology and Literature"). In Sigmund Freud's view, the creative urge is a sublimation of sexual instincts or excessively powerful instinctual needs, referred to as "excessive libido" (*Introductory Lectures on Psycho-Analysis*, 467; 429), which is a largely imperceptible inner drive or energy striving for meaningful expression. The creative urge surfaces in day-dreaming, a "half-way region" that Freud explains as a continuation of childish play and fantasizing in the adult, as well as a form of wish-fulfillment (*Lectures* 468; "The Relation of the Poet to Day-Dreaming"). Day-dreaming recalls the child's "wakeful sleep"; on the other hand, it refers to the instinct to reflect, to "'bend back and turn inward', away from outer stimuli in favor of psychic images" (Hillman, *Anima* 85), which is in turn related to the influence of *anima* (L. "soul" or "spirit") and the concept of inspiration.

Anima ranges in meaning from the image of the feminine in a male to the personification of the unconscious, to an archetype of life (a "life behind consciousness . . . from which consciousness rises," Jung 1940, 76), as given in the context of Jung's work and elaborated by like-minded scholars, particularly James Hillman (*Anima* 1985, which includes an extended bibliography on the topic). As an image of the feminine or accumulated experience of the feminine in a man, anima is personal and capable of assuming recognizable physical attributes in its various personifications, but in its archetypal essence it is the supra-personal "eternal feminine," represented in mythological figures such as Aphrodite, Selene, Persephone, Hecate, Athena, Koré, Pandora, Eve, and Sophia. As "matrix of all the divine and semi-divine figures, from the pagan goddess to the Virgin" (Hillman 153), anima possesses mysterious, unknowable dimensions, especially in its connection with fate. Indeed, psychologists emphasize the *unconsciousness* of anima, suggesting autonomy, spontaneity, ubiquity and collectivity in its functions and influence, in accord with its archetypal status. ("The archetype," Jung writes, "is essentially an unconscious content that is altered by becoming conscious and by being perceived, and it takes its color from the individual consciousness in which it happens to appear," "Psychology and Literature" 103). Thus anima influences moods, reflections, daydreams, complexes, and impulses, which may be projected onto a particular feminine being, for example, Beatrice, Laura, Mercedes, or Emma, or attributed to an unknown woman, an internal muse, correspondent breeze, or bird.

This archetype might be described as a breath of life, consistent with the etymological connection between L. *anima* and Gr. *animos* or *anemos,* meaning "wind," and the Gr. *psyche,* meaning "soul," and *psychein,* "to breathe": of "a life behind consciousness." She might also be understood as a mediatrix to the unconscious, Hillman explains with reference to Jung's mention of a "bridge to the unconscious" (*Psyche and Symbol* 336), as "She mediates the ceaseless movements of interiority" (Hillman 1985, 138). For lack of a real bridge, anima influence usually depends on its particular attachments, whether masculine-feminine pairings, mother-daughter relationships, or the dialectic between collective and individual.

> Anima-consciousness favors a protective mimicry, an *attachment* to something or someone else to which it is echo . . . . So, we think of her in notions of attachment with body or with spirit, or in the mother-daughter mystery, in the masculine-feminine pairings, or in compensation with the persona, in collusion with the shadow, or as guide to the self (*ibid.* 23).

An attempt to define *anima* entails consideration of *animus,* especially with regard to the *syzygy,* the archetypal image or divine pair of the maternal Eros, associated with relationships, and the paternal Logos, characterized by rational spirit and reason, which are, Jung remarks, "the foundation stones of the psychic structure" (*Psyche and Symbol* 19), reflected in mythological pairs such as Zeus and Hera or Aphrodite and Apollo, as well as the queens and kings in fairy tales. Although the meaning of anima is apt to be limited by the contrasexual implication of its pairing with animus (for example, in Jung's opposition of irrational moods and femininity in men to irrational opinions and other "quasi-intellectual elements" in women, *Psyche and Symbol* 16), it also gains some clarity by its juxtaposition to rational spirit and reason. Hillman suggests that one might think in terms of tandems, sequences and couplings like mythological pairings, instead of oppositions, with regard to anima and animus, for they compensate one another and are interrelated rather than opposed to each other. The *syzygy* inheres in the experience of men and women individually as well as interpersonal relationships. For instance, in the process of writing about the phenomenology of anima, Hillman comments that he has to take up an animus position: "if anima has been the subject of investigation, animus has been the investigator" or "if animus has been the logos plan and activity of making words serve critical discrimination, anima has been feathering those words and guiding their direction with her fantasies" (1985, 171). If the anima is evident in tandem with the ego, the discerning, rational, objective dimension of the psyche, the animus might be correlated with the ego. Hillman observes that "the qualities of *animus* in Latin—activities and functions of consciousness, attention, intellect, mind, will, courage, arrogance and pride—are those which we nowadays in somewhat different terms attribute to the ego. Indeed, it seems that much of what psychology has been calling the ego is the animus-half of the syzygy" (*ibid.* 179). By infusions of vitality, soul, irrationality, illusion, and imagination, anima complements animus and compensates for what might be lacking in ego consciousness.

In his discussion of inspiration (Chapter 13, "On Inspiration," in *Psychoanalytic Explorations in Art,* 1952), Ernst Kris considers the influence of preconscious mental activity without reference to *anima* as he surveys the topic from its ritualistic enactment in primitive societies to modern-day clinical interpretations. He highlights the process of externalization, whereby what comes from inside (impulses, wishes, fantasies) is thought to come from outside, from supernatural or divine sources. This process involves the mechanisms of projection and introjection, corresponding to notions of anima as "projection-maker" and "illusion-maker" (Hillman), which Kris relates to the action of "blowing on" and its reverse, "inhaling": meanings inherent in *inspiration*. His discussion also points to the relativity of passive and active states in an experience that revolves on alterations of consciousness or changes of mind: the passive state that receives or succumbs to inspiration is in turn an enthusiastic state prone for active elaboration of a spontaneous idea or vision. With the "bursting of boundaries between conscious and unconscious," confusion between inner and outer, passive and active, is inevitable. This is reflected in metaphors for inspiration: bird and angel versus interior paramour, or the correspondent breeze, which suggests an interchange between inner and outer processes.

Unconscious influences on the urge for self-expression are seldom explicit in literary representations of artists unless they are presented metaphorically, as in Franz Kafka's *The Metamorphosis*. Gregor Samsa, suffering what he calls the fantasy of his transformation into a monstrous bug one morning, is figuratively deflated, de-animated and obstructed in his path to self-expression by this stunning transformation, in reversal or adverse effect of the inspiration to be gotten from unconscious sources. As a result of social pressure to work as a traveling salesman, contrary to his poetic, aesthetic sensibility, amply suggested in the novel by his love for Greta's violin playing and his exquisite monologues, he is brought to the pathetic state of crawling on walls and ceiling and feeding on scraps. His transformation might also be taken as a kind of rebellion, bringing shame to his family by satisfying their low expectations to the utmost. Literary criticism explains Kafka's figurative image of the bug, with reference to the author's diary and letters, as an extended metaphor of a contemporary (early twentieth-century,

Prague) bourgeois view of the artist as an outsider, metaphorically a monster or parasitical vermin (Corngold 81-82). In other words, Kafka elaborated a myth of the artist based on a popular perception of the artist exclusively on the bodily plane, derived from the prejudices, preconceived opinions, and ignorance current in the collective psyche (what is "in the air" or the collective unconscious). Opinions and prejudices are among the aforementioned "quasi-intellectual elements" that Jung attributes to the *animus* in women, but they may be found in society at large as, likewise, *anima* or lack thereof may characterize a particular community at a particular time.

Kafka was probably unaware of the multi-valence of his metaphorical bug; he was unsatisfied with *The Metamorphosis,* he wrote in a letter to his fiancé. As indicated by the overwhelming acclaim of his work and its numerous meaningful interpretations, the author touched on archetypal patterns relevant to religious experience, folklore, and wisdom literature: punishment for pride and self-assertion, retribution, sacrifice, exile, father-son relationships, and sibling rivalry. Other than an artist-writer, mirroring the author, Gregor is seen as a tragic hero or antihero, prodigal son, Christ figure, rebel or outsider. At the same time, Kafka's surrealistic portrait affords humor, parody, farce, and tragi-comedy in the Samsa family drama. It offers the consolation to be had from illusions, specifically the illusion of Gregor's inferiority in his family's perspective (and by extension, society's), which is a projection on their part.

Literary rendition of unconscious influences is more often momentary and fleeting, like the epiphanies in Joyce's *A Portrait of the Artist as a Young Man* and Cather's *The Song of the Lark* that are revealing of anima influence. Anima attaches to the ordinary girl wading in a rivulet, whom Stephen perceives as a marvelous seabird and likens to the "wild heart of life" (Joyce 171). Anima inheres in the voices calling "Hello Stephanos! Here comes the Dedalus!," announcing the artistic path that is Stephen's destiny. In Cather's novel, Thea Kronborg intuits the spirit of ancient cliff dwellers permeating the canyon which she explores during her summer in Arizona. She perceives the fragments and shards of pottery that she finds as fragments of the cliff-dwellers' desire, which merges with her own hitherto unconscious yearning when she identifies her own creative urge with the human creative endeavor at large, partaking in *anima mundi*. Thea's awakening to vocation, like Stephen's, is shown to entail unconscious mental activity that Jung terms "the natural mind" (CW9, I, par. 167, n.5, quoted in Hillman 87), "where we do not think but are thought" (Hillman 1985, 85), which correlates with anima and the instinct to reflect. Thus reflection, moved by anima, stimulates consciousness of one's own life and soul (*ibid.*).

We find instances of retreat from normal activities, meditation and reflection on impressions and experiences, suggestive of connectedness with unconscious sources of inspiration. In Cunningham's *Lost Son,* Rainer continually seeks isolation in his quarters to reflect and be ready for inspiration that unpredictably brings spurts of creativity, suffering intermittent periods of lack thereof. Zack McCoy, in Updike's *Seek My Face*, is said to have secluded himself in the barn that was his studio for hours in preparation for painting, to have been entirely focused on work-in-progress and disconnected from other activity. Similarly, Lily Briscoe (Woolf's *To the Lighthouse*) resents intrusion on her concentrated efforts to render her vision on canvas. Woolf provides a window on Lily's mind with the interior monologues that revolve on her painting at dinner and leisure walks by the sea, as well as at work with brushes and palette. These monologues consist of reflections on people and place, insights, and memories, in addition to deliberations over the composition of her painting, that is, a stream of *consciousness.* But there is also an influx of emotion, the "love for this all" that motivates her urge for self-expression in painting, for Lily is particularly disturbed by intrusions of the masculine, rational mind (of Mr. Ramsay or Mr. Bankes) on her feeling-toned, synthetic, feminine mode of thought. As Lily's painting is primarily a tribute to Mrs. Ramsay, to whom she relates as a daughter, we may infer the influence of anima in its attachment to the mother-daughter mystery and its association with the realm of the mothers, the wellspring of creativity according to Jung.

The clearest avenues to unconscious motivation of self-expression are provided by portrayals of artists as day-dreamers, involving anima in attachment to masculine-feminine pairings, that is, women in an artist's life. James Joyce's account of Stephen's interior life of reverie in *A Portrait* is a prime example. Stephen appears a day-dreamer early on, in the interval between his childhood and adolescence in Dublin. He is a watchful observer, absorbed in his thoughts and detached from other boys' games. He immerses himself in the imaginary world of books. Reading Alexandre Dumas' *The Count of Monte Christo,* Stephen broods upon the figure of Mercedes, imagining another Mercedes and other moonlit gardens in which she would appear. ("He wanted to meet in the real world the unsubstantial image which his soul so constantly beheld," Joyce 65.) At a children's party, the real scene yields to interior images as Stephen associates Emma Cleary's glance with a tale he had heard in the past, in reality or in fantasy: "He heard what her eyes said to him beneath their cowl and knew that in some dim past, whether in life or in reverie, he had heard their tale before" (69). The verses Stephen dedicated to Emma "told only of the night and the balmy breeze and the maiden luster of the moon" (70), featuring *anima* as the mythical Luna instead of his meeting with Emma at the party or their ride on the tram. Stephen's musings and daydreams of Emma precede and influence the epiphanies on the strand; they also anticipate his awakening one morning in a flurry of roseate images that translate to lines and verses of the villanelle he dedicates to E.C. ("Are you not weary of ardent ways?"). Stephen is recurrently shown turning inward, day-dreaming and reflecting on his experiences along his path to verbal self-expression.

In an artist novel that is a virtual sequel to Joyce's *Portrait,* Vincas Mykolaitis' *In the Altars' Shadow* (Lithuanian *Altorių šešėly*), Liudas Vasaris, seminarian and priest, becomes the poet he was meant to be with the aid of anima influences, anonymous and known. The inner conflict concerning vocation, which Stephen resolves in adolescence, persists in Vasaris for over a decade of his adult life as a result of social pressure on the one hand and his passivity and super-ego dominated character on the other. (Entry into the seminary was often a pretext for obtaining a higher education among early twentieth-century villagers in Lithuania.) The resolution of his conflict, or the gradual awakening to vocation, is initially inspired by an unknown woman during mass in the cathedral, at whose sight Vasaris experiences an urge to make his mark in the world and a kind of depth opening within, suggesting latent and obscure dimensions of his personality. This woman, illuminated by sunlight streaming through stained-glass windows, seems "like a vision divested of an earthly woman's reality" (Mykolaitis 60), as it were a revelation of the eternal feminine. Subsequently, the resolution of Vasaris' inner conflict is facilitated by his relationships with Liucija, Baroness Rainacke, and Aurelija, who prod and open Vasaris to life and experience, enriching his poetic imagination and inner life of reverie. They are real women, who seek romantic or realistic relationships, but in Vasaris' mind, they function primarily as vestiges of "his Unknown" in the cathedral, bearing similar influence, in accord with the principle that anima is conceived in tandems. The women awaken and stimulate latent facets of Vasaris' personality, imperceptibly steering him toward the secular path of artist that is his destiny.

Liucija (Liuce) is the flirtatious niece of the canon of a parish neighboring Vasaris' homestead, the girl next door. She is in a position to serve coffee to Vasaris, to jest and converse at dinners hosted by her uncle. She visits the seminary on holidays with her uncle. On one occasion Liuce plays with the surname *Vasaris,* meaning "February" in Lithuanian, altering it to *pavasaris,* meaning "spring," and its diminutive *Pavasarėlis,* "Little Spring"—an endearing nickname, perfectly suited to Vasaris' instinctive identification with nature whenever he is outside the walls of the seminary. During summer vacations, Liuce accompanies the youthful seminarian on walks to his favorite place, "Dawn Hill" (*Aušrakalnis*), where they enjoy vistas of the countryside and the fragrance of wildflowers. Liuce gathers bouquets and weaves garlands as she tries to compete with the milieu for Vasaris' attention. At the turn of Vasaris' fourth year at the seminary, she is the life of a party on this hill, a wreath of hands joined in song, dance, and games. She is the embodiment of playfulness, spontaneity, and summer joy in the early phase of her relationship with Vasaris.

Baroness Rainacke offers diversion to Vasaris during his years as vicar in the village of Kalnynai ("mountain range"). She is first glimpsed galloping on a horse, leaping fences on the vast grounds of the Rainacke estate, where she later leads Vasaris on the round of her French garden and orangery. She embodies social graces and aristocratic entertainment when she hosts afternoon tea for the clergymen and festive events for the community. The Baroness invites Vasaris to make use of the manor's library; she draws him into her boudoir to hear his latest poems, to discuss literature and Epicurean philosophy. Formerly an actress in Poland, the Baroness is a sophisticated playmate as she entices the vicar to secular pleasures and forges through a layer of his asceticism. Yet the Baroness, like Liuce, is the stuff of Vasaris' day-dreams and reveries, inspiring courtly love and idealistic poems.

There are several indications that Liuce and Baroness Rainacke are assimilated in Vasaris' mind to "his Unknown." When Liuce, wearing a shawl instead of a hat, attends Vasaris' first celebration of mass, the young priest is awed by her resemblance to the woman in the cathedral, usually seen draped in a shawl. Conversations on life and beauty with the Baroness would influence muddled thoughts and obscure intuitions in Vasaris, recalling the subliminal depth that opened up at the sight of "his Unknown." In the vicar's poems, symbols of an unattainable ideal merged with images and attributes of his real acquaintances: the pilgrim's path was illumined by a bright star or warmed by the sun, and a distant castle seemed to be modeled on the Rainacke manor. These allegories were clearer to his fellow clergymen as implicit love lyrics than to Vasaris, who persistently projected his inner ideal, "his Unknown," onto his immediate relationships.

Moreover, Mykolaitis' portrayals of Liuce and Baroness Rainacke suggest aspects of the non-human or half-human mythological shapes that traditionally personify the archetypal *anima*. The Baroness is referred to as a witch on her horse by the housekeeper of the vicarage in Kalnynai. She appears to possess the keen eyesight of a witch when she observes Vasaris' gait and posture as becoming typically priest-like but his physiognomy and face as yet unaffected, or when she foreshadows future events in mentioning the possibility of Vasaris' resignation from the Church. In the role of temptress, the Baroness is Eve; as conversationalist and advisor, she alludes to the wisdom of Sophia or the Old Wise Man, with whom anima is associated. Liuce bears resemblance to the elfin nature of nixies (water nymphs) in her mischievous moments, when she says and does the opposite of what she intends and later explains that it was a little devil in her. The open-air episodes in which Liuce appears, particularly on Dawn Hill, exude "anima-air," pertaining to tempests, internal weather, "enthusiasm and inspirations" (Hillman 145), and so suggest Liuce as one of the creatures of air, like butterflies, angels, birds, and "stinging winged things" (*ibid.*), as well as anima in its literal association with breath and wind.

Early on, when Vasaris juxtaposes thoughts of his Unknown with attempts to block Liuce from his mind, the author comments that Vasaris would not believe if someone told him that "She [his Unknown] is the cause, the other [Liuce] only an effect; She is the spring, the other a mere current; that She is the essence, and the other, only one of a thousand manifestations. Until he relinquishes this one [his Unknown], his defenses against the other are futile" (Mykolaitis 60). Vincas Mykolaitis, writing in the 1930's, might have been familiar with C.G. Jung's studies of the unconscious mind, but the protagonist in his fictive autobiographical portrait is unaware of the influence of *anima* as mediatrix to his unconscious, interfering with his accurate feelings for women: as illusion-maker and projection-maker as well as guide to the self.

Vasaris' relationship with Aurelija (or Aukse, "Goldie") is preceded by a decade of study and travel abroad, behind the scenes of the novel, that factually liberates him from church ideology. When Vasaris returns to Lithuania, literary reputation in tow, he finds himself at the center of cultural life in the interim capital, Kaunas, joining a group of artists, writers and intellectuals that includes Aurelija. Vasaris and Aurelija are co-performers one evening: she fills the atmosphere with beautiful melodies before he reads from his latest play. An accomplished pianist and well-educated woman, Aukse is a likely soul mate for Vasaris (anima as bearer of his inner image of the feminine); a realistic woman, she is also interested in having a family. However, in the framework of Mykolaitis' novel, she serves primarily to mitigate Vasaris' inner conflict, which is again aggravated by family expectations and social pressure to maintain the obligations of priesthood. Proceeding in the footsteps of Liuce and Baroness Rainacke, at times reminiscent of these women in her spontaneous friendliness and behavior as conversationalist, Auksė patiently guides Vasaris toward integrity and the secular path that befits his character.

The influence of anima as source of inspiration and guide to self in Mykolaitis' novel supports his portrayal of a romantic poet and a modern artist, typically concerned with self-expression, as opposed to serving a collective ideology. Unlike previous poets and writers in Lithuanian literary history who thrived within the frame of church ideology, whom Vasaris cites as models in his conversations with the Baroness, Vasaris eventually feels shackled by church dogma and his responsibilities as a clergyman. He is essentially a Romantic rebel, requiring freedom to find and express his inner "I". He is Romantic in his identification with nature, exquisitely expressed throughout the novel, from his first return home from the seminary to his perambulations of the woods adjacent to the Rainacke estate, to his nocturnal excursion on the sand dunes by the Baltic Sea on a respite from his routine in Kaunas. Vasaris is implicitly a nature-worshipper, inadvertently possessing the sensibility of his pagan ancestors, who perceived nature as animated being and personified it as the Earth Mother. This vein of religiosity is consistent with Vasaris' fascination with the eternal feminine that reveals itself in several women in his experience, stirring his unconscious depth and his urge for self-expression.

In *Art and Artist,* Otto Rank refers to the Romantic as "pioneer and earliest specimen of the individual artist-type, whose art ideology is the cult of personality with its idea of liberty" (83). The urge for self-expression, which Rank conceives as an urge for immortality in terms of collective notions of soul and collective standards of art in previous epochs, becomes in the modern artist "an individual will-to-form" (78), further described as "a human derivative of the biological life-impulse" (84). This "will-to-form" might be understood as an assertion of one's particular way of seeing, thinking, and feeling about phenomena and problems in human experience in a medium of expression as well as one's choice of subject matter. Thus self-expression inheres in "objective" art, whether poetry, painting, or the performance of a given musical score. Unique personality is perceptible in Rilke's poems about things, Strickland's paintings of Tahitian landscapes, Briscoe's rendition of her experience at the Ramsays' summer home, and Kronborg's performances of Wagner roles, as well as Stephen Dedalus' and Liudas Vasaris' love lyrics, which are directly self-expressive in the Romantic tradition. On the other hand, will-to-form might be taken more literally, as an assertion or extension of personality in one's chosen medium of expression, whereby personality becomes the end of expression rather than a medium or vehicle for the expression of an object (idea or experience) in the artwork.

Direct assertion of personality is especially noticeable in John Updike's fictional portrait of Jackson Pollock, *Seek My Face*. Zack McCoy strives to develop a personal style, thereby to make his mark within "Abstract Expressionism," the prevailing art movement of his time in the United States, *ca.* 1940-1960. Interestingly, this movement recapitulates the trend from abstract to concrete expression, which Rank observes throughout the course of Western art history, replacing earlier progression from abstract expression of soul to concrete expression of reality with a progression from abstract expression of experience (or soul or reality) to concrete expression of self. Zack's experimentation with ways of being *in* the painting epitomizes concrete expression of self; it demonstrates "individual will-to-form" as an extension of personality in one's art.

Updike's novel unfolds as an extensive interview between a journalist and Zack's widow, Hope McCoy, in her Vermont home amid scenic mountains and valleys. The focus of conversation on Zack as person and painter is complemented by commentary on twentieth-century art, particularly the trends prevailing in New York from about 1930 to 1960. Zack is described at the outset as possessing "a desperate creative drive" (Updike 41): other than fame and wealth, he wanted to distinguish himself by a signature style. Abstract Expressionism provided a felicitous current for his yearnings, for self-expression was the fashion since the 1930's. "We weren't so much interested in the craft or the finished product as in what the painting did for the painter. That was the thing, back then, that everybody talked about—getting the *self out*, getting it on canvas. That was why abstraction was so glamorous, it was all *self*" (Updike 44). Hope mentions various concepts of self-expression discussed by her former teachers and colleagues, such as the surrealistic notion of letting the unconscious speak, or the aesthetic, sensuous aspect of the world as a means to condense feeling into an object of perception (45) or collage, in which the arrangement of scraps depended on feeling and an interplay of mind and body. Zack was conversant with these concepts while he sought to develop his own method of transferring his self to his paintings.

In the huge barn which Zack transformed into his studio in the Long Island Flats, he had room to experiment. Beginning with pastel, almost transparent water colors, he proceeded to pour and drip paint from a tube, producing clotted, textured, variegated effects. Alternately moving the canvas about on the easel and taping it to the barn floor, Zack encircled the canvas, drawing in the air, dripping and spattering paint in the process. Dripping was not random; Zack contemplated a composition for days beforehand and deliberated over his intentions. He is described as being decisive and intense in the process of painting. He was meticulous with his medium as he was precise with techniques, learning to thin paint exactly and choosing tools suitable for his purposes—sticks, dried brushes, kitchen implements. Zack's unique approach to painting attracted publicity. "This beautiful torso in black T-shirt, the tight dark jeans, the bald head, the intensity" (90) would be seen in *Life* magazine and in movies. Zack's painting procedure, involving ways of being *in* the painting, was perceived as an act, as performance art. But the personality on camera differed from the recluse in the barn, whom Hope remembers as being serious in self-exploration and self-expression, as cherishing the sincerity of the creative process.

In reminiscing about her former husband, Hope refers to Zack as a child, noting the innocence of his movements around the canvas and his childlike immersion in the *doing* (103). She says that his reflection was limited to the framework of his canvases, implying that he was nothing other than an artist. Zack also demonstrated childishness by his impatience in gratifying desires, for instance, by temper tantrums or stamping his feet. Occasionally, Zack was violent, in drinking too much, brandishing a brush in the air, or driving recklessly. (*Violence,* a psychologist remarks, derives from the Latin *vis,* meaning "life force"; it is likened to the natural force of plant life that resists repression. According to Renaissance doctors, violence is a manifestation of Mars, associated with the expression of individuality as well as anger, Moore 127). Zack's uncontained energy, like his urge for self-expression, exemplifies things "of the creature," with which the representation of artists in Updike's novel is suffused. "Of the creature" was a Quaker phrase voiced by Hope's grandfather for what was "too much, too human, too worldly, too selfish and cruel. War was of the creature. Lust and intemperence of course, yet reason and excessive learning and disputation, too. The arts . . . were of the creature, howls for recognition and singularity" (Updike 7).

As suggested by Updike's characterization of Zack McCoy, featuring childlikeness, sensuality, and violence, along with an obsession to make his mark in the world of art, the urge for self-expression is a basic drive or need in the individual, recalling excessive libido in Freud's terms. Zack McCoy bears some comparison to Hurtle Duffield, whose drive to paint everything he sees and knows never wavers, and to Charles Strickland, who subsists mainly on painting in harmony with his inner vision; more distantly, to Lily Briscoe, obsessed with expressing her love for the Ramsays and the Isle of Skye on canvas. Artist novels that relate the urge for self-expression to vocation, talent, genius, or gift (Joyce, Cather, Cunningham, Maugham, Mykolaitis) confirm the deep, innate nature of this urge. By associating the depth with mysterious origins, divine or subconscious, which tend to be less determinate than the natural force of plant life, they also point to the vulnerability of the creative urge and the challenges it poses. Talent might remain subliminal if not discovered and nurtured. When vocation is not clear and insistent—as in the adolescent Stephen, Vasaris, or Gregor—there are social pressures and conventional perspectives to frustrate the artist's creative needs. Stirrings of the unconscious in the form of day-dreaming and anima influence serve to rouse the urge for self-expression and strengthen the artist's awareness of vocation and personal talent.

With regard to the *literary* portrayal of artists, we find that the urge for self-expression, variously creative drive or creativity, is often linked, literally or symbolically, with the four elements—earth, air, fire, and water—which symbolize wholeness in nature and therefore suggest a yearning for wholeness and individuality on the part of the artist. The epiphany in Joyce's *A Portrait of the Artist as a Young Man* occurs in *plein-air* on a "day of dappled seaborne clouds." The girl whom Stephen perceives as a marvelous seabird is a creature of air, water, and earth; ignited by her image, Stephen glows with creative fire. The turning point in Cather's *The Song of the Lark* is Thea's summer sojourn in Panther Canyon, where her routine of bathing in the stream, basking in the sun, and exploring the rock cliffs precipitates her awakening one afternoon to the stirring of melodies from within and her affirmation of the vocation of singer. In Woolf's *To the Lighthouse*, Lily's self-expression, like Mrs. Ramsay's and the children's, elicits the symbolism of a spurting fountain and flowing water, associated with creativity in general. The *anima* images that motivate Vasaris' urge for self-expression in Mykolaitis' *Altars* are announced or accompanied by sunlight (in the cathedral), open air (Dawn Hill), country landscape (the Rainacke estate), and the seacoast (the site of his meeting with Auksė one summer holiday). In Cunningham's *Lost Son*, Rilke travels throughout Europe, away from cities—eastward to Russia, southward to Rome and the Ligurian Sea, northward to Sweden, westward to Copenhagen—in search for land, sunshine, and sea air conducive to good health and creativity. Ostensibly homeless and restless because of his unachieved childhood and reluctance to take an ordinary job, he is also portrayed as being at home in his numerous quarters, from Paris rooms to castle at Muzot: in the condition of the elements, moving, changing, and transforming, yet burdened with consciousness.

Self

Nature is conducive to yearnings for wholeness and longings to express one's self and individuality ("indivisibility" from the L. *individus*), as shown by the Romantic poets' dialogues with and monologues about nature. Take, for instance, William Wordsworth's "Lines Composed a Few Miles above Tintern Abbey" (1798), where nature is described as "The guide, the guardian of my heart, and soul / Of all my moral being" (ll. 110-111), for conceived not only as visible scenery but also a manifestation of world harmony, informed by divine presence; or Percy B. Shelley's "Ode to the West Wind" with its plea, "Make me thy lyre, even as the forest is" (V, l. 1); or Ralph Waldo Emerson's paeans to nature as the source of our health and wholeness because it is itself "of one pattern made" ("Xenophanes" 1. 6), likened to an unbounded stream going "Through flood and sea and firmament" ("Two Rivers" 1.7).

In twentieth-century psychoanalytical theory, nature is the domain of the unconscious, or objective psyche, that functions as compensation for consciousness ("the objective psyche is . . . a realm of nature . . . part of nature's secret," Jung observes, 1940, 101); therefore, it is propitious in the exploration and discovery of "self," which comprises both conscious and unconscious components of the personality. C.G. Jung defines the "self" as "a wholeness beyond the reach of consciousness" and "a totality of conscious and unconscious psyche," as well as "the center and circumference of the conscious and unconscious system"—with the disclaimer that it is a "mere postulate" and "a purely delineating concept" (Jung 1940, 176; 191). The "self" elucidates itself in empirical ways, for example, in dreams, occasionally by spontaneous images of a quaternity or a *mandāla* (Sanskrit for "circle"), which are symbols of unity and totality as well as order and reconciliation (Jung, *Psyche and Symbol* 30). As a wholeness transcending consciousness, the self can only be experienced in its parts or aspects because the human self is imperfect in comparison with the God image that is a model of self, encompassing uniqueness and universality, unitemporality and eternity, in the quaternity by which the unconscious formulates itself.

Jung's concept of the self and the objective psyche, or unconscious, of which it partakes (whereby it is an objective factor) is suggested by the Romantic poets' objective attitude toward mind and self, indicative of the existence of mind and imagination apart from the conscious ego. In *Biographia Literaria* (Chapter XII), considering in turn the perspectives of natural philosophy and transcendental philosophy, Samuel Taylor Coleridge speaks of an "ulterior consciousness" on the one hand and "self-conscious spirit as will" on the other, in each case arriving at a concurrence or coinstantaneity of the subjective and objective (Coleridge 1817, 168, 185, 174), so that subject and object presuppose each other (*ibid.*, 183). The identity of subject and object is indicated by the image of a wheel, with rays proceeding from center to circumference, which pertains directly to Coleridge's discussion of organicism but also corresponds with various symbols of wholeness cited by Jung and one of his definitions of "self." Similarly, Percy B. Shelley maintained that "Poetry . . . is at once the center and circumference of knowledge" (read "poetry" as self-knowledge or self-expression) and considered the "self" as "an atom to a Universe" ("A Defense of Poetry," 30-31). Geoffrey Hartman, a scholar of Romanticism, comments on the poets' objective attitude toward self, of the mind perceived as "a daimon . . . a respondent and secret sharer," likely to be associated with the spirit in nature with which poets converse, or with God speaking through nature in the Transcendentalists' view.

> The theme engaged by the great Romantics is that of a general . . . progress of imagination, of which the artist is a mediator. He reveals in what relation he stands to his own mind—which presupposes for mind (or imagination) an existence apart from ego. Authentic self-consciousness includes a strongly objective attitude toward the self: the mind is seen as a daimon . . . a respondent and secret sharer (Hartman 1973, 39-40).

A self apart from and greater than the artist's personal psyche and ego is implied by Van Wyck Brooks' discussion of self-expression ("The Doctrine of

Self-Expression," 1932), which maintains that a "progressive identification of the personal with the universal" is key to the artist's character. Writing before the publication of C.G. Jung's theory of the collective unconscious, Brooks voices similar ideas in his adumbration of the universal dimension as a "reality behind appearances" that is sought by the artist; thus he also suggests a quest for self beyond the reach of consciousness.

> His [the artist's] search is to express not himself . . . but his sense of something that exists in himself, something not personal but universal . . . something like 'the reality behind appearances'. To express not his own feeble or defective emotions but his conceptions, his apprehensions of that reality, felt through his emotions—that is the object of his search . . . . He feels himself a man, certainly, and at the same time an agent, a spokesman, a witness of the reality, greater than himself, of which his own spirit is a constituent part (Brooks 1932, 131-32).

In his study of nineteenth-century artist novels, *Ivory Towers and Sacred Founts* (1964), Maurice Beebe proposes a "divided self" as one of the recurrent patterns that form a model of artistic character. (The other patterns, interrelated with the "divided self," are "ivory towers," referring to artists who work in isolation, drawing from their inner resources—therefore an equation between art and religion more than experience; and "sacred founts," referring to artists who create on the basis of their experience, thus live more fully than others and continually struggle to balance life and art.) Beebe cites numerous examples of artists' "doubles" and instances of artists' experiences of being "outside" themselves or observing themselves. Separation between person and creator is exemplified by George Eliot's "second self," who wrote her novels; Joseph Conrad's crediting the production of his work to fictional characters as well as his unconscious, and by writers' use of pen names in general (Beebe 9). Beebe finds theoretical support for his notion of the "divided self" in C.G. Jung's comments on art and artists, which present the creative person as a duality, consisting of a human being with a personal life and an impersonal creative process, of which the former is an instrument or agent:

> Every creative person is a duality or a synthesis of contradictory attitudes. On the one side he is a human being with a personal life, while on the other side he is an impersonal creative process . . . As a human being, he may have moods and a will and personal aims, but as an artist, he is 'man' in a higher sense—he is 'collective man'—one who carries and shapes the unconscious psychic life of mankind (Beebe 10, with reference to C.G. Jung, *Modern Man in Search of a Soul*. Tr. Stanley Dell and Cary F. Barnes. London: Kegan Paul, Trench, Trubner, 1945, pp. 194-95.)

Beebe refers in turn to Jung's concepts of psychological and visionary art, the former proceeding from personal experience and the personal unconscious and the latter from the collective unconscious ("Psychology and Literature").

These eclectic but convergent views shed light on the elusive artistic selves in twentieth-century artist novels. The Romantic poets, by relating to the spirit in nature and speaking of mind and imagination in objective terms, lend credibility to the existence of the "objective psyche," which is otherwise explained by Jung as the collective unconscious, the source of our archetypes or universal images (including "self" along with *anima*, mother, father, trickster, old wise man, *et al.*). Van Wyck Brooks' perspective on self-expression as a "progressive identification of the personal with the universal" suggests that the quest for self is essentially a quest for universal meaning, shared by all (but the duty of artists to express), thus also a quest for relatedness. Maurice Beebe's discussion of the "divided self" provides numerous literary examples and support for psychological theory while indicating multiplicity in the patterns he finds. With regard to the "divided self," there seems to be abiding interest on the part of artists in twentieth-century portraits to reconcile artistic self and person, or the creative endeavor with personal life, even if this reconciliation calls for the subordination of personal life to creativity, of ego to self and to the experience of the totality of one's personality.

As noted above (according to Jung), the "self," conceived as a wholeness transcending consciousness, can only be experienced in its parts or aspects. In the literary portraits, the self is revealed empirically, by images or aspects of wholeness, or symbolically, by the perception or creation of symbols of wholeness. Self is expressed in the art work as well as perceptions and experiences during the growth of an artist that prefigure the art work. An avenue for intuitions and expressions of self is often provided by nature, for it is thought to be the realm, or transmitter, of the objective psyche, which comprises self. Another recurrent influence on expressions of self in the portraits is the artist's childhood, which has been described as open to the transcendent dimension, or, for lack of a representation of childhood, the child persisting in the mature artist, "an eternal child, something that is always becoming, is never completed" (Jung 1940, 284). Therefore, we find the most remarkable expressions of self in artist novels that represent both childhood and maturity, featuring a vital *puer* or *puella* in the adult artist, with M. Allen Cunningham's *Lost Son* and John Updike's *Seek My Face* in the fore. Dodie Smith's *I Capture the Castle* offers an interesting amalgam of child and adult in the adolescent narrator, Cassandra, who is also Smith's persona. Her childish, fairy tale vision of the castle enhances the reality she records with larger-than-life, archetypal dimensions (with characters suggestive of typical characters in fairy tales, as noted in Ch. 1, "Childhood"), so that Cassandra, a participant in the life of the castle, is a modern-day princess with a universal dimension as well as the precocious author of the story she records, reflecting Smith's youthful self.

An experience of self facilitated by the natural milieu is evident in the scene on the strand in Joyce's *A Portrait of the Artist as a Young Man*. At the beginning of this scene, Stephen is moved by a subliminal "elfin prelude," with a pattering of animals (symbolic of the spirit in nature according to Jung) to the rhythm of his inner music. Shortly thereafter, he envisions the winged form of Daedalus in the clouds, symbolic of his artistic self, and, walking onward, perceives a girl wading in the rivulet in the form of a wonderful bird, an *anima* image. The epiphany of Stephen's self on the strand might be taken as a pre-figuration of later developments (of the master craftsman who authors *Ulysses*) beyond the scope of *A Portrait*, for an integration of anima theoretically precedes the development of self. However, an integration of the anima perceived in the bird girl is indicated by the swoon to which Stephen succumbs after an invigorating walk, wherein he envisions a splendid flower opening in successions of unfolding petals—apt to be a mandāla image, thus a reconciling symbol, as well as an image of life, creativity, or the universe. (Jung cites mandālas with "a star, a sun, a flower, a cross of equal branches, a precious stone" at the center, among his historical models, *Psychology and Religion* 97.) In any case, this dream image appears to be a culmination of the sense of wholeness Stephen experiences on the strand, therefore a complementary image or variation of the brimming bowl to which Stephen is compared at the close of his education at Clongowes College and another image (beside the winged form of Daedalus in the clouds) of Stephen's newly discovered self.

In Cather's *The Song of the Lark,* Thea Kronborg proceeds from intuitions of a "friendly spirit" in the sand hills of Moonstone, Colorado, to communion with the spirit of ancient cliff dwellers in Panther Canyon, Arizona, where she recognizes her own spirit as part or parcel of a greater world spirit and senses the interconnection between her vocal art and human creativity in sum. Relation between herself and other selves, between personal and universal, is essential for her musical career because her voice and personality form a vessel for the expression of ideas and themes in musical scores other than her own. Thea's project is to develop the vessel to full potential, with musical standards and cultural ideals in mind, which she does throughout her childhood and years of musical training in Chicago. The clearest declaration of this project is given at the end of Thea's summer in Panther Canyon when, observing an eagle's flight, she exclaims, "O eagle of eagles! Endeavor, achievement, desire, glorious striving of human art!" (Cather 269) with confidence in herself and her decision to further her musical studies in Germany. Birds are symbolic of "thoughts and flights of mind," of "fantasies or intuitive ideas," Jung comments. The eagle, like the raven and the *lapis* (stone) or the hermaphroditic *rebis* represented with wings, is an alchemistic symbol signifying premonition or intuition, and all these symbols "depict the state of affairs that we call the self, in its role of transcending consciousness" (Jung 1940, 189). In addressing the eagle, Thea voices an intuition of her higher self as well as a desire to explore the limits of her self.

Rainer M. Rilke's search for wholeness, or quest for self, is enhanced by his incomplete, "unachieved" childhood, as represented in Cunningham's *Lost Son.* Initially equated with a longing for home, wholeness is sought in other people and places until Rainer realizes that it is solitude he needs to explore the limits of his expansive poetic self. He writes in his diary, "We must become human beings. We need eternity, because it alone gives our gestures room; and yet we know ourselves to be bounded by tight borders. We must, therefore, create an infinity within these limits—even here, where we no longer believe in boundlessness" (Florence Diary, 1898, quoted in Cunningham 294). As we know, Rainer eventually finds himself in isolation at the Castle at Muzot, Switzerland, where he writes *The Sonnets to Orpheus* in 1922, every one of which speaks of transcendent wholeness. As suggested by his dedication of *The Sonnets* to Orpheus, the god of music who retrieves his deceased wife, Eurydice, from the Underworld only to lose her on the return journey but to retain traces of the transcendent sphere in his exquisite art, Rainer's poetic self resonates with the myth of Orpheus. Rainer's interest in the transcendent realm of spirit accords with the philosophical and religious orientation of "Orphism," which is essentially an affirmation of the invisible world.

Instead of an explicit identification with Orpheus, like Stephen's identification with Daedalus in Joyce's *A Portrait*, Cunningham features several numinous experiences attesting to Rainer's intuitions of transcendent wholeness as well as his interest in the realm of the deceased. One of the earliest of these is Rainer's encounter with the sprawling acacia in an Alpine forest, which impresses him as animate being (spirit in nature or God speaking through nature) as it proceeds to transform itself to phlegm in his brain, whether by a will of its own or the poet's receptive capacity. Later, during his summer at Borgeby-gård in Sweden, Rainer investigates the chapel and crypt on the Nordlind estate, where he sees through a disintegrating portrait of the Chamberlain to his past life and character. After one of his Rodin lectures in Berlin, Rainer perceives the figure of his deceased father entering the auditorium momentarily and tipping his bowler hat in greeting (*cf.* Ch.2, "Receptivity," pp. 58-9).

In Paris, Rainer reaches out to people on the streets, to animals and flowers in the Zoo and Gardens, all of which interest him by their essences, or their reality behind appearances. He follows a spastic man to the St. Michel bridge, shielding him from onlookers' ridicule. He approaches peddlers with trays of shabby paraphernalia and mixes with invalids at the Hôtel Dieu, a hospital for the poor. At night he dreams of a homeless woman who was ousted from her bench at the Luxembourg Gardens. These episodes represented in *Lost Son* indicate an extraordinary sensibility that obligates him to express his empathy in poems, alongside the beauty he observes in his surroundings. Though spoken individually in the *New Poems* and *The Sonnets,* all beings and phenomena are felt and praised as integral, interrelated parts of a great unity, like the branches and tendrils of the ramifying tree that is a visible manifestation and symbol of transcendent spirit or deity.

With a few exceptions, the "self" in the representations of painters is best gleaned from the artwork, an empirical way, analogous to dreams, in which self comes forth. In Maugham's *The Moon and Sixpence,* Charles' inner vision of a distant isle amid blue seas and vast skies, where he might work in solitude, in harmony with nature, is suggestive of both center and periphery of his self. Also relevant is Charles' concern with eternity and its subtle rendition in his painting. The significance of his vision and his concern with eternity is articulated later by an observer's, Dr. Coutras', response to the murals Charles painted on the walls of his cottage in Tahiti, featuring primeval scenes as of the beginning of the world. The human beings in these murals seemed to belong to heaven and earth, the trees infused with a mystery and spirit that evaded the doctor. In a word, the vision was sublime

(Maugham 230). We also have Dr. Coutras' descriptions of a still life of fruits, in which the colors were at once opaque and translucent, static and vibrant, like the terrain Charles inhabited that flared with color in daytime and was supremely quiescent at night. The mixture of sensuality and spirituality in Charles' art reflected aspects of his person noted by the narrator: the curiously "spiritual sensuality" of his face and the crude, "primitive" outward demeanor of an artist wholly dedicated to the expression of his inner vision. As shown in the paintings, particularly the translucent aspect of their earthly, material contours, this vision comprised intimations of eternity in human life—indeed, a universal dimension of self, attained through the painter's faith in his inner vision.

Surprisingly, there are points of comparison between Charles' painting in Maugham's *The Moon and Sixpence* and Lily's in Woolf's *To the Lighthouse,* different though their personalities may be. Lily paints on an island—the Isle of Skye off the coast of Great Britain—surrounded by vast skies and the waters of a blue bay beyond the edge of the lawn where she places her easel. In her painting, envisioned as having a light, shimmering surface and a solid base, Lily aims to express the daily miracles and illuminations that brighten community life, centering on terra firma in the person of Mrs. Ramsay. While the illuminations pertain to the motifs of light and sight, to eyes and their individual beams and rays in Woolf's novel, they also intimate heavenly light or the translucence of eternity in everyday life.

In a conventional perspective the integration of light and darkness, surface and depth, in Lily's painting indicates an interrelation of masculine and feminine principles, the former traditionally associated with light and sky, the latter with darkness and earth (as in myths of sky gods and earth goddesses). Perhaps this is Lily's achievement, expressive of her "self," but unintentional and unconscious because the author's emphasis is on the process of interrelation and integration typical of the feminine mode, following from the feminine values of relation, love, and community. Lily's painting is motivated by her love and admiration for Mrs. Ramsay, which reflect Woolf's at least partial or subliminal identification with Mrs. Ramsay; Mrs. Ramsay is both the main character in Woolf's novel and a central figure in Lily's painting. The kind of surface and depth Lily wishes to represent in her painting is superficially analogous to Mrs. Ramsay's personal beauty, comprising exquisite facial features and depth of character, but in view of Mrs. Ramsay's recurrent reflections on the darkness she senses beneath her experience (for instance, her remark "Beneath it is all dark, it is all spreading, it is unfathomably deep" or the comparison of herself to a "wedge of darkness," Woolf 62-63) and Mr. Ramsay's immersion in the life of intellect, surface and depth pertain to the interrelation of masculine and feminine principles, shown in the exemplary relationship between Mr. and Mrs. Ramsay and latent in the artist's (Lily's and Woolf's) androgyny. Thus the feminine creative mode and feminine values affirmed by Woolf via Lily's painting are integral parts of the larger feminine self that is interrelated with its masculine counterpart.

We see no completed artwork in John Updike's fictional portrait of Jackson Pollock, *Seek My Face*, but we find clues to the painter's self in his person and approach to art. Updike features the process of painting, especially Zack's innovative techniques of dripping and pouring paint as he moved around the canvas and drew in the air in an effort to get his self into the painting. Zack's method of painting, compared to the practice of Indian sand painters, was designed to convey the unconscious dimension of psyche, in accord with prevailing tenets of abstract expression that were influenced by Surrealism. Considering Zack's self-expression, we may also remember his widow's, Hope's, remarks about Zack's childlikeness and his fervent interest in natural phenomena, like the rhythm of the ocean or the change of colors in spring, which amounted to Zack's identification with nature: "spring came . . . In the dunes, there were all these tiny pink blossoms . . . The ocean . . . softened in color, became a mild china blue. Zack was ecstatic. I could hardly get him to come indoors" (Updike 79-80).

Hope occasionally mentions the dominant colors in Zack's drip paintings as well as the impressions she had in viewing them, of peace, balance, and calm, sometimes a "spinning feeling" (101). She refers to the process of naming paintings according to the moods evoked or the motifs related to natural phenomena. For lack of substantial description of the artwork, we may turn to Jackson Pollock's painting, to which Updike's portrait adheres like a glove. Pollock's paintings, submitted to fractal analysis in order to confirm the authenticity of previously unknown works, resulted in a fractal dimension similar to that of natural phenomena, like mountains, rocks, or fern leaves (as discussed at more length in Chapter 10). The "chaos" associated with Pollock's painting turns out to be analogous to the geometry of the natural world, and his signature style equivalent with nature's "fractal signature." These findings correlate with Updike's portrayal of Zack as a natural being as well as the aesthetic theories cited in the novel (particularly Hermann Hochmann's "push and pull" and Roger Merebien's reference to the "aesthetic" as "merely the sensuous aspect of the world . . . not the end of art but a means . . . of getting at . . . the infinite background of feeling," Updike 45).

We may conclude that Zack identified with nature to the extent that he became a medium and transmitter of the unconscious, as nature is considered to be in the Romantic perspective. Or that he emulated nature to such degree that, instead of representing it through his individual prism, like most artists, he attempted to simulate nature and to simply *be* in his paintings rather than depict a chosen scene or object, or express a particular vision of nature. Thus his self shows forth in a spectrum of color combinations and a variety of patterns that convey moods, feelings, and states of mind during his painting process rather than intimations of transcendent wholeness. Expressive of a return to nature in an era of industrial progress and technology, highlighting process in a society focused on products and ends, Zack's unique signature style attained legendary status, not to mention popularity and fame resulting from publicity in *Life* magazine.

In each portrait the self is shown in parts or aspects of itself, for, in transcending consciousness, the self cannot be fully grasped or fathomed, only intuited and sought in attempts at self-expression. The whole self approximates divinity, as indicated by C. G. Jung's discussion of Christ as symbol of the archetype of self ("Aion," in *Psyche and Symbol* 34 *ff.*), a God image that is perfect in its embrace of individuality and universality, unitemporality and eternity (visualized as axes of a *quaternio*)—to which the psychological self aspires. The artist, deemed unusually sensitive and open to the transcendent sphere, may be able to render universal and eternal dimensions of human experience by way of empathy with fellow human beings and communion with world soul or spirit, and thereby to attest to the interrelatedness of all beings, as well as the potential largeness of the individual self. Rainer makes considerable progress in this direction; nevertheless, he describes himself as an "eternal beginner." Thea admits that she has a long way to go to reach "the level of her source" that is her measure. The difficulties and contradictions that Stephen experiences en route to recognizing his artistic vocation speak of the challenges he will face in exploring the boundaries of his self and realizing his potential. By identifying with nature, Zack implies the imperfection of the human condition or his sense of the impossibility of otherwise getting to "the infinite background." Charles, having completed the murals that best convey a vision he has harbored for decades, asks that these murals be destroyed after his death, as if to suggest that he had reached beyond himself in painting a sublime, primeval scene. No matter the age of the artist or extent of career represented, each portrait presents the artist as a traveler on an endless quest for self.

-CHAPTER 4-

Kinship with Nature

The artist novels offer an abundance of visually exquisite scenery for the reader's imagination to conjure: the Kohlers' garden, a spacious strand, Alpine forest, desert canyons, Swedish countryside, the Isle of Skye, Long Island countryside, and tropical landscape. Moreover, these settings are represented as animate places with vitality in their constituent parts, like whispering flowers, fructuous air, talking trees, powerful rocks, or fertile, luxuriant earth. It is no wonder that they stimulate the senses, serving to refine aesthetic sensibility, or that they evoke an urge for self-expression. But one may ask why certain places are conducive to revelations and transformative experiences that influence creativity and the discovery of individual aims, aesthetic agenda, or concepts of beauty.

We have noted previously, in Chapter 3, that in psychoanalytical theory, nature is the domain of the unconscious, or objective psyche, and is therefore propitious for explorations of self, conceived as "a wholeness beyond the reach of consciousness" (Jung 1940, 176). Now we side with nature and the point of view of ecological psychology as well as traditional lore, which posit the presence of spirit in nature. This spirit, comprised of ancestral spirits and nature spirits that dwell in woods and wild places according to folklore, might explain the Romantic poets' dialogues with nature more directly than psychoanalytic theory; likewise the harmonizing and communing with nature that we find in artist novels. Spirit of place may guide, or more precisely *inspire,* poets and artists, like all people, to the discovery of their particular gifts or individual aesthetics and so facilitate their participation in world spirit, *anima mundi*, of which spirit of place partakes. As evidenced in the literary portraits, this kind of inspiration ranges from revelations and transformative experiences to insights and intuitions that imperceptibly influence an artwork or musical performance.

In his book *Nature as Teacher and Healer* (1992), which includes a survey of the lore and literature of place, James Swan comments that "the spirit of a place is the result of the interplay between the spiritual world and nature, and the collective product of the interactions of the people of that area too" (225). While the physical elements of place adhere to a particular geographical location, the spirit presumably has universal qualities and appeal, for our heroes and heroines find kinship and inspiration in locations far from home, where they go by chance as well as by choice.

In Willa Cather's *The Song of the Lark,* Thea's vacation at the Ottenburg ranch in Arizona begins with her ride from the train station in Flagstaff, from plateau downward through pine forest, that anticipates her immersion in spirit of place all summer. As she leans back in her seat in the democrat wagon (a light wagon, usually with two seats and a top) and sees snow-covered mountain peaks disappearing behind rows of sun-streaked pines, she is greeted by "the thrilling blue of the new sky and the song of the wind in the *piñons"* (Cather 247-8). The scene exudes vitality not only by its breathtaking natural phenomena but also the presence of the spirit of Navahos, who once inhabited this area of Northern Arizona, as suggested by Cather's comparison between trees and Navahos in the opening section of Part IV, "The Ancient People," in her novel:

> The San Francisco Mountain lies in Northern Arizona, above
> Flagstaff, and its blue slopes and snowy summit entice the eye
> for a hundred miles across the desert. About its base lie the pine
> forests of the Navahos, where the great red-trunked trees live out
> their peaceful centuries in that sparkling air .... The great pines

stand at a considerable distance from each other. Each tree grows alone, murmurs alone, thinks alone. They do not intrude upon each other. The Navahos are not much in the habit of giving or asking of help. Their language is not a communicative one, and they never attempt an interchange of personality in speech. Over their forests there is the same inexorable reserve. Each tree has its exalted power to bear (Cather 247).

The presence of ancestral spirit remarked here prefigures Thea's numerous reflections on the ancient cliff dwellers of Panther Canyon, stimulated by her explorations of the rock cliffs and her walks along canyon trails. (The ancient people, referred to as Pueblo Indians in the fiction, are identified in the Notes as "The Sinagua, a member of the Hakataya regional group of prehistoric inhabitants of the American Southwest," with peak development *ca.* 1125-1215, Harbison in Cather 425.)

Thea is never truly alone in her days of solitude and restful retreat in Panther Canyon, for the spirit of nature is felt in every one of its facets. The rock rooms in the cliffs, maintained by sun and wind, are lined with "tough little cedars that twisted themselves into the very doorways" (250) and emitted their fragrance into the chambers. As Thea lies in her niche on warm blankets, she can hear "the strident whir of the big locusts" and "the light, ironical laughter of the quaking asps" (251). The slope downward to the stream is populated by yucca, cactus, and pale dwarf trees that provide the hot rock with shadow. At the base of the canyon, "a thread of bright, flickering green" consisting of cottonwoods, makes for "a living, chattering screen" (250) by the stream in which Thea bathes each morning.

The spirit of the canyon is also felt in its entirety, as if it were an animated being with moods to be reckoned with, fleetingly compared to an old man with rheum. On most days the atmosphere of the canyon was cheerful and hopeful, especially at sunrise, when

The red sun rose rapidly above the tops of the blazing pines, and its glow burst into the gulf, about the very doorstep on which

Thea sat . . . . The dripping cherry bushes, the pale aspens, and the frosty *piñons* were glittering and trembling, swimming in the liquid gold. All the pale, dusty little herbs of the bean family . . . became for a moment individual and important, their silky leaves quite beautiful with dew and light (264).

When accosted at night or in stormy weather, the desert creature was apt to come forth as sullen or frightening. On their descent from the cliffs one night, Thea and Fred confront a dull, indifferent, or malignant being, characterized by chill and darkness; the voice of the stream is now "hollow and threatening" (263). On another occasion, caught by rolls of thunder, they wade through turbid atmosphere along cliffs that appear murky green, then purple:

The yuccas, the cedars, and *piñons* stood dark and rigid, like bronze. The swallows flew up with sharp, terrified twitterings . . . the light changed to purple. Clouds of dark vapor, like chlorine gas, began to float down from the head of the canyon and hung between them and the cliff-houses in the opposite wall . . . . The air was positively venomous-looking, and grew colder every minute. The thunder seemed to crash against one cliff, then against the other, and to go shrieking off into the inner canyon (Cather 271).

Such a range of wilderness, hardly cozy and quaint beyond Thea's niche in the rock cliffs, is presented as a scene conducive to new awakenings, sensual and spiritual.

The stark contrasts inherent in the Arizona desert, exuding its particular spirit, summon to mind the changing rhythm of the tropical terrain inhabited by Charles Strickland in Maugham's *The Moon and Sixpence*. As seen by Captain René Brunot on his visit with Charles and Ata in the fold of a mountain that held their home, this corner of paradise, flaring with warm, exuberant colors and the fragrance of mangoes and cocoanuts in daytime, came to rest at night, with a scent of white flowers and serenity proportionate to the intensity of its diurnal vitality. The supernatural beauty of this place intimated the world of spirit as well as another dimension of consciousness to the visitor: "It was a night so beautiful that your soul seemed hardly able to bear the prison of the body. You felt that it was ready to be wafted away on the immaterial air, and death bore all the aspect of a beloved friend" (Maugham 212). Brunot voices the aspect of eternity in this tropical terrain that harmonized with the painter's inner vision and therefore wielded influence on his art.

In M. Allen Cunningham's *Lost Son,* we find the gentler rhythm of the Swedish countryside at Borgeby-gård, where Rainer M. Rilke resides one summer. Here the calm and stability of cultivated farmland are disrupted, the mild air penetrated, by pealing rain on the evening of Rainer's exploration of chapel and crypt on the edge of the estate. The chapel with its caving roof, unprotected from the elements for years, houses not only spiders and a stork but also the spirit of ancestors, as we may gather from the poet's entry into communication with portraits of the deceased Chamberlain and his wives. The transcendent moments of this episode, eliciting the Orphic dimension of Rainer's self, inspire the completion of *The Cornet,* concerning the poet's own ancestor, Christophe Rilke.

Such powerful places as Panther Canyon, Tahiti, and Borgeby-gård call for personal adjustment to the natural milieu previous to encounters with its spirit in the form of revelations or intuitions of another dimension of consciousness. In terms of ecological psychology, one must "bioentrain": "harmonize with the external field until inner biological rhythms and fields become identical with external ones" (Swan 205). With a few exceptions, the process of harmonizing with nature is taken for granted or abbreviated in the artist novels because the focus is on the *effects* of kinship with nature. In *The Moon and Sixpence,* we hear about Charles' inner vision and the finding of its counterpart in Tahiti, but the bioentraining is a *fait accompli* when Captain Brunot visits Charles and describes the island paradise. Rainer's meditative perambulations of the Swedish countryside—open pastures, hills, streams, and abundant woods that "enfold" him—are interrupted by travel to Copenhagen, an episode in his liaison with Lou Andreas-Salomé (Cunningham's *Lost Son*). Stephen's harmonizing with nature on the day of his walk on the strand is a matter of minutes (Joyce's *A Portrait*). The literary representations may reflect the predominantly urban culture of their authors or the popular view of an attainment of kinship with nature as something antiquated, belonging to the customs of traditional societies or "primitive" peoples. In Smith's *I Capture the Castle,* Cassandra prepares for Midsummer Eve rites with reference to a folklore manual, which prescribes libations as a gesture of respect for spirit of place, herbs to ward off evil spirits, wildflowers for garlands (symbolic of the circle of life), and dancing around the fire to enhance the feeling of unity with nature. Her observance of this ritual is associated with her childhood with Rose, as by society it might be attributed to the childhood of the human species. Yet it is a joyful adventure, like Topaz's communing with nature on the mound that is a source of strength and vitality for her creative spirit.

Harmonizing with nature is occasionally implied in the artists' embrace of natural milieu for the sake of health, or wholeness. The beneficial influence of spirit of place on creativity is then correlated with its conduciveness to health. Thea's vacation in Arizona is initially intended as a cure for depression and fatigue consequent to her bout with tonsillitis, as well as a change of scene from Chicago weather. Lily's visit with the Ramsays on the Isle of Skye is a form of recreation that is also auspicious for painting. In Rainer's experience, the summer at Borgeby-gård is so recuperative that it becomes creative: "Everything about the place is recuperative—and to such a degree that it must all . . . become *creative* as well" (Cunningham 275). Stephen's walk on the strand proceeds from a feeling of vigor and a burst of youthful energy adequate to an appreciation of the splendid day ("a day of dappled sea-borne clouds"), such that the attunement of his inner self to outer scene facilitates revelations of his identity and life itself. Through Stephen's experience of wholeness, harmony, and radiance on the strand, and its translation to aesthetic theory with reference to St. Thomas Aquinas, Joyce verbalizes a pattern of human interchange with nature that is implicit in Cather's *The Song of the Lark* and might be inferred in numerous other portraits.

Thea's attainment of harmony with nature at Panther Canyon is virtually equivalent with her experience of wholeness. Upon arrival in Flagstaff, she surrenders to the new environment: "The personality of which she was so tired seemed to let go of her. The high, sparkling air drank it up like blotting paper . . . . The old fretted lines . . . which defined her,—made her Thea Kronborg, Bower's accompanist, a soprano with a faulty middle voice,—were all erased" (Cather 247-8). She relaxes her ego consciousness, relying on her sensitivity and receptivity to stimulation in the environment until the health she gains brings forth an integration of body, mind, and soul that attends her best, for harmonious, days in the canyon. Contrary to her routine in Chicago, Thea's vacation in Arizona consists of pastimes suited to her personality and the natural milieu, requiring minimal effort and planning. At every step of her routine in Panther Canyon, Thea is enveloped by the elements, which signify wholeness in nature. She is refreshed by water in the stream each morning, as well as a breeze moving about the branches of shimmering cottonwoods. As she climbs upward to the rock cliffs, she breathes pure air that sustains her in more ways than one. Lying in her niche in the cliffs, she is warmed by sun-baked rocks beneath her blanket and sunlight surrounding her, making for heat therapy that brings slumber. In her waking hours, she is entertained by chirping birds, lizards leaping about the rocks, and an array of cactus and chokeberry blossoms amid strata of earth-colored rock formations.

When Thea begins to explore the rock chambers for relics of the ancient cliff dwellers' art, the canyon becomes a source of nourishment for mind and soul: a cultural museum of sorts with the advantages of an outdoor facility and primary location. Thea has opportunity to handle fragments of pottery and utensils, to surmise their original forms and the ways in which they were used on the premises, thus to participate imaginatively in the life of the ancients and to reflect on their creative spirit and intellectual capacity. The spiritual connection, proceeding from intuition and breathing the same air, yields a sense of belonging to the cultural continuum, therefore a new perspective on her role and responsibility in this theater. The intellectual reflection, especially the perception of herself as a vessel for voice, comparable to the function of pottery as vessel for food and water (respectively source of life and element of life) refers on the one hand to Thea's notion that voice is essentially vitality, resulting from her sensual awakenings in the canyon; on the other, to the connection she now feels with the ancient people, whereby her particular vocal talent is a part of a whole, interrelated with all other creative endeavor. These strands of mental and spiritual integration appear to be inextricable from the physical recreation she enjoys at Panther Canyon.

As in Stephen's experience on the strand, the wholeness, or integration of body, mind, and soul, that Thea attains involves a sense of harmony with nature. If we take Stephen's and St. Thomas Aquinas' definitions of wholeness, harmony, and radiance as guidelines, "harmony" is the consonant relation among parts of a complex whole (as well as the relation of part to whole and whole to part), so there cannot be wholeness without harmony or harmony without wholeness. Much as wholeness and harmony are preliminary to Stephen's epiphanies, Thea's experience of integration and attunement to natural milieu precipitate her definitive awakening to artistic vocation, her new insights, and self awareness, signaled by her address to an eagle one morning. Furthermore, the radiance that Fred notices in Thea on the occasion of his visit to the ranch recalls Stephen's radiance upon his identification with the winged form of Daedalus in the clouds. Whereas the scene on the strand in Joyce's *Portrait* is concentrated in one day, the Panther Canyon episode in Cather's *Lark* progresses over two months, offering more information about the process of Thea's harmonizing with nature as well as her receptivity to spirit of place.

When Cather portrays Thea surrendering her personality to the pine forest en route to the ranch and later to the elements in the canyon, recurrently mentioning her passivity and lassitude during the early part of summer, she sets the stage for subconscious influences on Thea's mind via nature. Thea's inactive state at Panther Canyon is somewhat comparable to Rainer's withdrawal to isolation to let impressions gestate within him, Zack's meditation in the barn, and Lily's requirement of privacy in her station on the edge of the lawn. Thea's experience shows that submission to the mysterious spirit of nature as well as its palpable stimuli is eventually rewarded by greater vitality of body, mind, and soul: enhanced consciousness or even entry into another dimension of consciousness.

The interchange between artist and nature consists of an alternation of conscious effort and musings, which appears to be fortuitous but with a purpose intimated in the ensuing changes of perception. As it were the spirit inhabiting nature demanded further effort on the part of the artist to make something of his or her gifts. The artist is challenged to express these gifts, to bring forth inner visions, and re-create the discovery of one's individual part in the wholeness of nature. This is what the artists in the literary portraits are intent on doing, especially in a series of portraits that is concerned with aesthetics rather than socially or politically engaged art. In secular terms, they try to fulfill their obligations to nature and humankind; in religious terms, to God, as they reach for higher selves and standards intuited in transcendent moments.

We find traces of religious experience in the artists' interchange with nature, as in Stephen's exclamation "O heavenly God!" when transfixed by the sight of the bird-girl in the rivulet, or blends of secular and religious attitudes, reflecting individual concepts of religion, such as Rainer's veneration of living beings—human, animal, or plant—and belief in the afterlife inherent in his acceptance of the transcendent sphere. Most often we find parallels between secular and religious experience, implicit or explicit, inviting the reader's discernment of one or the other according to his or her convictions. On the one hand, there is Cather's *The Song of the Lark* and Woolf's *To the Lighthouse*, where religious beliefs might only be inferred. On the other, in Maugham's *The Moon and Sixpence* there is an explicit parallel, presented by means of various narrators' perspectives on Charles' creative personality and his painting, particularly as these manifest themselves in the isle of his dreams, Tahiti, as a result of the harmony attained between Charles' inner vision and the tropical terrain.

One segment of the parallel between religious and secular experience, concerning Charles' pursuit of painting and adventure in the South Seas in sum, is voiced by Captain René Brunot, a middle-aged Frenchman who befriended the painter on his business trips to Tahiti and admired his art. Brunot feels sympathy with the painter on the basis of his own work in creating a plantation where there was barren desert in the nearby Paumotus. He shares the search for beauty with Charles ("We were both aiming at the same thing . . . Beauty," he says, Maugham 214) although their individual means of expression differ: clearing brush, cultivating land, and building a house for the family versus expressing visions of beauty on canvas. Brunot admits he couldn't have achieved all he did without his belief in God, comparing his own Catholic faith with Charles' faith in his vision and his artistic vocation. Brunot regards Charles as an eternal pilgrim, "haunted by a divine nostalgia" (215).

The parallel between secular and religious pilgrimages is resumed in Dr. Coutras' response to the murals he sees in Charles' cottage, painted during the last few years of his life (a fictive invention on Maugham's part, with no counterpart in Gauguin's artwork). The murals represented a primeval forest in a tremendous, mysterious composition that awed and amazed the doctor. The wall paintings were both sensuous and spiritual, strange and frightening, evocative of associations with magic or the occult pertaining to "the hidden depth of nature" (227); the forms and colors of the composition changed forever the doctor's perception of human beings and natural phenomena. In a subsequent account of his impressions to the English narrator, Coutras likens the murals to "a hymn to the beauty of the human form . . . and the praise of Nature" (230) with earthly and heavenly dimensions, as well as a vision of the Garden of Eden. He compares his impressions of Charles' murals with his feelings upon visiting the Sistine Chapel in Rome, where he was confronted by the sublime. He sees the composition in both secular and religious light: a parallel, the lines of which are interwoven in Charles' "primitive" vision that harks back to a time with no distinctions between secular and religious realms.

Dr. Coutras' mention of imagery of the Garden of Eden in the murals recalls Captain Brunot's description of Charles' and Ata's corner of paradise in the fold of a mountain as an enchanted place, with "the beauty of the Garden of Eden" (210). The murals, which Coutras interprets as a fulfillment of Charles' vision and his life's purpose, were undoubtedly inspired by the Tahitian landscape and the spirit of the island, to the extent that these resonated with his inner vision. The aspect of the Garden of Eden is an expression of the universal dimension of Charles' self while the combination of sensuality and spirituality, as well as the strangeness of the composition, have to do with Charles' signature style that marked his painting from the start but was more pronounced when his inner rhythm accorded with the outer rhythms of the environment. Thus Coutras' responses to the murals offer commentary on their individual and universal dimensions, parameters more relevant to a discussion of the influence of place on artistic endeavor than changing distinctions between secular and religious perspectives. In sum, the universal dimension coincides with the religious aspect—both of which pertain to "a reality behind appearances" in Van Wyck Brooks' words for the universal dimension—while the parallel between religious and secular experience with regard to Charles' painting is formed in the eyes of a beholder, such as Captain Brunot or Dr. Coutras in Maugham's novel.

As indicated by Charles' remarkable achievements in Tahiti, Thea's insight into her vocal art in Panther Canyon, Stephen's discovery of a system of aesthetics on the strand, or Rainer's acute perception in the Swedish countryside, the attainment of harmony with nature is conducive to artistic growth along with enhanced awareness of self as individual and self in relation to community or cosmos. Harmony, an adjustment of inner rhythm to external rhythm, as well as the consonant relation of part to whole and whole to part, inevitably consists of an affirmation of individual rhythm and one's unique part in the scheme of multiplicity in unity that characterizes the realm of nature as well as the cultural continuum. While nature is an avenue for the exploration of self in the sense of progression to its universal dimension, it is also a source of inspiration for individual aims, projects, or conceptions of beauty, by virtue of resonances between inner and outer rhythms and patterns, concurrences of the subjective and objective, or the principle that like attracts like. In his chapter titled "Personal Power and Nature," Swan presents a similar perspective in the words of Rudolf Steiner (philosopher, scientist, educator, 1861-1925): "If we enter deeply into the nature of the living world, we naturally begin to create in such a way that what we apprehend inwardly in the spirit can take on the most manifold outward forms" (Swan 228, with reference to Steiner's Lecture of Sept. 28, 1921, *In Partnership with Nature* 1981, 40). Nature is sufficiently diverse to be a mirror for everyone.

The discovery of these individual aims or aesthetics, as well as their development and refinement in a particular medium of expression, make for the aforementioned reciprocation in the artist's interchange with nature. The bond with nature might be mediated by other sources of inspiration, notably personal relationships (that may involve *anima* or *animus* influence), as shown in Rainer's relationship with Lou, Thea's with Fred, Lily's with Mrs. Ramsay, or Stephen's with Emma Clery. On the other hand, kinship with nature might be disturbed by personal relationships and social obligations, to the detriment of the latter and eventual isolation of the artist, as seen in the life stories of Rainer and Charles, unique poet and revolutionary visual artist, respectively, who valued their artistic gifts and individuality above everything else.

From the standpoint of the artists' relation to nature, the selves they express are subliminal identifications of inner visions or images with their counterparts in the realm of nature; in other words, they are individual appropriations of principles, patterns, or images in nature that are universal but have special attraction to their perceptive capacities. Examples of patterns and principles adapted by artists in the literary portraits are transformation, radiance, vitality, integrity, vibrant stasis, and the interrelation between surface and depth. The process of identifying inner with outer refers to the relation of microcosm to macrocosm, voiced in Joyce's *Portrait* and implied in Cather's *Lark*. These novels suggest, on behalf of other portraits, that the artists' individual projects and interests stem from identifications of inner and outer images in childhood and depend on individual circumstances, experiences, and chance events, as well as the urge for self-expression and self-confidence that are strengthened in episodes of communing with spirit of place.

Rainer, who is extraordinarily open to the transcendent sphere, sees all phenomena and beings on a continuum of temporality to transcendence, so he assumes the project of describing their essences, or the spiritual dimension of their being, which is the universal dimension. The objects of his poems become symbolic of a whole greater than themselves and are consequently fuller, richer, and more significant as particular parts of a whole. A tree in the Alpine forest is symbolic of the objective psyche in nature; the panther in the Paris Zoo evokes the predicament of all caged wild animals; the hydrangea in the Gardens suggests evanescent beauty and life as well as the heavens when its blue merges with the horizon. Every phenomenon is transformed by its relation to the whole, which includes the transcendent realm: by the influence of the invisible on the visible, or in S. T. Coleridge's explanation of symbols, the translucence of the eternal in the temporal, the general in the especial. Transformation is therefore the principle of nature that dominates Rainer M. Rilke's poetry and underlies his individual style (epitomized in the *Elegies* and *Sonnets to Orpheus*), as suggested by M. Allen Cunningham's *Lost Son*.

Among the painters, Charles Strickland also relies on his inner vision more than outer reality in his painting, for he is concerned with the expression of an aspect of eternity in his art. When his inner vision finds its objective correlative in the tropical terrain of Tahiti, his self-expression is facilitated by the natural milieu. The effect of vibrant stasis that he achieves in his painting, for instance, in the still-life of fruits gifted to Dr. Coutras that combined opacity and richness in its colors with a lustrous, translucent quality, reflects the coalescence of serenity and exuberance on the tropical island, images of which he had harbored in himself since his apprenticeship in Paris (Somerset Maugham's *The Moon and Sixpence*).

Lily Briscoe is interested in the interrelation of surface and depth in nature and wants to express it in her painting because, like Mrs. Ramsay, with whom she sympathizes, and the author, Virginia Woolf, whom she impersonates in *To the Lighthouse,* she intuits the dark basin of reality beneath the flutter of daily activity, conversations, and appearances. As a woman, Lily is attracted to relationships in general, but as a woman visual artist, she identifies with the relation between the blue waters surrounding the Isle of Skye as well as blossoming hedges on the lawn and the base of the island, a volcanic mountain. The geometrical relation is mirrored in Mrs. Ramsay's person, with beautiful outward features resting on a solid, earthy matriarchal character. In Woolf's novel, there is a parallel between the beauty of her main character and scenery on the Isle of Skye, represented in Lily's painting by abstract shapes for Mrs. Ramsay and a tree, within a composition designed to reveal a light, shimmering surface anchored in a solid base.

In John Updike's *Seek My Face,* Zack McCoy identifies with all of the natural phenomena surrounding him: with the variety and vitality of nature, as opposed to a recurrent pattern or principle. His ecstasy in springtime, when he sees the colors of the ocean mellowing and the days on Long Island lengthening, presumably expresses his Dionysian aspect that pertains especially to spring. By his innovative techniques of pouring and spattering paint onto canvases, Zack expresses his various moods, feelings, thoughts, and sense impressions as if these were natural phenomena. His paintings, from pastel watercolors to black and white biomorphs on canvas to primary colors in abstract compositions, reflect nature's variety, with its alternations of dark and light, density and transparence, calm and turbulence, height and depth, fluidity and rigidity—and these in a multitude of nuances resulting from the rhythms of his body as he moved around the canvas with paintbrush or tube.

The radiance Stephen Dedalus experiences on the strand upon awakening to his artistic vocation correlates with the radiance of color and light in nature, imaged in the opening flower he envisions in a swoon toward the end of this scene in James Joyce's *A Portrait.* The correlation is mediated by Stephen's perception of a girl wading in the rivulet as a marvelous seabird, an *anima* influence. However, the bird was a symbol of inspiration, a conveyor of the breath or spirit that anima literally signifies, before the psychological concept was formulated and given a range of meanings, from the image of the feminine in a male to the archetype of psyche and archetype of life, as well as mediatrix to the unconscious. From a "primitive" perspective, Stephen's perception of the bird-girl, by which he is awestruck, is a moment of intuiting the spirit in nature. After some brisk strolling along the beach, when Stephen is processing the revelatory image, he falls into a swoon, which emphasizes the subliminal quality of his perception, or altered dimension of consciousness that is preliminary to kinship with nature. ("Kinship ties between person and nature originate" with "glimpses into another dimension of consciousness," Swan comments, 116.) The vision brought by the swoon, of a splendid flower with layers of petals, crimson to pale rose, emitting light as they unfold in succession, is an image of life or the creative principle or the universe symbolized in a flower, but for Stephen it is essentially the radiance he has associated with feminine beauty and the element of St. Thomas Aquinas' aesthetic theory that he would find most interesting. The vision of the flower might be taken as a part of Stephen's self, a mandāla image, because it is an image of nature with which he identifies and therefore appropriates to his poetry and aesthetic theory.

Thea Kronborg in Willa Cather's *The Song of the Lark* attunes her singing to whatever lyrics or musical scores she performs, from the whispering flowers in a song by Heine to the throes of semi-divine Norse heroines in Wagnerian opera. One might say Thea identifies with nature in sum, or with nature's variety, but it turns out that her achievements rest on her integral approach to musical performance: her effort to sing for the idea that ties a song or score together, so that all subsidiary parts, with their nuances and accompanying gestures, follow from her comprehension of the whole. Her integral approach recalls the principle of harmony, the consonant relation among parts of a whole (as well as the relation of part to whole and whole to part), pertaining to organicism in nature. Thea appears to have intuited organicism and harmony since her childhood, when she explored the sand hills beyond Moonstone and enjoyed leisure hours in the Kohlers' garden; therefore, she gains so much during her summer in Panther Canyon, where she has a chance to experience wholeness and harmony sensually while basking in the elements; spiritually and mentally, by communing with the spirit of place and reflecting on the life and art of the ancient cliff dwellers.

While the principles and patterns are universal and might be adapted by many artists, the particular ways in which they resonate with a certain personality (a "self") and the manner in which an artist adapts them to his or her means of expression make for unique styles in writing, signatures in painting, and presences in musical performance. The individuality inspired by kinship with nature and identifications with facets of nature also demonstrates an artist's urge for self-expression and unique aesthetic sensibility (related to sensuality or receptivity), which is usually formed in childhood. Thus Willa Cather's notion of a vessel as metaphor for art and artist, described as a sheath or mold to hold an element of life, might be applied to all artists who appropriate and mold a pattern or principle of nature according to their experiences and perceptions, producing original artwork.

-CHAPTER 5-

Creative Work

To complement the notion of artist as day-dreamer or visionary, there is the reality of art—the poem, book, painting, musical or dramatic performance—which entails effort and labor in its making. The work of art is usually twofold, consisting of an inner, mental process of germination and growth of an idea or vision, and the formation of the vehicle for its expression in words, elements of visual composition, or musical sounds. Mature works of art might be preceded by decades of preparation and practice in a chosen medium of expression, nourished by inner growth and cultivation of a particular talent. If the most characteristic trait of an artist is the urge for self-expression, the most typical behaviors are experimentation with the possibilities of a medium of expression and laboring over technique with wholehearted dedication to one's craft. Therefore, artists might seem to be living in a world of their own, a magic circle and a smithy, of both dream and drudgery, as they do occasionally in the literary portraits.

When we think of workers in literature, we may conjure the miners represented in Émile Zola's *Germinal* (1884), the meat packers in Upton Sinclair's *The Jungle* (1906), or peasant farmers and laborers in the social realism of the former Soviet era (c. 1944-1988). Work and workers are the subject matter of these slices of life in a particular place and time. By contrast, in the artist's novel—a variation of the *Bildungsroman,* a novel about character development—the subject matter is an individual artist's growth, life, or career, which is apt to be romantic in post-Romantic literature. It will feature adventures in space and time as well as odysseys in an artist's inner landscape, exotic settings, and romantic relationships. Yet an artist's work is the *raison d'être* of this literary genre and its attention to the personality that has charmed society by its writing, painting, or singing. If we look closely at the adventures that comprise setting, character, and plot, we find work as the artist's challenge, or action, as in drama, necessitating the resolution of conflict between the urge for self-expression and social expectations, or between one's dedication to creative endeavor and commitment to family. Work, as challenge or action, is the wheel at the center on which everything else revolves (beyond an artist's childhood), which is to say that work is the theme or at least a recurrent motif, adhering to other narrative elements in an artist novel.

Work is a recurrent motif as both an artist's challenge and art, for art is often equated with work. Take the Latin word for work, *opus,* pl. *opera,* used to number artists' works, especially musical compositions; Jung's consideration of *opus* as imaginative work, or the alchemists' use of *opus* for the chemical work of producing gold, elixir, or the philosopher's stone from various raw materials due to their association of the word with soulful, mindful endeavor (as Moore explains in *Care of the Soul,* 184-5.) In M. Allen Cunningham's *Lost Son,* art and work are juxtaposed when creative work is referred to as a lifting of longing "into art, into work" (344). The emblematic image of a variously positioned hand is seen at the head of each chapter in Cunningham's novel, a hand by itself or with notation of the place and time in Rainer M. Rilke's life represented in the chapter. The molding, shaping, flexible hand was probably inspired by the sculptor Auguste Rodin, Rilke's erstwhile mentor, whose motto was *"toujours travailler"* ("always to work"), but it also signifies the poet's hand, which relays the work of eyes and heart to written words. In Willa Cather's *The Song of the Lark,* Thea's study of music is recurrently associated with her power of application, her habit of charging at difficulties, and her effort to master musical scores. Lily Briscoe in Virginia Woolf's *To the Lighthouse,* Hurtle Duffield in Patrick White's *The*

Vivisector, and Charles Strickland in W. Somerset Maugham's *The Moon and Sixpence* are depicted continually working on their painting, thus pursuing their artistic aims and realizing their visions.

Theme, as opposed to subject matter, tends to be an invisible wheel, requiring inventiveness on the part of authors to convey its importance. In the twofold process of work, the inner, pertaining to heart and soul, mind and spirit, is by nature secretive and obscure. Like the *anima*, it will attach to someone or something: to characters in a relationship, to settings and plot episodes. By an author's legerdemain, including all manner of indirection and implication, productive work comes forth as a dimension of the various narrative elements. The process of work may be expressed by interior monologues as well as dialogues; by reminiscences and flashbacks as well as commentary on what occurs behind the scenes of a narrative plot; by shifts in narrative point of view (between first, second, and third person) to obtain both subjective and objective perspectives on the creative process. The subtle methods used to express creative work suggest its all-consuming nature while they complement the direct description of artists immersed in their craft.

Cather's *The Song of the Lark* attaches the theme of work and art to various lessons—piano and voice lessons as well as life lessons—made palatable by their settings and participant characters. ("Lesson," incidentally, is one of the definitions of theme in a literary work.) Thea's early musical training and introduction to song are highlighted by their location, Fritz and Paulina Kohlers' home and luxuriant garden on the outskirts of Moonstone, and Thea's demanding but generous teacher, the unforgettable Professor Wunsch, uttering forth commands with a distinctly German accent or passionately proclaiming desire and imagination. In Chicago, Thea's hard work is witnessed and rewarded by the attentions of Andor Harsanyi, the one-eyed Hungarian concert pianist reminiscent of Odin (god of wisdom, knowledge, and poetry in Teutonic mythology). Although Thea's voice lessons with Madison Bowers are behind the scenes, we are given ample clues to their value and effectiveness by Thea's long hours in Bowers' studio, where she plays accompaniments for other students in order to pay for her own two brief lessons per week; by her lunch hour duets with the debonair Fred Ottenburg and performances in Chicago society, which demonstrate progress in her voice training. This order of persistent struggle followed by enjoyment of the fruits of labor recapitulates the rhythm of music lessons in Moonstone, progressing from the churning of scales and chords to leisure singing and conversations in the Kohlers' garden.

Thea also learns about the interdependence of art and work when not directly studying piano or voice but rather observing life around her or taking stock of her progress and circumstances. As an adolescent in Moonstone, she rebels against the resignation and complacency she sees in church groups, her siblings, and the singers with whom she competes at community events, opposing striving and serious effort to the prevailing mindset. In Chicago, she is cognizant of the fact that it was the price of a life (the railroad engineer's Ray Kennedy's life insurance for six hundred dollars) that brought her to the city, so she is determined to do her best in the course of advanced musical training. During her summer in Panther Canyon, Arizona, while following the trails worn by ancient cliff dwellers or handling shards of pottery in rock chambers, Thea reflects on the hardship and struggle of the ancients' way of life. She appreciates the intricate handiwork required to mold clay vessels and embellish them for aesthetic effect, superfluous to their use for holding water or food. When Thea reaches stardom at the Metropolitan Opera, she remarks to her old friend Dr. Archie that her work (her art) inevitably becomes her personal life: "It's like being woven into a big web. You can't pull away, because all your little tendrils are woven into the picture. It takes you up, and uses you, and spins you out; and that is your life" (Cather 378).

In Cunningham's *Lost Son,* work partakes in particular settings, where the poetry that Rainer cultivates lives with him and shares his rooms, so to speak, as he labors in solitude. The most work is had in Paris, at 11 *rue Toullier,* 29 *rue Cassette,* and finally a ground-floor room in the antique Hôtel Biron at 77 *rue Varenne* (an eighteenth-century convent converted to a boarding house for artists). In Paris, with its Luxembourg Gardens, Notre Dame, National Library, and Zoo, Rainer receives the most and gives forth the most: *The Book of Images,* the *New Poems,* the main part of *The Notebooks of Malte Laurids Brigge,* the final edition of *The Lay of the Love and Death of Cornet Rilke,* and more. Paris is the city which Rainer comes to love despite its difficulty. It is the gravitational point of his continual journeying, to which he returns after visits to Germany, where his wife, Clara, and daughter, Ruth, settle; after travels to Italy, Sweden, and Denmark, and lecture tours throughout central Europe—until he is prevented from returning by the politics of World War I and his Austrian passport. In a letter to Clara, he writes, "It seems to me . . . as though Paris must still give me a work . . . . Each must find the center of his life in his work, and grow outward from there in radial manner, as far as the work will go" (April 8, 1903, quoted in Cunningham 236).

Rainer inhabits a series of cottages in artists' colonies, private estates, and Mediterranean villages, which are conducive to a mode of life centered exclusively on work and its rhythm of in-gathering and outpouring. At first he shares a cottage with his wife and daughter in Westerwede, adjacent to an artists' colony in Worpswede, Germany. Here Rainer reworks the sixty-six Russian prayers basic to *The Book of Hours.* After several months in Paris (1902), Rainer journeys southward to Italy, finding sanctuary in Viareggio on the Ligurean Sea: a chapel-like balcony room in the Hotel Florence and a beach hut for in-gathering, weather permitting. In counterpoint to the storms and gusts that descend on the village, Rainer surges with creative energy, producing thirty-four poems in a week. "Sheltered there . . . Rainer gives release to the rage of new work" (231). The following year, Rainer and Clara retreat to the Roman *campagna,* the Villa Strohl-Fern (an artists' colony named for its Alsatian founder), where they take separate lodgings for the sake of their individual creative endeavors. But with the onset of fever and grippe, invasions of ants from the garden bridge on which Rainer's cottage was built, and Rainer's mother's, Phia Rilke's, three-week Roman holiday, this abode yields only one month of productive work: February, when Rainer conceives of his alter ego, the poor young poet Malte, with whom he would struggle over four years. "For the rest of February Rainer clung to his day labor, working, working, an anchorite in his garden cottage, preparing his own meager meals of groats and vegetables but nourished entirely in another way" (Cunningham 256). He was nourished by memories, reveries, images, and ideas, we may surmise, and by the creative process itself.

Back in Paris, Rainer is invited to work as secretary for Auguste Rodin and to avail himself of a newly outfitted guest house on the sculptor's estate at Meudon, the Villa des Brillants overlooking the Sèvres Valley (gestures of appreciation for Rainer's monograph on Rodin, recently translated into French). Although Malte must be kept in abeyance while he tackles Rodin's correspondence, Rainer finds intervals to prepare for a lecture tour and begin the "sculptural" poems that proceed from observation at the Gardens, the Zoo, and Rodin's Pavilion de L'Alma. In the company of the master sculptor, Rainer is bound to the discipline of creative work, figuratively making of himself a hand, a vessel, that will hold work patiently and gradually bring it forth ("Has one come anywhere near acquiring the strength to grasp and shape all that surrounds one?—to make of oneself a hand and mold it all to serve one's art?" 211).

Rainer gives credit to the various rooms that shelter him over the years, from modest quarters in Paris to comfortable cottages and spacious castles. On an afternoon walk in Paris with Paula Modersohn-Becker, Rainer identifies a window at 11 *rue Toullier* as Malte's residence, indicating the immortalization of this address in his fictive *Notebooks*. The *Duino Elegies* are named for the Duino Castle near Trieste, on the Adriatic Sea, where Rilke worked under the patronage of Princess Marie von Thurn und Taxis in 1912 and wrote the first few Elegies. Duino having been demolished during World War I, the *Elegies* were completed at the castle in Muzot, Switzerland, and Rainer is shown stroking the stone wall of the castle tower in gratitude: "that glorious February evening in Muzot when the poet will step from his tower, the ten Elegies at last complete, and stroke the bastion's stone wall in thanks" (431).

Albeit influenced by characters and settings that animate the artist, work is inevitably a component of plot, the story line or episodic sequence in narrative that is usually the main vehicle of theme. Plot features phases of an artist's growth, including early training when childhood is represented; it highlights creative activity and achievement in maturity. In artist novels, plot is typically motivated by the artist's effort to realize creative potential, which consists of practice and sometimes a search for felicitous circumstances to this end. Like heroic adventure, the story line of artist novels might feature a call to action and a significant point of departure that determine ensuing episodes and further creative work. We have Thea's departure for Chicago in Cather's *The Song of the Lark,* Rainer's for Műnich in Cunningham's *Lost Son,* and Charles' for Paris in Maugham's *The Moon and Sixpence.* The latter demonstrates artistic work as motivator of plot most clearly, for Maugham's story begins with Charles' sensational exit from his stockbroker's position, family, and social circle in London in order to pursue painting in Paris.

Maugham's fictive portrait of Paul Gauguin is indeed dramatic, involving incessant struggle with poverty in addition to the main challenge of painting that propels him to Paris and beyond. Charles lives in Paris for approximately six years, learning to paint and working out his individual style. Initially an apprentice at the studios in Montparnasse, he soon strikes out on his own, figuring out techniques by trial, error, and persistence. His only concerns are a supply of paints and canvases, a meager room, and enough food to subsist, be it a liter of milk and loaf of bread per day. When funds run out, he takes odd jobs, such as house painting or guiding English tourists through Parisian night life, for his strikingly original canvases fetch only about sixpence each. Charles is described as never ceasing to work at his art and never satisfied with his accomplishments relative to his inner vision. Indifferent to comfort, surroundings, people, and their opinions, he is totally absorbed in the process of realizing his vision in painting. However, his vision subsumes a longing for a place compatible with its strange harmonies, where he might work with body and soul in unison. He yearns for "an island lost in a boundless sea, where [he] could live in some hidden valley, among strange trees, in silence" (Maugham 83)—which he would find in Tahiti. Before leaving Paris, Charles shows a friend, the English narrator in the novel, about thirty of his works, to the latter's perplexity and incomprehension. The peculiar colors and forms were intended to convey something, but he knew not what; their author appeared to be aiming for some inscrutable Nirvana (166-7).

Charles' journey to the isle of his dreams begins in Marseilles, a crossroads for travel in all directions. Here, in the company of sailors, vagabonds, and beachcombers, he drifts from the friars' *Asile de Nuit* (Asylum of the Night) to the streets and to sailors' boarding houses, working intermittently as stevedore or painter, until he answers to a call for a stoker aboard a tramp bound for Australia. Thus he works his passage to Tahiti via Sydney and Auckland, arriving at his destination "with a box of paints, an easel, and a dozen canvases" (197), according to Captain Nichols, who also made his way from Marseilles to Tahiti.

The story of Charles' life and art in Tahiti consists in reminiscences of persons who had come into contact with him—Tiaré Johnson, Captain Renè Brunot, and Dr. Coutras—in dialogue with the narrator, who travels to the South Seas several years after Charles' death. Tiaré, landlady of the Hôtel de la Fleur, tells of the match she arranged between Charles and Ata, a native woman, and their settling in a bungalow in a remote fold of a mountain. Here they lived off the produce of the land, and Charles could devote himself to painting, his work resonating with the exuberant colors of the luxuriant paradise. Captain Brunot and Dr. Coutras had the privilege to see work-in-progress on their visits with Charles. When he came to diagnose an illness, Dr. Coutras found Charles painting a still life of fruits; later, Charles was absorbed in painting the interior walls of his house with splendid primeval scenes. These murals would be burned after Charles' death, at his request, presumably because he had satisfied his creative urge, burned out "the passion that fired him" (82), and realized his vision. (The pictures acquired by Captain Brunot and Dr. Coutras would yield their daughters' dowries.) Charles' composite portrait drawn by the series of narrators indicates creative work as Charles' mode of life, therefore motivator of episodes in his life, which revolve increasingly on the mere process of painting.

From the artist's perspective, the creative endeavor is valuable in itself, regardless of the fate of the finished work. Creative work satisfies the urge for self-expression that pertains to vitality or joy of life but not necessarily to a means of subsistence. So artist novels inevitably include some record of creative process or work-in-progress while a number of them highlight extensive process. For example, Joyce offers Stephen's composition of a villanelle, the poem dedicated to Emma Clery, from its conception in daydreams to its distillation in words, lines, and verses one morning. Cather reveals Thea's procedure in the interpretation of a few songs and operatic roles. Cunningham represents Rainer's preliminary work on *The Notebooks of Malte Laurids Brigge* and a few of the New Poems. Updike elaborates Zack's experimentation with ways of being *in* his paintings. Lengthy process is shown when an artist's creative endeavor represents the author's process of writing the novel, as seen in Lily Briscoe's painting from beginning to end of Virginia Woolf's *To the Lighthouse* or Cassandra Mortmain's keeping of her journal throughout Dodie Smith's *I Capture the Castle*. Cassandra's journal is practically equivalent with Smith's novel, and her work is downplayed in favor of the adventure, intrigue, and romantic relationships she records. On the other hand, Lily's art features a medium different from the author's, so it is more effective as an analogy. Lily's painting process is a significant thread of the plot in *To the Lighthouse,* interwoven with episodes in the life of the Ramsay family and their guests on Skye, together making for the theme of the interrelation between the reality of art ("this other thing, this truth, this reality," Woolf 158) and the reality of family and community, comprising their respective activities and interests. The portrait of an older poet, Augustus Carmichael, complements Lily's and contributes to the reality of art in Woolf's work.

A guest at the Ramsays' retreat on the Isle of Skye one summer, Lily is very observant of her surroundings and hosts, very receptive to impressions of ambience and individual behaviors. She is portrayed with senses alert, straining to see the colors and shapes of natural objects, relating affectionately to Mrs. Ramsay and the nine children, taking walks along the seashore with a co-guest, the botanist William Bankes. She is forthwith in love with the people and milieu, motivated to express her feelings and experience in painting, her way of communicating and reciprocating the joy she receives. Lily immerses herself in the mental process of envisioning her experience in terms of an arrangement of form and color on canvas. Once she sets up her easel at the edge of the lawn and applies the first brushstroke, she faces the challenge of bridging the gap between planning dreamily and rendering her vision on canvas. Her work is certainly twofold, consisting of inner mental process, proceeding from heart and mind, and the manual process of painting with brushes and palette (both conveyed in large part by Woolf's interior monologues). Away from the canvas, at dinner or walking by the sea, Lily continually revisions her composition, deliberating over the position of the tree or the shape by which to depict Mrs. Ramsay: circular dome or triangle? After all, there were many ways of seeing an object, itself changing with the play of light or rendered malleable by the observer's feelings. Lily's flowing train of thought and fluttering emotions, set in contrast to the definite outlines of male discourse, particularly Mr. Ramsay's, reflect Virginia Woolf's fluent, winding, incrementally repetitive prose style. Lily's work develops intuitively, with trust in the inner urge, the motive of her painting, to determine its organization.

Lily's creative endeavor proceeds as daily routine, a series of ups and downs in the struggle to bring forth her vision. It is valid and meaningful as process, regardless of the outcome of the completed work. Lily's painting is her activity and mode of life, less personal and more focused on beauty than others'. While Mrs. Ramsay knits socks for the lighthouse keeper's family and looks in on the poor in the village, nurtures her children, engages in matchmaking, or plans dinners, Lily is working by her easel, mixing colors, dipping into her palette, and applying brushstrokes on canvas, thus caught up in the reality of art. She is fastidious and resolute in her application, moving green, blue, and violet according to her vision or figuring how to connect masses on the right with those on the left, eventually positioning the contours of a tree (the tree of life and art) at the center of her composition. Lily's decision about the tree occurs toward the end of her first summer visit with the Ramsays, and her painting has yet to be finished.

"Time Passes" (the title of Part II of Woolf's novel), and Lily resumes her painting a decade later when she returns to Skye at Mr. Ramsay's invitation. While Mr. Ramsay and the children carry out their long-postponed expedition to the lighthouse as a tribute to Mrs. Ramsay, who has passed on, Lily completes her painting, inspired by vivid memories of

Mrs. Ramsay—her beauty, her strength, her role as guidepost to family and guests. Memory consolidates Lily's thoughts and unifies her shifting vision. She begins to lay on red and gray as if spontaneously; she draws another line in the center of her composition and proclaims the picture done.

"It would be hung in the attics, she thought; it would be destroyed. But what did that matter?" She has had her vision, Lily says (Woolf 208-9). She has satisfied her urge for self-expression and confronted time and change by preserving her experience with the Ramsays in her chosen medium of painting. Lily's art work bears similarity to other modes of life and activity that might be frustrating for lack of felicitous results or definite meaning. Mrs. Ramsay's matchmaking does not necessarily result in a good marriage. Two of her brightest children suffer untimely death on account of illness or war, yet her family lives on. In a scale of achievement represented by the alphabet, Mr. Ramsay reaches Q, approximately, and he strives for R. In *To the Lighthouse,* the importance of process in art recalls emphasis on the journey as opposed to the destination in life generally, as voiced in poetry from Homer's *Odyssey* to Constantine Cavafy's "Ithaca" and numerous other renditions of this theme.

Lily's painting and Mrs. Ramsay's social work are essentially comparable with regard to their motives and purpose, granted ostensible differences in means of expression and desired effects. While Mrs. Ramsay knits socks to produce something useful and comforting for the lighthouse keeper's children, she also expresses her friendship with members of the community. Her dinners provide family and guests with the pleasure of conversation and cheerful ambiance: soul food as well as nourishment for the body. Lily's painting might seem useless by comparison, especially if destined to collect dust in an attic, but the pleasure it has afforded Mr. Bankes and passers-by who chanced to see her work-in-progress, or the tribute it pays to the Ramsays, is no less than the effect of an elegant dinner table or the *Boeuf en Daube* recipe that enhances the taste of beef and vegetables. Lily's stated motive in painting is her love for "this all," similar to Mrs. Ramsay's motive for social work and bringing family and community together. Mrs. Ramsay's work, like Lily's, is an expression of her individual vitality—her sensuality, soulfulness, and emotion. While Mrs. Ramsay serves life around her, Lily celebrates life and by celebrating, also serves the general good, the "human gain" in Woolf's words.

We may find work interesting by virtue of its influence on an artist's personal life story, that is, in motivating plot, relationships with other characters, and setting in a novel; in yielding adventure and leading to exotic places in a few instances. Creative work has such wide-ranging influence because of the challenge it poses for the artist, that of promoting self-expression and realizing talent in the face of conflicts of values or difficulties posed by limiting circumstances or social milieu. In a word, the challenge is the assertion of one's individuality by transforming inner visions, images, and ideas that have been brewing indefinitely into art work. Therefore, the theme of the growth of the artist is apt to become the theme of creative work, eliciting an equation between art and work. Virginia Woolf's juxtaposition of the reality of art with the reality of family and community in *To the Lighthouse* brings forth the theme of creative work more clearly than other novels, by the effect of contrast as well as analogy. Her comparison and contrast between Lily's painting process and Mrs. Ramsay's social activities expresses an appreciation for the different ways in which creativity and individuality may be asserted and fulfilled. In fact, Woolf's novel serves to remind us of the affinity between the artist novel and the novel of character development as it shows basic similarities between the artist and other people who are engaged in productive work.

Nonetheless, creative work retains an aura of mystery associated with divine gift, creative spark, or inspiration. Whether creative work is at the center of an artist's portrait (as in Woolf's *To the Lighthouse*), the periphery (as in Smith's *I Capture the Castle*), or in between, it is only partially revealed in the literature. Given inroads into an artist's mind and creative process (as by Cather, Cunningham, Joyce, and Woolf), we can appreciate the effort and dedication involved in the realization of an art work, yet the work itself remains obscure to varying degree. Along with work per se, literary portraits indicate artists' longings, ideals, and perceptions, which tend to revolve on concepts of beauty that distinguish the finished work of art or musical performance. This is true of autobiographical and partly autobiographical portraits (Joyce, Cather, Smith, Woolf), illuminating as confessional accounts, as well as fictional portraits (those of Gauguin by Maugham and Pollock by Updike) and fictional biographies (of Rilke by Cunningham), which are based on research and firsthand appreciation of their subjects' art. Consequently, we proceed to Part II, an attempt to glean the aesthetics that elucidate creative work in the novels while they also refer to experiences in childhood, sensuality, self-expression, and kinship with nature.

PART II

Aesthetics

The aesthetic interests and concepts of beauty discussed in Part II elicit aspects of the artists' selves, previewed in Chapter 3, as they evolve from yearnings and longings to verbal, visual, or audible artworks. Artist novels tend to be short on description of the artwork and long on the artist's growth, including milestones in the development of individual aesthetics, which are also informative about particular aims and interests. We may rely on these milestones to glean individual aesthetics, as for James Joyce's *A Portrait of the Artist as a Young Man*, or juxtapose episodes in an artist's life with glimpses of the artwork, digressing occasionally, particularly in the case of fictional portraits, to primary sources that are referenced in the fiction, for example, Paul Gauguin's and Jackson Pollock's paintings, to observe distinctive styles.

The aesthetics and concepts of beauty revealed in the current selection of novels reflect patterns and principles inherent in nature: radiance, vitality, integrity, vibrant stasis, the interrelation of surface and depth, change, and transformation. For the most part, they stem from the artists' kinship with nature, especially the experience of harmony with natural milieu, which appears to inspire self-expression and stimulate creativity. This provenance is most directly indicated by Zack McCoy's identification with nature in John Updike's *Seek My Face*. In artist novels that represent childhood and feature scenes of sensual and spiritual awakening in the midst of nature, we see that aesthetic concerns may begin with perceptions in childhood, which are later retrieved and affirmed by experiences of kinship with nature. In other words, encounters with nature awaken aspects of their selves that were dormant for a while. For example, Stephen Dedalus appreciates radiance in the form of light throughout his childhood, and his interest in radiance as a form of beauty is kindled again in the scene on the strand. Although we do not hear about Charles Strickland's childhood in Somerset Maugham's *The Moon and Sixpence*, we know that the painter harbored an inner vision of a distant tropical isle for decades before his identification with the terrain of Tahiti that served to elucidate his aesthetic of vibrant stasis. In Virginia Woolf's *To the Lighthouse*, Lily Briscoe's aim of rendering a bright, shimmering surface on a solid base in her painting is influenced by her relation with Mrs. Ramsay as well as her observation of the natural milieu on the Isle of Skye. This novel demonstrates that aesthetic concepts derived from nature might be filtered through personal relationships and other sources of inspiration, such as cultural and traditional ideals. An interweaving of ideals with natural models is shown in Thea's aesthetic of integrity, as well as Rainer's aim of transformation and Cassandra's project of embellishing the daily life of the castle in the process of keeping her journal.

Change, or transformation, obviously a principle of nature, reflected in art throughout the ages, is both the most simple and the most complex among aesthetic concepts. In Dodie Smith's *I Capture the Castle*, change is associated with a vision of the castle in spring, which accords with Cassandra's fairytale vision, and it is effected by a concerted effort on the part of artistic characters to ameliorate their life in the castle, thus to maintain the spring vision in the face of difficulties. On the other hand, the change that M. Allen Cunningham offers as Rainer's aesthetic aim in *Lost Son* is the result of long, accumulated experience on the part of the poet: of his inner journeys and outer journeys, his embrace of the transcendent sphere as well as the imminence of nature, and his numerous new beginnings, inspired by dialogues with angels, soul-mates, mentors, trees, and flowers. However, both Cassandra's and Rainer's persistent striving for the achievement of their aesthetic aims is "childlike" with regard to the unshakable faith the characters have in their visions or ideals, and to the challenges they pose for adults' status quo.

Note on omissions:

A few novels that were briefly discussed in Part I are omitted in Part II due to a lack of information about the artwork or other indications of aesthetic concerns: Vincas Mykolaitis' *In the Altars' Shadow,* Franz Kafka's *The Metamorphosis,* and Patrick White's *The Vivisector.*

-CHAPTER 6-

Dodie Smith, I Capture the Castle: the Embellishment of Reality

Dodie Smith's childlike narrator, Cassandra Mortmain, has no stated agenda in keeping her journal other than teaching herself to write and having fun in the process. She has fun because she is a participant in the daily life of the castle that she tries to "capture," and this life bears traces of her first impression of the castle as one in fairy tales. Cassandra assumes Smith's rose-colored glasses, designed to romanticize her subject matter, but she does so imperceptibly, for, being childlike, she consistently heightens reality by the play of imagination and, being a competent adolescent narrator, she presents the author's rose-colored vision as reality. Consequently, in this novel, illusion merges with a reality enhanced by color, music, poetry, and drama—a romanticized reality—making for a world of possibility and promise.

As suggested by the title of Smith's novel, the setting is key to Cassandra's project. An old castle in the English countryside is as real as it is exotic and virtually distant in time, as amenable to romantic values as it is in dire need of restoration. So it was when discovered by Cassandra's father, James Mortmain, on a house-hunting expedition after the success of his first book and lecture tour. Attracted by a round tower on the horizon, James followed a long winding road to the signpost "To Belmotte and the Castle Only," there turning on a lane overgrown with brambles and hedges (reminding Cassandra of the Prince wending his way to Sleeping Beauty), leading to grey stone walls and towers reflected in the emerald water of a moat surrounding the castle. Across the bridge was a gatehouse with nail-studded oak doors beside a large house of herring-bone brick with lattice windows and an attic gable (a kind of "Hansel and Gretel" house, Cassandra thought). The interior of this castle proved to be a disappointment, with layers of wall paper or paint covering the original woodwork, false ceilings, partitions in the spacious kitchen, and a moldy smell pervading the rooms. But James could see the Tudor and Stuart splendor beneath the Victorian additions. He focused his attention on the mullioned windows, imagining the view in summer, with fields of wild flowers and wheat stretching far beyond the moat.

James obtained a forty years' lease from the owner, Mr. Cotton of Scoatney Hall, and with his permission, proceeded to restore the castle to its original glory, partly medieval, mostly seventeenth-century. (The house itself, built in the time of Charles II, was grafted on to a fourteenth-century castle, built by a Norman knight, Etienne de Godys, whose name stayed with the castle and nearby village: Godys End, abbreviated to Godsend. The original name, Belmotte, associated with the mound, or motte, was reserved for the tower on the mound.) Before the work began and before addressing the need for heat and electricity, James collected antique furniture appropriate for the old castle: beauty before utility. One spring day his family moved into the spacious rooms with shiny wood paneling and freshly curtained windows, with views of flower beds and swans gliding in the moat below.

About eight years later, the castle is almost bare of furniture, yet full of color. James' versatile young wife, Topaz, is cynosure in the project of embellishing daily life in the castle: she paints, plays the lute, sews for the family, improvises entertainments, and communes with nature in her leisure. She is seen floating through the rooms in a velvet orange tea gown, blending with the wood paneling as well as the ginger cat, Abelard, and the golden wheat fields outside the windows. When Topaz avails herself of green dye to refresh the wardrobe—nightgowns, sheets, and James' cardigan for good measure—she simulates an early spring. Cassandra's sister, Rose, models the old silk tea gown with flowing sleeves, now sea-green, on the staircase and Topaz is heard strumming a tune on her lute, "Green Sleeves," when Neil and Simon Cotton, heirs to Scoatney Hall, appear on the scene. In preparation for a visit with the Cottons at Scoatney, Topaz fashions yards of pink muslin for Rose and a white frock with blue sash for Cassandra, reserving a clinging grey, Grecian-shaped dress for herself so as not to outshine her stepdaughters.

There is music in the air, and poetry. Topaz and Rose spring clean to the tunes of "The Isle of Capri" and "Blow the Man Down" and birds chirping by the open windows. A grand piano, too old and heavy to be sold off, stands in the drawing room for Rose to play. When Topaz and Rose are away in London, Cassandra enjoys the portable wireless, a gift from Stephen, an orphan who lives with the Mortmains, who also presents her with verses of poetry written in beautiful script, telling of lilies, roses, violets, and budding love—no matter that they're copied from George Herbert or Robert Herrick. Soon Cassandra has a gramophone and wireless combined, received from Simon Cotton along with a blue and gold leather-bound manuscript book for her journal.

As Cassandra proceeds to fill her Six-Penny Book, Shilling Book, and Two-Guinea Book with the record of daily events at Godsend, we may notice a progression from magical rites to romantic comedy, particularly a plot concerning mistaken identities, reminiscent of Roman and Shakespearian comedy: from ritual to romance, with some farce and melodrama interspersed in the episodic sequence. The drama begins with Rose's rite vis à vis the gargoyle above the kitchen fireplace, for lack of a Devil's Dyke or Well in the vicinity. Hoisted up a rope by her younger brother, Thomas, and Stephen, Rose voices her desire: "Heavenly Devil or devilish saint / Grant our wish, hear our plaint, / Godsend Castle a godsend craves" (Smith 47). Well nigh synchronously, Neil and Simon Cotton arrive at the castle, which they do not recognize as their own. They are searching for help to dislodge their car from the flooded, muddy lane leading to the castle when they alight on the scene of Rose descending the staircase in the velvet tea gown, accompanied by lute-playing. It seems that the ritual charm is effective;

however, the initial attraction between the Cotton brothers and Mortmain girls is trailed by disappointment, for the path of true love is never smooth in fairy tales. The Cottons are repelled by Rose's affectation and conspicuous forwardness as well as Cassandra's "conscious naiveté" on the occasion of their next meeting.

Reunion occurs on Rose's and Cassandra's return from their excursion to London to retrieve the wardrobe bequeathed to them by their great aunt Millicent. Nearing the end of the train ride, at the station before King's Crypt (the one for Godsend Village), none other than Neil and Simon board the train. To avoid them, Rose gets off the train and runs across a dark field in the long fur coat she has been wearing for warmth. Taken for a bear on the loose, she is pursued by troops in arms until Neil recognizes her voice and rescues her. Rose's impulsive flight compensates for her previous affectation and fuels conversations, endearing her to Neil Cotton once again. Ensuing entertainments at Scoatney and Godsend offer further occasions for rendezvous and peripeties in plot: Rose enchants Simon while Cassandra amuses Neil. In the event of supper at Godsend Castle, Cassandra is complicit in the confusion among partners as she tries to prolong her sister's interview with her new friend, engaging Neil in conversation and a circuit of the chilly waters of the moat.

While Rose is in London, arranging her trousseau with Topaz and Mrs. Cotton, Simon checks in at Godsend Castle in the course of his rounds between the London flat and Scoatney Hall. He brings Cassandra presents—chocolates, gramophone, notebook—as to his future sister-in-law, whom he considers a wonderful child. On Midsummer Eve he finds Cassandra on the mound, lighting a fire in preparation for the ritual she has observed with Rose for years. Far from thinking her "consciously naïve," as he had once described her, Simon takes interest in the celebration and all its paraphernalia: garland, cakes, port, herbs, and salt. He joins her in dancing round the fire, circling it seven times. The call for more wood brings the pair to Belmotte Tower and a view of the castle enveloped by moonlight and mist, another dimension of the romantic ambience of the evening, which proceeds to a candlelit supper at Scoatney Hall. Suffice it to say that

Simon is unconsciously naïve in kindling his friendship with Cassandra, and she, though versed in folklore, is innocent of the love charms and pairings associated with Midsummer Eve rites when she bids them farewell as to childhood games.

Dramatic episodes in the life of the castle have affinities with play, as do Topaz's dressing up, the playing of instruments, the recitation of verses, and Cassandra's joyful preoccupation with her journal. These creative activities and pastimes are opposed to serious work, earning capacity, and the mercenary world of London, as if the Mortmains were "playing castle" in an illusory world of their own, at least for the duration of Cassandra's fairy tale-inspired journal. Real work is out of place and time in this context. James Mortmain *was* a successful writer, we are told, and by the end of the novel, he appears to be planning another original scholarly work; in the meantime, he is experiencing writer's block, doing crossword puzzles, and reading detective novels. Topaz *was* an artists' model in London. Rose is *in*competent in housework and gardening. Thomas is usually *away* at school in King's Crypt. The remarkably industrious Stephen works on a nearby farm *outside* the castle, obtaining produce and dairy products for the Mortmains.

Nevertheless, the Mortmains are sufficiently connected with the "real" world of work and productive activity to be credible as a mid-twentieth-century English family. They are on good terms with the Vicar of Godsend Village and with Miss Marcy, the librarian, both of whom are sources of good advice, enriching conversations, and books. Interchanges with the Cottons, who have returned to England from the United States, refresh memories of James' lecture tour in the States and his former success as a writer. Evenings at Scoatney Hall bring the Mortmains into contact with Londoners while they further romantic relationships. All of these people support the values of art, imagination, love, and nature by which the Mortmains live and encourage their creative pursuits. The Vicar purchases a few items from Aunt Millicent's bequest, providing temporary income in addition to moral support. Miss Marcy volunteers to run errands in the village. The Cottons not only overlook their tenants' unpaid rent but entertain them and present them with hams for the holidays. Simon volunteers to write a critical essay on James' first book, *Jacob Wrestling*. Leda Fox-Cotton, a guest at Scoatney, offers Stephen employment in London. There is evidently mutual attraction between outsiders and insiders, and no animosity between them. The community welcomes friendship with the inhabitants of Godsend Castle and expresses interest in their mode of life.

As noted at the outset, Cassandra, the narrator of the journal that is Smith's novel, is both childlike and sufficiently sophisticated to be the author's persona and assume her rose-colored glasses. The playfulness of creative activity at Godsend Castle therefore reflects a mixture of childlike and adult perspectives. In the child's view, there is no clear dividing line between the real and the imaginary: the fairy tale vision of the castle informs the Mortmains' daily life at Godsend, intimating a world of unlimited possibility, which is attractive and uplifting to the immediate community. The validity of the childlike perspective precludes an appearance of vanity and irresponsibility in the Mortmains' carefree way of life while it highlights the positive and edifying aspects of illusion (lit. "in play," *in>il* + L. *ludus*). At the same time, Cassandra conveys an adult perspective, which is romantic with a grain of salt in its differentiation between the real and the imaginary. Cassandra is aware of the leaking roof, the faded curtains and shabby furniture that have replaced authentic antique pieces, the lack of variety in the family's diet, but she does not let these shortcomings diminish her enchantment with the castle or her vision. She counteracts Rose's habitual despondency and pessimism about the family's predicament as she encourages her sister's rite with the gargoyle or prolongs her tête à tête with Simon. She is cognizant of her father's experience of writer's block and its effect on the family's livelihood; however, she considers his talent and promise intact. She appreciates Topaz's cooking, sewing, and housekeeping as much as her lute-playing, painting, and dressing up, for she recognizes all these activities as ways of embellishing the reality of daily life.

As a result of the combination of perspectives, childlike and mature, the color, music, drama, and journal keeping are not only enjoyable in themselves, like play, but also a means to counteract the disillusioning effects of time, to cure boredom and despondency, and provide mental and spiritual sustenance for the participants, in a word, to kindle the joy of life. Dodie Smith's entertaining narrative makes the point (a Romantic tenet) that art celebrates life and serves life, upholding the corollary view that life, with its variety and vicissitudes of fortune, is worth living and celebrating. This theme, naïve and taken for granted in the child's attitude, is reinforced by the adult perspective and its acceptance by the community.

Smith's aesthetic concept, shown by the infusion of creative activity into daily life at the castle, which in turn influences her "rags to riches" plot, is essentially change effected by the play of imagination. Her rose-colored glasses, motivating her characters' persistent efforts to improve the status quo, recall Wallace Stevens' motive for metaphor, which is a desire for "the exhilaration of changes" and a refreshment of "the ABC of being" (stated more subtly in his poem "The Motive for Metaphor" as well as "The Man with a Blue Guitar" and other poems that explore the relation between reality and the imagination). In *I Capture the Castle,* the equation between change and art holds for change effected by poetic activity that is partly contrived and partly serendipitous, proceeding from both desire and receptivity to the environment. It is a basic and general aesthetic concept, which is ideally available to everyone and might be achieved in a variety of media. As it is an aesthetic concept primarily in the sense of "perceptive" (from the Gr. *aesthētikos,* "perceptive," and *aisthanestai,* "to perceive, to feel"), it is preliminary to most other concepts of beauty offered in artists' novels.

-CHAPTER 7-

Willa Cather,
The Song of the Lark: Integrity

Beauty in *The Song of the Lark* is both an ideal and a reality: something we long for and cherish, like excellence, honesty, or love, and an aspect of the phenomena we experience or perceive in nature and humanity. In the sphere of art and artists, which is the focus of Cather's attention, the ideal and the real are bound up with each other, interconnected. Manifestations of beauty reflect certain ideals pertaining to art or artistic endeavor, and the ideals are a measure of real beauty. As might be expected in a romantic novel about the growth of an artist, the ideals are lofty. Beauty partakes of the ineffable: "what one strives for [in art] is so far away, so deep, so beautiful . . . that there's nothing one can say about it" (Cather 381), reflects Cather's heroine, Thea Kronborg. Beauty is associated with the refinement of a sense of truthfulness in the artist; with feeling, passion, dedication, and spirit—all more easily perceived than described or prescribed. Beauty is perceived in a child's voice, in the performance of a Mexican serenade, a song by Grieg, and operatic roles whenever the ideal is glimpsed in the practice of art, particularly vocal art.

Various remarks on beauty aside, what Cather demonstrates in her portrait of Thea is beauty in the process of an artist's growth and the unfolding of musical talent, as suggested by numerous comparisons between the youthful singer and nature's blossoms. When Thea comes into her own, into full possession and expression of her musical gift, she is likened to a tree bursting into bloom (the standard of nature being a Romantic tenet as well as a Classical one). And this, the fulfillment of one's creative potential, is the intersection of the ideal and the real that is foremost in Cather's novel: it is the challenge in the dramatic action and the culmination of the theme of the artist's growth. The attainment of the ideal of fulfillment is essential to the splendor of Thea's eventual performances at the Metropolitan Opera, perceived variously as personality, color, passion, explosive force, and projecting power. There is no final word on the beauty of her performances, but if the ideal is fulfillment of one's creative potential, then real beauty is the extent to which Thea can bring her talent and person to the interpretation of a musical score. In other words, the concept of beauty Cather maintains is integrity, or fullness, in artistic expression.

Thea's growth proceeds in the stages of childhood, adolescence, and early maturity, which comprise several milestones in the development of her potential as a singer. These are presented as an incremental repetition of a theme with variations, the theme being her musical talent, its discovery, affirmation, and reaffirmation; the variations are the people, places, and fluctuating circumstances that influence her personal and artistic growth. Alongside the piano and voice teachers we encounter, there is Mrs. Kronborg, who assesses her daughter's talent and personality expertly; Thea's Aunt Tillie, protective of her niece in the event of family disputes; Dr. Howard Archie, the family's physician in Moonstone, who singles out Thea as his favorite, encourages her ventures, and boosts her confidence at every turn. Later guardians and guides include Fred Ottenburg, who recognizes Thea's talent and provides opportunities for the enrichment of her personality in Chicago and Panther Canyon, Arizona; and Oliver Landry, Thea's accompanist during years of musical training in Germany, who also turns up in New York. For her part, Thea is faithful to her musical gift, once she apprehends her calling or uniqueness, and responsive to her teachers and friends who support the concerted effort of striving toward an ideal of fulfillment. Cather's digressions from the main theme to the multifaceted circumstances of Thea's life and the local color of each, to histories of places and people that touch Thea's, provide her romance with a credible realistic framework. The author's admission of the play of chance and irony in her story makes for complexity in the pattern and renders Thea's progress all the more remarkable.

The initial discovery of Thea's vocal gift by Johnny Tellamantez when, at age six or seven, she alights at his doorstep to listen to his guitar and repeats the melodies "just-a beautiful" in his account, apparently had no effect on the Kronborgs. Thea qualified for participation in the church choir whether or not she had talent, for singing in church was a matter of course for a Methodist minister's daughter, and piano lessons were a family tradition on her mother's side. Thea studies piano with Professor A. Wunsch, a German musician who has made his home with Fritz and Paulina Kohler on the outskirts of Moonstone after some travelling with an unsuccessful orchestra. She walks over the sandhills to the Kohlers to receive expert training in the scales and chords, études by Czerny and Hummel, and Clementi sonatas. When Thea is declared talented by her teacher, she is set to more piano practice at home. Her repertoire is varied by musical scores from Dr. Archie's library, like Carl Maria von Weber's "Invitation to the Dance" or C. W. Glűck's "Orpheus." After lessons, Thea revels in Mrs. Kohler's hospitality and entertains her by singing church hymns.

On Thea's thirteenth birthday one Saturday in June, Wunsch teaches her Heinrich Heine's "Im leuchtenden Sommermorgen" ("In the soft-shining summer morning") as they stroll in the Kohlers' garden amid fragrant lindens and luxuriant flower beds after the piano lesson. Thea demonstrates an ability to listen and to memorize lines quickly, and she repeats the verses with exquisite feeling and inflection in her voice, as if simulating the whispering of flowers featured in the lyrics. "It was a nature voice, Wunsch told himself, breathed from the creature and apart from the language, like the sound of the wind in the trees, or the murmur of water" (Cather 69-70). These impressions of Thea's voice reflect images of his pupil previously brought to mind: when Thea sang for Mrs. Kohler, she seemed to him like "a yellow flower, full of sunlight" or a "thin glass full of sweet-smelling sparkling Moselle wine," its bubbles lightly dancing and bursting (29). Wunsch proceeds to examine Thea on the meaning of Heine's verses to stimulate her mind. He speaks of spirit and imagination, and the heart that is of the essence of art, like rhythm in music; of desire, that conquers all difficulties. He reminisces about singers he had heard, artists with standards and good taste, waxing purple with the passion and enthusiasm he had for authentic art. Though vaguely understanding the drift of Wunsch's thoughts, Thea is stirred and excited. She can identify with desires and inspirations in her own life, which for the time being she attributes to a "friendly spirit" or companion that responded when summoned and made everything "more interesting and beautiful" (71): a kind of fluctuating movement of her inner self, a comforting sureness experienced in solitude or in the company of teachers or friends, like Johnny or Dr. Archie. On this day Thea walks homeward over glittering sand hills with fresh awareness of her musical gift and a sense of both the pleasure and the challenge it offered.

Subsequent turning points in Thea's growth during her teen years are gains fueled by losses. When Thea begins to conduct piano lessons at age fifteen, she soon finds herself taking on Professor Wunsch's pupils, for her teacher succumbs to his habit of drinking, which causes a scandal in the small town, and must of necessity move on. Her present goal of becoming a fine piano teacher, no doubt inspired by Wunsch, is supported by family and friends, especially the railroad brakeman Ray Kennedy, who cherishes Thea as his future sweetheart. Ray's notion of piano training in Chicago to benefit Thea's career in Moonstone is ironically actualized by the sum of his life insurance, six hundred dollars, which he designates for this purpose as he expires after a railway accident.

The scenario in Chicago resembles that of Moonstone, with variations and augmentation in all its components. Thea obtains the position of soprano in Mr. Larsen's Swedish church; she also sings at funerals occasionally to maintain her livelihood in the windy city. She boards in the home of Mrs. Lorch, where she has a spacious room with piano and fireplace—like the parlor back home—in addition to nourishing meals and moral support for long hours of practice. She studies with a concert pianist, Andor Harsanyi, who finds her the most stimulating and most tiring of his students, the most intelligent and most ignorant, given the limited cultural resources of her hometown. Instead of the Kohlers' home and garden, Thea explores the Art Institute on Michigan Avenue, where she is particularly attracted to an equestrian statue, exuding strength and vitality, and upstairs, a painting titled "The Song of the Lark" (Jules Breton, 1885) of a peasant girl in a wheat field, illumined by early morning sun. These artworks are among the things she identifies as hers, as belonging to her or resonating with her soul. She attends symphony concerts, which inspire her with desire to devote herself to art.

As previously in the company of Prof. Wunsch and the Kohlers, Thea's voice is rediscovered at leisure with the Harsanyis one evening. Upon disclosure of her position in a church choir, Thea submits to singing a few hymns after supper: "Come Ye Disconsolate" (Mrs. Kohler's favorite) and "Rejoice, for the Shepherd has found His Sheep" from her audition for Mr. Larsen. When Thea recalls a few verses from Glück's "Orpheus," the hidden treasure in her, or "hidden creature," surfaces again, with marked effect on its audience. Mr. Harsanyi shoots up from his chaise longue with a turn on his heels that his wife recognizes as a sign of intense interest or sudden resolution. He asks Thea to repeat the aria, then leads her through various keys, observing a voice that lay on her breath, a relaxed throat, and a very individual quality in the voice. Later he reflects, "It was like a wild bird that had flown into his studio," beating "its passionate wings" (Cather 160), a wonderful voice!

Before long, Harsanyi would recommend a voice teacher and give up his prize student, encouraging Thea to direct herself along the path of a vocal artist, one best suited for her particular talent. Their farewell conversation the following May Day, referred to as a "greeting," echoes Thea's exchange with Wunsch on her thirteenth birthday, but now the subject is Thea's vocation rather than art and artists in general, the thing in *her* that has to do with beauty and power. Harsanyi speaks to Thea of the need to find herself, "to emerge as yourself (178). Imagination, spirit, and intelligence, which he sees dominating technique in her piano playing, are advantages in vocal training.

Whether by force of habit or admiration for her teacher, or the difficulty of being truthful and facing more challenge and uncertainty, Thea is reluctant to agree to the recommended change. Harsanyi pleads on behalf of a gift of the gods, which she is not quite ready to acknowledge or prefers to hold in abeyance. As Harsanyi had said, "Every artist makes himself [or herself] born" (150), and this process is only at the stage of germination in Thea.

Although we have little information on the voice lessons Thea has with the expert in vocal training by the name Madison Bowers, we see Thea's vocal talent asserting itself and her personal beauty increasing in proportion to the nurturing of her musical gift. When Thea plays accompaniments for Bowers' other students, she becomes exasperated with the pretentious women, lacking in artistic standards ("those instinctive standards which are called ideals," 219), who frequent Bowers' studio and whom she must accommodate in her playing. Thea's countenance is fixed in a squint as she accompanies the florid Mrs. Priest, apt to be singing off pitch, or when Jessie Darcey voices A at the point of B-natural in "Ave Maria" and corrects this with B-flat. We see Thea participating in musical evenings with Chicago society, where she impresses her hosts with the first real voice they've heard in this city and appears to them like a Swedish summer, her milky white skin adorned in pale rose silk with silver butterflies.

During summer vacation in Moonstone Thea calls on Johnny Tellamantez for the lyrics of a serenade he used to sing, "Rosa de Noche," and is invited to a Mexican ball next day, an occasion to dance and sing with really musical people. The evening culminates in an impromptu concert with Thea's performance of Mexican part songs with Johnny, a trio from "Il Trovatore," and a sextette from "Lucia di Lammermoor." Thea is inspired to excel by her open, receptive audience and in turn leaves them awestruck or sighing. The melodies carry over the gulch, where the Kohlers delight in Thea's soprano voice that "shot up like a fountain jet" amid other voices and "played in and about and around and over them, like a goldfish darting among creek minnows, like a yellow butterfly soaring above a swarm of dark ones" (199). "*Ach, wunderschön*" ("exceedingly beautiful"), Mrs. Kohler whispers; "*Ja, schön*" ("yes, beautiful"), Fritz agrees.

Thea's physical appearance is adequate to her voice. The Ramos cousins, seeing a Scandinavian girl for the first time, find Thea's fair skin and shining yellow hair dazzling, fit for paradise: "*Blanco y oro, semejante la Pascua!*" ("white and gold, like Easter!"), they exclaim. In conversation with Dr. Archie, Thea presents a taller, towering version of her former self and a new determination that startles her old friend: "She was beautiful as his little Swede had never been, but she frightened him . . . . A light seemed to break upon her from far away—or perhaps from far within" (Cather 206), the gleam in her eyes like a diamond drill-point. From the context of their dialogue, about wanting and attaining and the possibility of failure, it is clear that Thea is coming to terms with the direction Harsanyi had pointed out, flaring with the desire Wunsch had extolled.

When Thea's verve is all but extinguished by routine at Bowers' studio next year, by Chicago weather, and a bout with tonsillitis, Fred proposes a vacation at his family's ranch in Arizona: basking in the sun might return her normal color. Among the milestones in Thea's growth as an artist and successive affirmations of vocation, her experience in Arizona the following summer is the most significant. Here she arrives at a definitive affirmation on her own, independent of others' advice, and this affirmation is comprehensive, involving body, mind and soul. Thea's daily sojourns in Panther Canyon, with a splash in the stream at the foot of the canyon and sun-bathing in her chosen niche of the rock cliffs, waken her senses and receptivity to the elements. The ideas in the songs that well up in her pertain to fragrance, color and sound rather than words, so that she begins to appreciate music in its sensuous forms and to experience voice in connection with mere vitality (a connection that Bowers had noticed in the ripples of her spinal cord when she sang with Fred, of which Thea was unaware). She remarks that voice *is* vitality, "a lightness in the body and a driving power in the blood" (257).

The physical revelations are complemented by Thea's spiritual communion with the ancient people who had once inhabited Panther Canyon and by her attempts to understand their culture and way of life. The refreshment afforded by the stream in this desert milieu brings home stories told by Henry Biltmore at the ranch of a way of life that revolved around the precious element of water, expressed in customs, ceremonies, and religion, and most evidently in the shards of pottery, formerly vessels for water, scattered about the rock chambers.

> That stream was the only living thing left of the drama that had been played out in the canyon centuries ago. In the rapid, restless heart of it, flowing swifter than the rest, there was a continuity of life that reached back into the old time . . . Thea's bath came to have a ceremonial gravity. The atmosphere of the canyon was ritualistic (Cather 254).

Walking along the trails blazed by ancient cliff dwellers, Thea intuits the life of women with children on their backs and jars in their hands, as if accessing collective memory. Examining fragments of their handiwork in the cliff chambers, she admires the exquisite designs on the shards, perfected beyond the requirements of usefulness and necessity. Thea remembers Ray Kennedy's accounts of expeditions to Navaho reservations and his reference to fragments of pottery as "fragments of their desire" (269), implying an obligation to do one's best in honor of this desire, for the sake of the human endeavor at large.

Yet another of Thea's reflections concerning the pottery shards suggests an image of the artist that Cather held as a model for her portrait of Thea Kronborg, also relevant to her concept of beauty. While splashing water on herself one morning, Thea exclaims to herself, "What was any art but an effort to make a sheath, a mould in which to imprison for a moment the shining, elusive element which is life itself—life hurrying past us and running away, too strong to stop, too sweet to lose?—The Indian women held it in their jars" (254-5). Applied to Cather's heroine and her musical gift, this hypothesis points to Thea's person as the human vessel for the expression of the life ("the elusive element") in the music she performs. The notion that the more refined the vessel, the more nurtured and molded, the better it will serve its purpose, anticipates the integration of body, mind, and soul that Thea attains at Panther Canyon as a result of her relation to the natural surroundings, her spiritual bonding with the ancient cliff dwellers, and new awareness of her part in the continuity of culture. The analogy of the vessel evidently marks a threshold in Thea's growth.

Thea is inspired and strengthened by the nearness of the ancient civilization, palpable in the dust of the rock cliffs. Traces of its life infuse her movements, daydreams, and contemplations while the natural setting refreshes her senses. She feels relieved of old habits and routines, in touch with her own vitality, core values and ideals. Like the flight of an eagle she follows one morning, signaling "endeavor, achievement, desire, glorious striving of human art!" (Cather 269), Thea's ideas become simple and clear, stirring her toward decisive action concerning plans for vocal training in Germany. When Fred visits and engages her in a hiking expedition, he notices the directedness of Thea's movements, the muscular energy, and extraordinary projecting power of her body as she waves from a distant ledge. He sees a beautiful transformation of the woman he met in Bowers' studio, an emergence of Thea the artist, as Harsanyi might have said.

The integration of personality Thea attains at Panther Canyon is basic to the splendid vessel for voice that she later presents in a range of operatic roles; the projecting power of her body from a distant cliff anticipates the power of her stage presence at the Metropolitan Opera in New York. But there is another component to the realization of an ideal of fulfillment, which connects this threshold in Thea's growth to the next, much as it links the surges of talent previous to the summer in Arizona: persistent struggle in the course of musical training. This component tends to be obscured in favor of the peaks in Thea's musical experience, in accord with the romantic *élan* of Cather's portrait. Thea's effort is often revealed indirectly, by witnesses and second-hand accounts, by letters and newspaper clippings from Germany, received by Mrs. Kronborg, Mrs. Kohler, Dr. Archie, and Thea's Aunt Tillie, for the decisive decade of study abroad is behind the scenes of the novel. However, Cather's round-about expression of Thea's industriousness, like indirection or understatement in poetry, might be designed to convey the central importance of the matter of practice in her musical media.

In Chicago, Thea impresses Andor Harsanyi with her power of work and way of charging at difficulties, which must increase with an expanding repertoire. Harsanyi observes Thea's struggle to overcome gaps in her previous training, her responsiveness to instruction, and eagerness to comprehend musical scores. Her approach is *organic*. Before rendering parts and passages of a score, she must grasp the main idea or theme, which will infuse all the parts and tie them together meaningfully. Once Thea discovers the gist of the song, the main idea, she practices it until her voice is adequate to the melody, and her delivery to the meaning of the lyrics. As Thea's learning of "Die Lorelei" after a piano lesson with Harsanyi alludes to her mastery of another song by Heine on her thirteenth birthday, when she not only repeated the lines but infused the lyrics with feeling and insight into the subject matter, we see a recurrent pairing of rigor in the piano lessons with expressions of personality in the training of her voice, the former facilitating the latter. The implications are that Thea's musical training and her personal growth must keep abreast of one another and that her integral, organic approach to the interpretation of musical scores correlates with the degree of integration of body, mind, and soul in her personality. These are confirmed by the entire episode of Thea's awakening to vocation at Panther Canyon, in the interim between her musical training in Chicago and her voice training in Germany.

The early years of Thea's decade in Germany are recalled by Oliver Landry, a singer and accompanist whose path abroad had intersected with Thea's. Conversing with Fred Ottenburg after Thea's performance in Wagner's "Das Rheingold" at the Met one afternoon, Oliver remembers playing the scene between Fricka and Wotan a thousand times, for weeks, until Thea found her line of interpretation and worked her voice into it, then changed and reworked her role, attaining a golden quality that distinguished Fricka as a goddess of wisdom instead of Wotan's jealous spouse, for which she is usually taken. Even as she practiced, Thea sang for the idea, trusting her breath and every gesture and movement of her body to follow nuances of meaning and shades of emotion expressed by the voice when it was attuned to the main idea of a score. Her idea might involve sensations, which she had discovered and prized in Arizona. For the role of Fricka, she brought forth the light of northern sunsets and the fresh colors of Swedish summer, though her clear and sunny Fricka was also modeled on her mother's Swedish visage and mannerisms.

On Friday afternoon at the Met, when the curtain falls on part one of Wagner's Ring cycle, the Volsungsaga, critics and admirers attempt to describe qualities of Thea's performance that made for a splendid Sieglinde. Was it projecting power? Explosive force? Dramatic temperament? Passion? (Cather 395) or the color and personality that are born in a singer, which Oliver Landry took for inherited memory or "a gift of the gods" (372)? In the author's view, Thea has simply come into possession of everything she had at the beginning—voice, imagination, intelligence, spirit, physical strength—and had been refining over the years. This afternoon, vessel and voice worked in perfect harmony, at the service of Wagner's music, as it were effortlessly rendering Sieglinde's role.

> Her inhibitions chanced to be fewer than usual, and within herself,
> she entered into the inheritance that she herself had laid up, into
> the fullness of the faith she had kept before she knew its name or
> meaning . . . . All that deep-rooted vitality flowered in her voice,
> her face, in her very finger tips. She felt like a tree bursting into
> bloom (395).

Thea's achievement resonates with lines in Wagner's lyrics when Sieglinde sings about the story of her life and tells "how the thing which was truly herself, 'bright as the day', rose to the surface" (393). In Thea this "thing," variously termed "the friendly spirit," "the hidden creature," and "the thing in her that had to do with beauty and power" (71, 162, 180) rises to the surface as a result of nurturing mind, body, and soul in order to sustain the talent and the rigorous training it demanded.

From Andor Harsanyi's perspective, Thea's excellent performance is merely sufficiency, ideally the norm rather than the exceptional event. When the curtain fell, he sighed, "At last . . . somebody with *enough!* Enough voice and talent and beauty, enough physical power. And such a noble, noble style!" (394). He suggests the obligation to do one's best for a given musical score (which Thea had apprehended in connection with the relics of cliff dwellers' art), as well as the prevailing tendency to fall short in the effort (as shown in Bowers' studio in Chicago). Taken as the fulfillment of an ideal, standard, or expectation, "sufficiency" is tantamount to Cather's concept of beauty pertaining to art and artists, which is the full expression of one's creative potential, making for integrity in the performance of a given song or musical score.

In conclusion, one might note that Cather contextualizes her concept of beauty in a wider sphere of socio-cultural standards that set the measure for the individual artist. Beyond the inner circle of family and friends, guides and guardians, involved in Thea's progress to stardom, Cather represents cultural milieu that is conducive to individual achievement. Limited as it is, the Moonstone standard keeps Thea on track and aspiring for more, especially through the influence of the books she reads and the romantic idealists she befriends. She finds a vibrant cultural sphere in Chicago, a sense of cultural continuity in the rock cliffs of Panther Canyon, and abroad, the German musical tradition, which prevailed in the West until the early twentieth century. Different standards along her path, like the complacencies in Moonstone communities and the pretensions of her "natural enemies" in Bowers' studio and the Metropolitan Opera, serve to delineate the standards of good taste and excellence in musical performance that inspire Cather's heroine and set the bar for which she reaches. Toward the end of the novel, when Thea reminisces about Moonstone with Dr. Archie and speaks of art as a way of remembering childhood, she refers to a stream reaching the level of its source ("The stream has reached the level of its source. That's our measure," 382). Taken metaphorically, the source of a river or stream may refer to initial endowment or musical gift, which implies heritage and in turn culture, or cultural memory. So we may understand why Cather depicts Thea in communion with the spirit of nature as well as a past civilization before sending her to Germany to study Wagner's operas, particularly the

Norse legends that partake in her own Swedish heritage; why she employs a German musician, Professor Wunsch, to instill the Northern European ideal of wholeness or comprehensiveness in art, modeled on organicism in nature.

-CHAPTER 8-

James Joyce, A Portrait of the Artist as a Young Man: Radiance

Stephen Dedalus' attraction to light is evident throughout his childhood and adolescence, before his experience of radiance on the strand and his association of radiance with "epiphany." Light appears in connection with warmth and color, evoking happiness, contentment, and creative energy in the context of everyday experience at home and school. Imagery of light, color, and warmth in *A Portrait of the Artist as a Young Man* gains clarity by its contrast with dark, colorlessness, and cold, together making for a backdrop of chiaroscuro in the dramatic action of Joyce's novel, not unlike the rhythm of day and night or the interplay of sunlight with mist, fog, and cold grey air. Therefore, we may sketch Stephen's growth as an inclination to light (and color and warmth), complicated by his adolescent experience of rebellion and conflict—also perceptible as an alternation between light and dark, or clarity and chaos—which is summarily resolved by Stephen's experience of wholeness, harmony, and radiance on the strand, featuring both natural light and spiritual manifestations. While Stephen's experience on the strand is basic to his theory of beauty, the various stages of his growth, replete with successive epiphanies, offer "the daily bread of experience" that is to be transformed to art, "the radiant body of everliving life" in his definition (Joyce 221).

The spectrum of light imagery begins with the ambiance of light, color, and warmth in Stephen's home in Blackrock, which he experiences both in reality and imaginative reverie during his school days at Clongowes Wood College. Thoughts of hearth and fire back home comfort Stephen when he is ill as a result of being shouldered into a cold, slimy ditch on the grounds of his school. When he anticipates Christmas vacation at home, he envisions colored lanterns in the hallway, chandeliers and old portraits garlanded with red holly and green ivy. The reality measures up to his musings and expectations, for he finds luminous décor and a glowing red fire at home: "A great fire, banked high and red, flamed in the grate and under the ivy-twined branches of the chandelier the Christmas table was spread" (27). Light also figures prominently at Clongowes College, a luminous castle framed by pale cold sky and pale grey air over the playground. Stephen delights in the castle lights, associating them with warmth and imagination kindled by stories: "It was nice and warm to see the lights in the castle. It was like something in a book" (10). He is drawn to the fire in the infirmary because it allays his chill and inspires reverie, as of waves in the sea at night, "long dark waves rising and falling, dark under the moonless night" (27) and a light shining in the pier head to welcome entering ships. In another reverie, he imagines the dwellings of peasants whom he sees at chapel on Sundays, the dark within their cottages lit by fire, becoming a "warm dark" (18). In the course of his daily routine Stephen observes various degrees of gaslight in the corridors of the castle and pale, grey, or sunny light in the windows.

An interplay of black, grey and white gradually overtakes the aura of light, warmth, and color that suffuses Stephen's childhood. Light may be reflected or not in people and phenomena of the environment. In the event of breaking his glasses on the cinderpath at Clongowes and subsequent punishment for his supposed idleness (pandy-batting on his hands by the prefect of studies), Stephen is struck by the lack of color and light in the prefect's visage: "his witegrey face and non-coloured eyes behind the steelrimmed spectacles" (52). The warmth and color at home cede to a dim atmosphere, with a "dull fire" and "weak light" shed by the lamp on the eve of the Dedaluses' move to Dublin. The atmospheric shift is marked by the train ride to Dublin with his mother, a "passage through the gloomy foggy city" (Joyce 65), and persists throughout most of his adolescence. In his early perambulations of Dublin, including walks to the docks and quays at the harbor, Stephen sees grey streets or muddy water at his feet and "lowering skies" above him. The dull grey city contrasts with sunny Marseilles, of which he had read, and fleeting impressions of sunlit streets in Cork, where he travels with his father.

The squalor that Stephen finds in Dublin as a result of his family's diminished standard of living is relieved by the festive lights of a children's party at Harold's Cross and excursions to the center of town, with its array of illumined shop windows. But it is Stephen's career at Belvedere College, his new school, that offers most diversion from the gloom, especially his participation in a play at Whitsuntide and later, the retreat in honor of St. Francis Xavier.

The evening of the Whitsuntide play is bright with stage lights as well as spiritual manifestations verging on epiphanies. The theater glitters with lanterns: "the light spread upwards from the glass roof making the theatre seem a festive ark . . . her frail cables of lanterns looping her to her moorings" (74-5). Stephen is elated as he anticipates his performance in the play and thinks of Emma, who might be in the audience. Memories of previous encounters with Emma flood his mind, so that he experiences a gamut of emotions, from "gloomy tenderness . . . in dark courses and eddies" (77) to an "invisible warm wave" (83) in his body at the reminiscence of their touch. This occurs in the midst of conversation with his friends, breaks in their jesting banter that brings previous taunts and insults to his mind ("Confess!"). Yet anger, malice, and resentment escape Stephen, and it is presumably the spiritual element in his day dreams of Emma and love that arms and protects him from darts of darker emotions this evening as in conversations past ("the adventure in his mind stood in no danger from their words," 78; "some power was divesting him of that suddenwoven anger as easily as a fruit is divested of its soft ripe peel," 82). We may see a subtly drawn analogy between forces of light and dark, constructive and destructive, in the minds and souls of students surrounding Stephen and the play of light in the atmosphere, with stage lights opposed to a dark auditorium and theater lanterns shining in dark evening air.

Joyce maintains an analogy between atmospheric effects and his hero's mental and spiritual states throughout the novel, reinforcing the correlation between inner microcosm and outer macrocosm established by the close of his education at Clongowes College. For example, in childhood (Blackrock), on one of Stephen's rounds with the milkman, "a dusk like that of the outer world obscured his mind as he heard the mare's hoofs clattering" (Joyce 64). In later adolescence, when Stephen enters the kitchen of his home in Dublin, the sight of his siblings adjourning from afternoon tea instills in him a blend of remorse and gratitude along with a recognition of all that had been given him and denied them. Accordingly, "The sad quiet grey-blue glow of the dying day came through the window . . . covering over and allaying quietly a sudden instinct of remorse in Stephen's heart" (163). In early manhood, on the morning of his awakening to a flurry of roseate images in his mind and lines of verse descending on his pen, Stephen experiences a crystallization of thought and feeling in a moment of clarity compared to "a point of light": "The instant flashed forth like a point of light and now for cloud on cloud of vague circumstance confused form was veiling softly its afterglow" (217). As it were the various phases of his life partake in a theatrical setting comparable to the one at Belvedere College.

The episode of the retreat in honor of St. Francis Xavier at Belvedere College is supreme in its evocation of light and dark, centering on the imagery of heaven and hell in Father Arnall's sermon, which is reflected in the states of Stephen's soul prior to and after the event. Father Arnall expounds on the exterior and interior darkness of hell that is opposed to the light of God, of hosts of splendid angels, and the Blessed Virgin. Hell is described as a dark reeking prison, for the everlasting fire of hell emits no light; it is "a never ending storm of darkness, dark flames and dark smoke of burning brimstone" (120). The exterior darkness, which torments the flesh, is complemented by interior darkness, resulting from torments of the spirit—by far the worse.

Arnall explains that every spiritual faculty is afflicted: "the fancy with horrible images, the sensitive faculty with alternate longing and rage, the mind and understanding with an interior darkness more terrible even than the exterior darkness which reigns in that dreadful prison" (130). Listening to Arnall's commentary on the pains of the damned, like the pain of loss and the pain of conscience, Stephen identifies the spiritual darkness of hell with his own recent fall into debauchery, sloth and lust, which he had likened to a "thick fog" encompassing his mind and the plunging of his soul "into a somber threatening dusk" (111). Slowly lifting himself by contrition and penance after the retreat, Stephen attains clarity of mind and purity of heart as by invisible grace. Nevertheless, the process from chaos and confusion to inner peace and happiness is embellished by light filtering through the blinds in the chapel, then an altar resplendent with candlelight amid bouquets of white flowers. When Stephen returns home, he finds white pudding with eggs and sausages on the shelf for tomorrow's breakfast.

Juxtaposing the highlights of the evening of the Whitsuntide play and the retreat in honor of St. Francis Xavier, we find correspondence between the power of love and spiritual light that make anger and malice fall away from Stephen the night of the play and the love of God, shown in piety and devotion, that purifies Stephen of sin after the retreat. A secular view of spiritual life is set beside a religious perspective, each attended by shades of light and dark, intimating good and evil as well as beauty and ugliness. This is one of several parallels between secular and religious views in the novel expressed by light imagery. Another is suggested by the allusion of "a point of light," a metaphor for the inspiration Stephen receives the morning he writes a villanelle, to the light entering the chapel window during the retreat "like a spear," gleaming "like the battleworn mail armour of angels" (116). Such analogies between the secular and the religious shed light on the difficulty of Stephen's choice between the path of a Jesuit and that of an artist, for beauty and light, which he has appreciated since childhood, are to be found in both. The correspondence between secular and religious experience also pertains to Stephen's concept of "epiphany," revelation or spiritual manifestation, as basic to art and to his notion of the ideal effect of art—"luminous silent stasis" in the viewer—which Joseph Campbell has discussed as a similarity between the way of the artist and the way of the mystic (Campbell 2002, 92-96).

If we consider Joyce's treatment of light in connection with color, which is essential to the concept of "radiance," we find increasing disparity between secular and religious realms. The splendid fire in the Dedaluses' home in Blackrock and the fire in the infirmary at Clongowes College, attended by the cheerful, red-haired Father Michael, contrast with the fire tended by the dean of studies at Belvedere, which is meager and kindles very slowly as the dean maneuvers candle butts among coals and shafts of paper, poking wan flames. Also opposed are the luminous chandeliers at home, reflecting in garlands of holly and ivy, and the dim light of candles in chapel and church. We may remember the color or lack thereof in persons and visages: the rosy complexions of Stephen's parents and Aunt Dante, becoming red during heated conversations, mirth and song, versus the "whitegrey face" and "non-coloured eyes" of the prefect of studies at Clongowes as well as the "shadowed face" and "mirthless reflection of the sunken day" (Joyce 160) that Stephen observes in the director of studies at Belvedere. The grey faces evoke shadow in the life of priests at the College, along with gravity, chill, and order. In considering the life of a Jesuit, Stephen envisions a pale, faded image of himself as "the Reverend Stephen Dedalus, S. J.": "an undefined face or colour of a face," its pallor possibly turning to "pallid brick red" (161), as seen on the faces of his mentors. On the other hand, when Stephen intuits the artist's path on the strand and conjures an image of Daedalus' winged form as model of himself, he is radiant from head to toe: "An ecstasy of flight made radiant his eyes . . . and radiant his windswept limbs" (169).

Whereas chiaroscuro is clearest in Joyce's portrayal of the Jesuit teachers at Clongowes and Belvedere, the retreat in honor of St. Francis Xavier, and Stephen's ensuing phase of piety, color is most evident in the secular environments of Stephen's home in Blackrock, his home in Dublin (especially when he attempts to ameliorate his environment with the funds from an essay prize and when he composes poetry), the natural milieu of the strand,

and Stephen's imaginative musings throughout the novel. As the latter elicit Stephen's aesthetic sensibility and awakening to artistic vocation, the allure of color appears to be a decisive element in his choice of vocation as well as an influence on his perception of the source of art and beauty in mundane life and his concept of the aesthetic purpose of art (stated, for example, in his definition "Art is the human disposition of sensible or intelligible matter for an esthetic end," Joyce 207). Stephen agrees with St. Thomas Aquinas that beauty is pleasing to the eye, and color is often a source of pleasure.

A consideration of color in *A Portrait* must include the phenomenon of flowers—real, imagined, and symbolic—strewn along Stephen's path from childhood to maturity. Stephen is introduced to roses by the song he hears at home about "wild rose blossoms" (7) and claims as his own, suggesting interiorization and variation: the stuff of song is fuel for the imagination. At Clongowes College, red and white roses on badges designating teams in a math competition stimulate Stephen's musing on a spectrum of rose colors and hues: "pink and cream and lavender," in addition to red, white, and maybe green amid wild roses (12). In his wanderings about Blackrock, Stephen identifies a whitewashed house and rose garden with Mercedes' home in Dumas' *The Count of Monte Christo* and imagines other gardens as sites of rendezvous with the girl. Visions of Mercedes and roses are lodged so deeply in the recesses of Stephen's mind that they recur spontaneously in his adolescence, offering solace in phases of restlessness. At the close of the scene on the strand, Stephen succumbs to a swoon wherein he envisions a luxuriant crimson flower—"an opening flower . . . breaking in full crimson and unfolding and fading to palest rose, leaf by leaf, wave of light by wave of light, flooding all the heavens with its soft flushes, every flush deeper than other" (172)—evoking both the epitome of real roses and the symbolic "book of life" or world symbolized by a flower, indicated by the questions that introduce Stephen's vision: "A world? a glimmer? or a flower?" (*ibid.*). This vision differs from Stephen's previous reveries of flowers by its lyrical quality and vivid imagery: it is a creative, imaginative response to experience, marking a turning point from the apprehension of beauty to the creation of art.

Stephen's vision of the crimson flower is sparked by the sight of a girl, perceived as a seabird and an angel (respectively an *anima* image and messenger or source of inspiration) and experienced as an epiphany of "the wild heart of life" (Joyce 171), presumably effects of her youthful femininity as well as his soulful appreciation of her beauty. The girl is unique and his experience is new, in depth if not difference from previous experiences of the feminine, so that instead of the habitual pairing of girl and flower, we find a transformation of his perception and experience in the luminous crimson flower, anticipating his later reference to the creative act as a "transmuting of the daily bread of experience into the radiant body of everliving life" (221). Nonetheless, the transformation bears analogy to reality: as the girl is radiant, for suffused in sunlight and glowing with health, so the imagined flower is radiant, indeed envisioned emitting waves of light; as the potent bird image enhances the girl (as conveyor of her essence or soul), so the symbolic flower expands the significance of the real flower. The beauty apprehended in the girl on the strand is similar to the beauty created in the crimson flower, which consists of an interplay of color and light, with the distinctive quality of the object increased by light—sunlight as well as the light of imagination, soul or spirit.

The significance of the sequence of imagery from the song about wild roses that Stephen hears in infancy to his vision of the crimson flower on the strand is elucidated by Barbara Seward's insights in "The Artist and the Rose" (1957, 1962), a discussion of the rose in connection with women, art, and religion. With regard to the song about wild roses, Seward associates the green rose that Stephen attaches to the song in his line "Oh, the green wothe botheth" with his "incipient creativity" as well as "the blossoming stage" of his growth, which is green in the sense of fertile and green in the sense of immature (Seward 169). Further, she relates the roses attributed to Mercedes in reverie to subsequent associations of roses with women, ideal and real, beginning with the link between white roses and the Blessed Virgin in his prayers (citing "his prayers ascended to heaven from his purified heart like perfume streaming upwards from a heart of white rose," 171). Consequently, she discusses Stephen's perception of the girl-bird in terms of comparison and contrast with Dante's vision of Beatrice, referring to Stephen's vision of the crimson flower as a "temporal image of Dante's rose of God" (Seward 173). Moreover, she remarks on Stephen's use of the adjective *wild* in connection with the girl-bird ("the wild heart of life"; "A wild angel had appeared to him, the angel of mortal youth and beauty," Joyce 171-72), which recalls the wild roses in the song he liked as a child and indicates the line of progression from the green rose Stephen conjured early on to the crimson flower he envisions on the strand. The latter is then clearly a complement to the green rose and a culmination of his "incipient creativity."

To elucidate the spiritual component in Stephen's concept of beauty—the soulful content or spiritual light implied in his concept of radiance, which in turn influences the "spiritual manifestation" essential to "epiphany"—we return to the convergence of secular and religious perspectives in Stephen's experience. This convergence, remarked in terms of analogies between spiritual light in secular and religious contexts (theater and church), is evident before and after Stephen's choice of the secular path of artist. It is indicated by Stephen's exclamation "Heavenly God!" after he gazes at the girl in the rivulet, which relates his experience of "the wild heart of life" to a perception of divinity and is apparently an intensification of his previous implicit worship of Eileen, Mercedes, and Emma. Stephen's reverence for girls, demonstrated by his irritation when friends spoke jestingly of Emma, stems from his spiritual experience of the feminine (the archetypal feminine, conveyed by *anima*), not entirely separable from his worship of the Blessed Virgin during his pious phase. The edifying, comforting effect of the Blessed Virgin is a variation of the inspiring and strengthening effects of the archetypal feminine. Thus we may find a conversion "from the worship of things divine to the worship of things earthly" in the scene on the strand (Seward 173). Later, Stephen's perception of the divine in the earthly is suggested in his deliberation over the connotations of *claritas* (radiance) in Aquinas' aesthetic theory, involving the possibility of symbolism or idealism ("the supreme quality of beauty being a light from some other world," Joyce 213) as well as the expression of "divine purpose": "I thought he might mean that *claritas* is the artistic discovery and representation of the divine purpose in anything or a force of generalization which would make the esthetic image a universal one, make it outshine its proper conditions" (*ibid.*). His words reflect his perception of the girl as a bird, an *anima* image, and its subsequent transformation in the image of an unfolding flower, symbolic of life and vitality.

Emphasis on Stephen's arrival at a secular orientation does not discount the influence of his Catholic upbringing and education in Jesuit schools on his perspectives on art and beauty. These schools provided moral and spiritual ground for his growth as an artist and reference points for the development of his own aesthetic theory. We find ample proof of Stephen's respect for his Jesuit teachers and the Christian doctrine they taught him, as well as his interest in the works of Cardinal Newman and St. Thomas Aquinas. Stephen defers to Aquinas' notions of *integritas, consonantia,* and *claritas* in defining the basic components of beauty in his own aesthetic theory. He applies the terminology of Christian liturgy and ritual to the creative process, likening inspiration to the Annunciation ("Gabriel the seraph had come to the Virgin's chamber," i.e., "the virgin womb of the imagination" in his conception of the villanelle, Joyce 217) and the creative act of transformation to the tasting of the Eucharist in communion (implied in "transmuting the daily bread of experience into the radiant body of everliving life"), which in turn assimilates the artist's role to that of a priest. Stephen's understanding of "epiphany" as "spiritual manifestation" might stem from the religious sense of the term, "appearance or manifestation of deity," specifically the manifestation of Christ to the gentiles, commemorated by the festival of Epiphany, January 6. In sum, it is likely that Stephen's familiarity with Christian doctrine, intended to lift the soul upward to heavenly light while bending it back to custom and tradition on earth, influences the ideal or romantic aspect of Stephen's theorizing about beauty and art at this stage of early maturity in *A Portrait,* as shown particularly by the confluence of the divine and the earthly in his understanding of radiance.

*　　*　　*

In the course of his first year at the University in Dublin, toward the close of the novel, Stephen converses with his friend Lynch about the topic of beauty in preparation for writing an essay about aesthetics. He traverses the topic from its premises, which are "the frame and scope of the imagination," to its end, which is the induction of a "luminous silent stasis of esthetic pleasure" in the viewer or listener (Joyce 208, 213), indicative of the aesthetic purpose of art (as opposed to the didactic, informative, or provocative) in his view. Stephen suggests the source of his concept of beauty in the manifold rhythms of life and organic nature, which partake in the rhythm of the universe and reiterate the interrelation of microcosm to macrocosm that he has intuited at various stages of his growth. He considers rhythm an essential quality of beauty, pertinent to "harmony" (*consonantia* in St. Thomas Aquinas' terminology), which is the "relation of part to part in any esthetic whole or of an esthetic whole to its part or parts or of any part to the esthetic whole of which it is a part" (206). To Lynch's prompt "If that is rhythm, let me hear what you call beauty," Stephen replies, "To speak of these things and to try to understand their nature and having understood it, to try slowly and humbly and constantly to express, to press out again, from the gross earth or what it brings forth, from sound and shape and colour, which are the prison gates of our soul, an image of the beauty we have come to understand—that is art" (206-7), implying an equation between beauty and art as well as a correspondence between the process of aesthetic apprehension and the creative process.

Stephen's concept of beauty is remarkably broad, for based on life-long experience. His awakening to the vocation of artist proceeded from keen aesthetic sensibility and the imaginative capacity he demonstrated since childhood, which are revealed in full force on the strand. In readiness to take the artistic path, for experiencing harmony between himself and the universe, he conjures Daedalus' winged form in the clouds, with which he identifies, and in readiness to create art, he perceives a girl in the likeness of a seabird, an inspiring *anima* image. In other words, he experiences revelations of his essential self and of feminine beauty, which he had yearned for and sought in the wanderings of childhood and adolescence. Stephen's ideas about art and beauty are also influenced by avid reading, with special interest in the Romantic poets and modern drama, particularly Henrik Ibsen, in addition to the writings of Church fathers. Stephen can relate to the components of beauty in Aquinas' aesthetic theory on the basis of his experience of wholeness during his walk on the strand, much as he had applied characters and scenes from Alexandre Dumas' *The Count of Monte Christo* to his own aesthetic experience in childhood and Lord Byron's poetry to his romantic reverie in adolescence. In theorizing about beauty, Stephen recapitulates phases of aesthetic apprehension in his experience, as he suggests to Lynch: "To finish what I was saying about beauty . . . the most satisfying relations of the sensible must therefore correspond to the necessary phases of artistic apprehension. Find these and you find the qualities of universal beauty" (Joyce 211).

If Stephen's phases of aesthetic apprehension culminate in the episodes on the strand, which comprise his experience of wholeness, harmony, and radiance, these must be the qualities of beauty to which he refers. Indeed, he emphasizes their importance for his own aesthetic theory in his subsequent explication of Aquinas' Latin terms (*integritas, consonantia, claritas*) for his friend. Stephen gives most attention to *claritas,* "radiance," with regard to both the apprehension of beauty and the intended effect of art:

> the instant wherein that supreme quality of beauty, the clear radiance of the esthetic image, is apprehended luminously by the mind which has been arrested by its wholeness and fascinated by its harmony is the luminous silent stasis of esthetic pleasure, a spiritual state very like to that cardiac condition which the Italian physiologist Luigi Galvani . . . called the enchantment of the heart (213).

Stephen speaks confidently on this point, for he has felt radiance in his glowing face and limbs at the instant of identifying with Daedalus and experienced the "luminous silent stasis of esthetic pleasure" while gazing at the bird-girl in the rivulet. And he had perceived radiance many times previously—in the hearth fire back home, in the colors of roses, and Emma's visage, for instance. According to the principle of conscious life cited by Jung (1940, 153), "There is nothing in the mind that was not first in sensation" (*"nihil est in intellectu, quod non antea fuerit in sensu"*). However, in Stephen's experience, as in that of numerous poets and writers, sensual experience is bound up with intuitions of the spirit, both of which precede intellectual formulations.

In his conversation with Lynch, Stephen comments that an application of Aquinas' terms suffices for his theory of beauty, but he needs new terminology for the creative process ("So far as this side of esthetic philosophy extends Aquinas will carry me all along the line. When it comes to the phenomena of artistic conception, artistic gestation and artistic reproduction I require a new terminology and a new personal experience," Joyce 209). He does not discuss the requisite terminology as he does Aquinas' aesthetic theory, but there are clues to his notions of artistic conception, artistic gestation, and artistic reproduction in his day dreams, interior monologues, and attempts at creative writing preceding the conversation with Lynch. The clearest of these clues are yielded, of course, in the scene on the strand, which is widely interpreted as a series of "epiphanies," with reference to Stephen's comments on the experience of an epiphany in *Stephen Hero*, the preliminary manuscript of *A Portrait of the Artist as a Young Man* (in print since 1944). So the "new personal experience" and "new terminology" appear to center on "epiphany," a showing forth or revelation, previewed in the course of Stephen's growth, with its numerous moments of awareness, insight, and clarity, culminating in the epiphany of Stephen's identity as an artist and an epiphany of "the wild heart of life" as a source of art.

The essential structure of *A Portrait* as a sequence of epiphanies and the importance of "epiphany" for Stephen's concept of art are indicated toward the close of *Stephen Hero* by Stephen's reflections on an impression he received while overhearing a conversation in the street:

> This triviality [a conversation between a young lady and a gentleman] made him think of collecting many such moments together in a book of epiphanies. By an epiphany he meant a sudden spiritual manifestation, whether in the vulgarity of speech or a gesture or in a memorable phase of the mind itself. He believed that it was for the man of letters to record these epiphanies with extreme care, seeing that they themselves are the most delicate and evanescent of moments (Joyce, *Stephen Hero* 211).

Stephen proceeds to explain to his friend (Cranly in *Stephen Hero*) that any object, say a clock that is routinely glimpsed, might occasionally show forth its essence and be perceived precisely for what it is, as a result of an exact focus of the spiritual eye. The example of the clock conflicts with Stephen's definition of epiphany as a "spiritual manifestation" unless he has in mind the perception of mystery, timelessness, or eternity behind the incessant rotation of the hands of a clock. On the other hand, it extends the concept to include moments of appreciation and clarity vis à vis phenomena of the environment as well as moments of spiritual rapport with animate beings. The broader concept supports Stephen's connection of epiphany with radiance ("It is just in this epiphany that I find the third, the supreme quality of beauty," *Stephen Hero* 211) and allows for the analogy between epiphany and light, or the figurative expression of epiphany by natural light, which Joyce maintains throughout *A Portrait of the Artist as a Young Man*.

-CHAPTER 9-

Virginia Woolf, To the Lighthouse: Integration of Depth and Surface

> Beautiful and bright it should be on the surface, feathery and
> evanescent, one colour melting into another like the colours on a
> butterfly's wing; but beneath the fabric must be clamped together
> with bolts of iron. It was to be a thing you could ruffle with your
> breath; and a thing you could not dislodge with a team of horses
> (Woolf 171).

That is how Lily Briscoe envisions her painting when she contemplates her
work-in-progress toward the close of Woolf's novel. The beauty she describes
inheres in the shimmering blue bay and splendid landscape of the Isle of
Skye, locus of the Ramsays' summer home. It also suggests Mrs. Ramsay,
outstanding for her exquisite facial features as well as her inner strength
and sternness. In the course of Lily's interior monologues concerning her
painting, we learn that it represents both of these: Mrs. Ramsay, whom Lily
admires and loves, and the natural milieu in which she delights during her
visit with the Ramsays. Lily strives to render her experience of people and
places: to express the object rather than the subject, but the object in her
own particular view, influenced by feeling.

Lily's style is "abstract expressionism," like Zack McCoy's in Updike's *Seek My Face*; however, it is objective abstract expressionism. Mrs. Ramsay is represented by a purple triangle and the landscape by an arrangement of form and color in which natural phenomena, abstracted and synthesized, are implied in their proximity to the contours of a tree at the center of the composition. Lily said she painted what she saw—the bright violet jacmanna, the gleaming white rocks, the massive hedge—for she was honest (Woolf 18). Yet her vision altered the hues and shapes of reality, making for a subjective *gestalt,* in which distinct forms of reality are blurred in order to emphasize depth and surface, and to allow for the expression of flecks of rapture and delight that ruffle the plane of appearances.

Lily's vision is embedded in the recurrent motifs of light and sight in Woolf's novel, which uphold the author's tenet that there are a myriad ways of seeing reality. Each person has a particular beam or ray along which to see ("Looking along his [Mr. Bankes'] beam, she added to it her different ray," 48), influenced in turn by variations in atmospheric light. For example, James, the Ramseys' youngest son, sees the lighthouse as "real" in daytime, with its tower and windows on whitewashed rocks, and "imagined," with a yellow eye opening and shutting, in evening mist. "For nothing was simply one thing" (186). Lily is portrayed trying to see people and places, "looking, straining, till the colour of the wall and the jacmanna beyond burnt into her eyes" (17). She wishes she had "fifty pairs of eyes to see with" (198) to better appreciate the Isle of Skye and to perceive the multi-faceted Mrs. Ramsay. "Love too had a thousand shapes" (192).

Among the numerous pairs of eyes and their spectacles and glasses in the novel, Lily's eyes are distinctively "Chinese" and "dim." She is an outsider, it seems, with an insider's perspective. In her painting position at the edge of the lawn, she is depicted "with the dim eyes and the absent-minded manner" (53), specifically at the point of Mr. Bankes' inspection of her painting-in-progress. Lily's dim eyes contrast with the clear blue eyes of Mr. Bankes, biologist and fellow guest as the Ramsays' summer retreat; her absent-minded manner betrays her confusion by Mr. Bankes' analytical questions about the effects of masses, light, and shadow in her painting, as well as their intrusion on her state of concentration on the painting. The dim eyes are associated with both an overwhelming of her vision by the general view and a diminishing of the general view by her unique vision: "subduing all her impressions as a woman to something much more general; becoming once more under the power of that vision which she had seen clearly once and must now grope for" (53). Dim eyes then have to do with the interplay of subjective and objective perspectives in her attempt to abstract facets of reality and express the depth of feeling that motivates her work. While the reality of Skye is predominantly light, marked by the lighthouse, depth of feeling is associated with the darkness beneath appearances: "Beneath it is all dark, it is all spreading . . . This core of darkness . . ." (62).

Lily's way of seeing partakes of a feminist perspective, that is, Virginia Woolf's, and a feminine creative mode that is highlighted in Woolf's portraits of Mrs. Ramsay and Lily Briscoe. Mrs. Ramsay is the model mother and matchmaker at the center of family and community, radiating a sense of stability, peace, and comfort as she organizes the coming together of family and guests, notably at dinnertime. She is positioned vis à vis Mr. Ramsay, the traditional male, continually demanding attention as he darts in and out, disturbing the peace, opposing reason to the "illusions" of love and imagination. For instance, when Mrs. Ramsay encourages James' anticipation of an excursion to the lighthouse, Mr. Ramsay remarks that stormy weather is bound to prevent it. While Mr. Ramsay and his protégé, Charles Tansley, talk of knowledge and dissertations, the women seek relationship and intimacy. Accordingly, Lily explores her relation to Mrs. Ramsay and her family, and in painting she strives to depict the object seen through the eyes of love, whereby it is whole and integrated, even if "unreal" (46). Lily's view contrasts with Mr. Bankes' scientific, analytical perspective. It is also opposed to the interests of a male artist, the elderly poet Augustus Carmichael, who writes impersonal poetry about distinct and definite things, "the desert and the camel . . . the palm tree and the sunset . . . [saying] very little about love" (195).

Love's shape is malleable and changing; so too are Lily's perceptions of the object to be rendered on canvas. Complex and subtle at its inception, contemplated at dinnertime and strolls by the sea, her vision changes when she picks up her brush. Lily sees Mrs. Ramsay in the august shape of a dome as she observes kinds of love around her, but this shape becomes a triangle in her visual composition. Therefore, the transition from conception and envisioning to work is especially difficult for Lily; it is a "dreadful" passage (19). Again and again she struggles to draw the first line on canvas and to subject mounds of paint on her palette to her will. Moreover, Lily is at risk of being interrupted by Mr. Ramsay or her solicitous companion, Mr. Bankes, or the Ramsay children. She is apt to hesitate in her application, frustrated on the one hand by her own fastidiousness and on the other, by lapses in confidence, for, as Charles Tansley maintains, "Women can't paint" (Woolf 48, 159).

Lily wishes not only to satisfy her creative urge but also to assert her social self in her art, involving moral and ethical dimensions of her personality. As a guest at the Ramsays' summer home, Lily is outstanding for her fine manners, tactful behavior, and civility. (We also hear about her obligations with her father at home on Brompton Road, which she keeps.) Lily is familiar with codes of behavior between hosts and guests, men and women, parents and children, and so apt to suffer from a lack of manners on the part of others, such as Charles Tansley, Mr. Ramsay's boastful student. Nevertheless, she acquiesces in Mrs. Ramsay's tacit request to bolster the male ego, to smile, and be nice in the face of impertinence, giving of herself for the common good. Lily's ethical awareness characterizes her artistic persona as well: she wishes to reciprocate the joy she is given by the Ramsays, especially Mrs. Ramsay, by expressing her love for the family and their summer home in her painting. Her motive of reciprocation signifies relation, regard, and respect among members of a community, in line with the ancient tradition of gift giving. Lily's expression of love is "part of the human gain" according to the author's commentary, voiced by Lily: "It was love, she thought [of Mr. Bankes' regard for Mrs. Ramsay] . . . distilled and filtered; love that never attempted to clutch its object; but, like the love which mathematicians bear their symbols, or poets their phrases, was meant to be spread over the world and become part of the human gain" (47). The ethical motive no doubt influences Lily's persistence and resolve to complete her painting.

The daily routine of setting up easel and canvas on the edge of the lawn is resumed ten years after Lily's first sojourn in Skye—after World War I, after the passing of Mrs. Ramsay and two of her children. Mrs. Ramsay has become a memory, yet clear and vivid. Lily's painting takes on new life as images in her mind, like spurtings of a fountain, spontaneously direct her brushstrokes. She proceeds to dip into her palette and cover the white spaces on her canvas with strokes of blue, green, and umber, at long last fulfilling her desire, expressing her relation to beloved persons and place.

The painting process is exceedingly long, for Lily is the author's double, or persona, and central character in Woolf's representation of "this other thing," the reality of art (158). Lily's presence throughout the novel, alternately painting and socializing with the Ramsays and their guests, continually observing the scene, indicates the interrelation of the reality of art and the reality of life—of family, community, and relationships, centered on Mrs. Ramsay—which is the basic theme of *To the Lighthouse*. Art, particularly Lily's painting and Augustus Carmichael's poetry, is shown to enrich daily life on Skye. Lily's painting is available for all to see; Augustus, though not as sociable as Lily, reads his poems after supper occasionally. On the other hand, Lily and Augustus draw inspiration from the Ramsay family circle and Mrs. Ramsay's ability to bring everyone together in felicitous moments, likely to linger in memory. The recurrent symbolism of the spurting fountain, signifying creativity, adheres both to artists and to members of the Ramsay family.

In one of her eloquent passages, Woolf speaks of "little daily miracles, illuminations, matches struck unexpectedly in the dark" (161), recalling epiphanies in James Joyce's stories and the concept of beauty as light or illumination. The "daily miracles, illuminations" in *To the Lighthouse* are inspiring conversations at dinner time or strolls by the sea; admirations and intimacies, as between Mr. and Mrs. Ramsay or Lily and Mrs. Ramsay; recognitions of love, of friendship, of summer joy in the children or joy in creative process—all of which entail a depth of feeling or thought. Woolf also mentions "pinnacles" in reality: "Here and there emerged from the mist . . . a pinnacle, a dome; prominent things, without names" (74). One thinks of Lily's first choice of a dome to represent Mrs. Ramsay in her picture, as well as the lighthouse, with which Mrs. Ramsay is identified in the course of the narrative. When Mrs. Ramsay's eyes meet its strokes of light—the "eyes" of the lighthouse—"it seemed to her like her own eyes meeting her own eyes . . . for she was stern, she was searching, she was beautiful like that light" (Woolf 63). Mrs. Ramsay is certainly a guidepost and a source of strength and comfort to family and guests. She is remembered as such, for toward the end of the novel, while Lily finishes her painting and Augustus Carmichael attains renown for his objective poetry, Mr. Ramsay and the children conduct their long-anticipated expedition to the lighthouse as a tribute to Mrs. Ramsay. Lily's painting attempts to express both the various spurtings of the fountain that make for illuminations of daily life and the solid ground that is a requisite for pinnacles and domes. Her intention to integrate surface and depth proceeds from the feminine creative mode that is concerned with relation or synthesis.

Lily's painting, described at the outset as "beautiful and bright . . . feathery and evanescent" but "clamped together with bolts of iron" beneath, reflects Woolf's representation of reality in *To the Lighthouse*. Daily life on Skye, effervescent with bright moments and miracles, is securely based in a traditional, rooted family surrounding Mrs. Ramsay. The portraits of family and community are embellished by the setting: the glistening sheen of the Isle of Skye that is situated, like all islands, on the foundation of a volcanic mountain, and is guarded in this context by a lighthouse. In painting, Lily strives for effects similar to the authoress' flowing, stream-of-consciousness style of writing and her interweaving of depth with surface as she alternates weighty interior monologues with light-hearted description of the daily pastimes of children and guests on the lawn, or their excursions to the beach and the village. Lily's vision, as well as the difficulty of its achievement on canvas, mirror Woolf's concept and work. Like a play within a play, Lily's picture is a microcosm of Woolf's novel, abstracted and transferred to a visual medium.

-CHAPTER 10-

John Updike, Seek My Face: Vitality

Zack McCoy, fictional counterpart of Jackson Pollock in John Updike's *Seek My Face*, attains renown for his signature style within the mid-twentieth-century American art movement of Abstract Expressionism. As indicated by Zack's efforts to be *in* his paintings by means of the techniques of dripping and pouring paint, his notion of a signature style is self-expression in the concrete sense of extending himself in the art work via the medium of paint. Zack conveys states of mind, feelings and moods, as well as bodily rhythms in his art, attaining visual effects such as balance, spin, peace, and quiet in his paintings: facets of himself in the process of painting or aspects of his self and personality. The publicity about Zack's "action painting" and "performance art," highlighting the vitality of the painting process, is to the point after all, for this process makes for his various signatures on canvas.

Updike's novel seldom mentions the visual images or subject matter of Zack's paintings that a reader might expect in order to gauge the range of his interests or his concept of beauty. Instead, Updike emphasizes Zack's personality and the painter at work, experimenting with methods of painting, which are essential to his concern with authentic self-expression. Updike achieves this focus by structuring his novel as an extensive interview between a journalist, Kathryn, and Zack's widow, Hope, for she would best remember her former husband personally and at work in the barn that was his studio. An artist in her own right and serendipitous critic of Zack's work, Hope McCoy is also a fine persona for Updike the art critic and connoisseur of art, a voice for the documentary dimension of the novel pertaining to Jackson Pollock's career. Hope's reminiscences contain ample commentary on twentieth-century art, particularly the trends prevailing in New York *ca.* 1930-1960. Citing the theories and precepts of her teachers and colleagues, she provides context for Zack's growth as an artist and clues to his aims and aesthetics in a more academic vein. Through Hope's first-hand accounts of the artist and his time, Updike weaves his portrait of a very individual artist with the seemingly anachronous aesthetic aim of expressing his particular vitality in his art.

Zack McCoy drew inspiration and ideas from numerous sources on the path to a style of his own. He practiced representational technique with the regionalist painter Thomas Benton before adapting to the self-exploratory methods current in the 1930's and '40's. He began to drip and pour paint in the 1930's when he was surrounded by Surrealism, which acknowledged the influence of dreams and the unconscious in art, automatism or stream-of-consciousness in artistic technique. He was impressed by the Mexican painter's Siqueiros' "messiness" and use of new industrial paints, and by the earth colors in the murals of Orozco. Eventually Zack joined a group of painters who saw themselves as revolutionaries, eager to undo millennia of convention in their pursuit of "abstract expressionism" instead of continuing to evolve methods of representation. According to one member of the group, Bernie Nova, "The purpose of abstract art is to convert color and shape into mental plasma" (Updike 49); by other accounts, the purpose was to catch the fundamental truths of life, to penetrate into the world mystery. The practical aim of the Abstract Expressionists was to get the self out, onto the canvas, and so to discover and invent ways of achieving this goal.

Hope McCoy speaks at length about Zack's endeavor to make his mark, particularly with regard to his techniques of applying paint to canvas. In the huge barn which he transformed into a studio outside their home in the Long Island Flats, Zack had room to experiment. After the war, *ca.* 1946, he produced clear pastel watercolors, their "peach and lime green and powder blue" (Updike 83) almost transparent as a result of free-flowing brushstrokes, but soon he blazed a trail to painting with the tube, dripping and pouring paint, creating clotted, textured, variegated effects, as well as "black-on-white biomorphs on canvas" (123). Moving a painting around on the canvas or taping the canvas to the barn floor, Zack began to draw in the air, letting paint trail and drip in his path, reaching the center of the canvas by spattering. He explored the qualitative aspects of color and learned to thin paint exactly in order to assert his intentions on canvas precisely. In pouring, he availed himself of a heavy impasto, adding sand, pebbles, and pieces of broken glass. He used sticks and trowels, knives, glass turkey-basters, and dried brushes to finish his paintings.

Zack's dance-like movements around the canvas demonstrated the body as medium of expression, along with the paintbrush. Movements of the body are a vehicle for instinctive and unconscious self-expression, complementing mind-directed technique; they allow for the indeterminacy and mystery that give life to art (14). While Zack admitted the influence of the unconscious, he usually contemplated a work for weeks, intuiting appropriate choreography before approaching the canvas. Hope remarks on his decisiveness and sureness in the dripping process and the "eerie control Zack had . . . a sense of balance, of balancing rhythms" (107), as opposed to mechanical or repetitive application of paint to canvas. As a result, his painting was likely to exude an overall effect of quiet and calm despite violent spatterings in its details. When body and mind work in unison, in focus and concentration, there is harmony, Zack would say; when he loses contact, the paintings become disorganized, and he would have to re-work the project.

Hope offers threads of aesthetic theory relevant to Zack's painting by her references to teachers and colleagues. She quotes Roger Merebian's comments on the trend toward abstraction and getting the self out on canvas:

> The so-called aesthetic . . . is merely the sensuous aspect of the world—it is not the end of art but a means, a means for getting at, let's call it, the infinite background of feeling in order to

> condense it into an object of perception . . . the impulse from the
> unconscious, the automatistic moment, is only a moment, a way
> to get the painting mind going—probing, finding, completing
> (Updike 45).

With regard to the composition of abstract painting, the play of lines, forms, and colors that elicits a spiritual dimension, for instance, the effect of peace noted in Zack's paintings, we have Hermann Hochmann's theory of "push and pull," which Hope reiterates more than once:

> He said when you put a single line on a piece of paper there is no
> telling what its direction is. But if you put a shorter line under it,
> the longer line moves, and the shorter one goes in the opposite
> direction. He said the piece of paper had now become a universe,
> in motion . . . when there was a third thing, as in music when
> two notes combine to make a third sound, this third thing was
> spiritual, non-physical, surreal (35).

As for colors, some recede and others advance, pushing and pulling in the picture plane, making for "color harmonics." Hope's theorizing implies that Zack was conversant with the phenomenon of "push and pull" and, generally, with "the life-giving zeal" embedded in the qualitative substance of a work of art (37). Therefore, when Zack is described as being absorbed in painting, he is immersed in the life of the painting (*cf.* Pollock's statement "The painting has a life of its own" from "My Painting," 1947).

Authentic self-expression for Zack depended on his concept of self as a natural being. He is quoted as saying, "I *am* Nature" (159). Zack likened his painting process to the method of American Indian sand painters, a ritualistic, rhythmical kind of expression, conducive to being in harmony with nature and in character with his own outdoor personality. When not absorbed in his art, Zack is portrayed reveling in the natural scenery of then rustic Long Island: walking the dog or bicycling for miles with Hope, planting a vegetable garden, moving the barn thirty yards uphill with a few fellows so as not to obstruct the views from the house. At the turn of spring and the mellowing of the ocean's blue, Zack was elated. He would explore the dunes and coastal marshes that were teeming with wild life and observe the movements of ducks and birds. Apparently at one with nature, he strove to express his own being and rhythm in his art rather than imitate the views he enjoyed at leisure. "His painting now had to come entirely from within" (83) and he, in turn, had to be *in* his painting.

Critics called Zack's art "action painting" and "performance art," highlighting the artistic act with its swirling movements and fiery gestures, as opposed to the finished product. With regard to his signature style, critical acclaim was vague ("self and beauty, beauty and self," 153) and Hope would hardly presume to analyze the paintings. The "drip paintings are beautiful . . . stunningly beautiful," she says; she also remembers the "skyey, spinning feeling" to the early ones (101). In her view, the dominant effect of his painting is quiet: "There was this peace, this balance, and calm in his paintings" (103). These qualities are related to Zack's mood in the barn, to the purity of his intent, and his total absorption in the painting process. The aesthetic effects of his canvases might also be related to the beauty of Zack's physique remembered by Hope in the way of personal attraction. "He was beautiful," she says, recalling individual features like the "knit of his face," with its "lovely low-relief episodes of muscle and dimples and planes" (54), his "leathery-soft" skin, "his natural and becoming baldness," his perfect ears, tight buttocks, and rounded calf muscles, and more importantly their unity, with "a swing to his body, a thrust . . . that used to take my breath away" (Updike 55-6).

To elucidate the various accounts of Zack's signature style in Updike's novel, I venture into secondary sources which complement the aesthetic theory and documentary material interspersed in the fictional portrait of Jackson Pollock: the recent application of stylometrics to Pollock's paintings and a monograph on the painter. First the research in stylometrics reported in Daniel Rockmore's "A Style of Numbers Behind a Number of Styles" (*The Chronicle of Higher Education*, 9 June 2007). Rockmore, a professor of math and computer science at Dartmouth College, presents the work of Richard

Taylor, artist and scientist, specialist in fractals and chaos and connoisseur of Pollock's art, who was called to investigate the authenticity of thirty-two previously unknown works, presumably by Pollock, discovered in a storage bin in Wainscott, Long Island, in 2005.

Rockmore explains that stylometry is a quantitative, mathematical analysis of consistency and recurrence of certain features and patterns in authorial style, which has had most success in literature in the twentieth century. Consideration of word frequency and usage stylistics of function words like pronouns, prepositions, and conjunctions is central to literary stylometry. Stylometric study of paintings has proceeded from an observation of recurrent fundamental forms and details in an artist's work—the depiction of hands, earlobes, or drapery, for example—to quantitative comparison of these forms and details by means of "wavelet analysis." This produces statistics on simple linear elements in a picture and permits the reconstruction of parts of a picture as a sum of various lines and patterns, for a picture is considered "an agglomeration of numbers or frequency patterns" (Rockmore B10). Wavelet analysis has provided a numerical signature for Peter Breughel the Elder's work, among others.

What critics had perceived as "chaos" in Pollock's paintings, Taylor saw as "the mathematics of fractal geometry" (*ibid.*), analogous to the geometry of the natural world, in which structures—fractals or fragments—repeat themselves to a quantitative degree according to the organic principle that a part contains components and attributes of the whole. The particular fractal dimension of natural phenomena, for example, "coastlines and mountain ranges, the branches within branches of a fern leaf, or our own circulatory or pulmonary system" (B11) is between one and two. Applying quantitative analysis to Pollock's drip paintings in 1997, Taylor found that the fractal dimension of the clotted paint was the same as that of natural phenomena, between one and two, and that there were fractal dimensions specific to periods of Pollock's work, from 1.4 in the early paintings to 1.7 in later ones. As the fractal dimension of both nature and paintings is termed "a fractal signature" or style, Pollock's signature style is comparable to that of natural phenomena.

In more recent work, Taylor has linked these fractal findings directly to the physical dance through which Pollock created his poured paintings. These new ideas relate the rhythms of his canvases to recently discovered patterns found in the quavering of motion produced by a body trying to maintain a delicate point of balance (Rockmore B11).

Rockmore comments that fractal analysis does not diminish Pollock's achievement or the beauty of his paintings but rather "reveals and amplifies it" (*ibid.*). His presentation of Taylor's work also pertains to aesthetic theory given in Updike's novel, for instance, Hochmann's remarks on the disruption of Renaissance perspective by the forces of "push and pull" and the effect of naturalistic space that is created "when the two-dimensionality of a picture is violated" (Updike 37). Rockmore's article ends with an undocumented quote from Pollock: "My concern is with the rhythm of nature . . . the way the ocean moves," which is consistent with Updike's portrayal of Zack as an outdoor personality at one with nature.

Leafing through Frank O'Hara's illustrated monograph *Jackson Pollock* (1959), we find swirling lines spreading and moving throughout a painting; the recurrence of intricate patterns with variations, symmetrical for the most part; and spectral color combinations, predominantly green, red-blue-yellow, grey, black and white. If not simply numbers, the names of most post-1946 paintings refer to natural phenomena or natural processes, for example, Autumn Rhythm, Summertime, Out of the Web, Lavender Mist, Scent, Shimmering Substance, Echo, Ocean Greyness, Greyed Rainbow, White Light, Moon Vibrations, Four Opposites, the Deep, White on Black, Black, White, and Grey.

In Updike's *Seek My Face*, Hope remembers naming pictures with Zack once the life of a painting had revealed its particular mood, atmosphere, or motif and made an impression on the viewer. Some were given the names of stars and galaxies, inspired by a star book Zack had given to Hope and by clear nights on Long Island, as well as the aforementioned "skyey, spinning" quality of the early drip paintings. A reddish painting was named

"Betelgeuse"; a cold-looking one, "Sirius"; another, blue and black, was called "Magellanic Cloud" (Updike 101-2). This is Updike's fiction, serving narrative interest and Hope's involvement in the naming process, but also pertinent to Zack's painting in the air and the swirling motion of his lines on canvas. Most paintings in *Seek My Face* were titled by their dominant colors or given numbers by the gallery owner, according to Jackson Pollock's practice and experience. In both the fictional portrait and the illustrated monograph, the essence of the paintings and their beauty in the eyes of the beholder comprise the spectacular play of lines, forms, and patterns, as well as their rhythm and balance, which may be recognized as vitality in the signature style.

-CHAPTER 11-

W. Somerset Maugham, The Moon and Sixpence: Vibrant Stasis

Maughams's fictional portrait of Paul Gauguin was inspired by his acquaintance with artists who knew and admired Gauguin during the year the author spent in Montparnasse (Paris), as well as his journey to Tahiti, the painter's beloved island, in 1917. One of the Parisian artists is undoubtedly represented in the novel by Dirk Stroeve, a Dutch painter who recognizes genius in Charles Strickland while most observers ridicule his art. Dirk is eloquent on the beauty in Charles' painting and beauty in general, which is to him the most precious thing in the world:

> Beauty is something wonderful and strange that the artist fashions
> out of the chaos of the world in the torment of his soul. And when
> he has made it, it is not given to all to know it. To recognize it,
> you must repeat the adventure of the artist. It is a melody that
> he sings to you, and to hear it again in your own heart you want
> knowledge and sensitiveness and imagination (Maugham 76).

Maugham heeded these words, heard or authored, in following the artist's adventure as far as he could with his persona in the novel, an English writer, and involving supportive narrators as witnesses of Charles' life and work in the main narrator's absence.

The English writer is less than enthusiastic about Charles' painting, but he is very much taken by Charles' extraordinary personality from their very first meeting in London, and he thinks that personality is paramount in an artist. His project is to demonstrate a connection between the person and his art by presenting a personal portrait and letting accounts of Charles' painting by others—especially Dirk Stroeve in Paris, Captain René Brunot and Dr. Coutras in Tahiti—complement descriptions of his person, indeed to explain the person, who is an enigma until seen in the light of his art. Thus the unique beauty perceived in Charles' painting is shown to reflect his personality. Like Zack McCoy in John Updike's *Seek My Face,* Charles is *in* his painting; however, he shares pictorial space with an isle of his dreams, an inner vision of a place where his body and soul would be in harmony, which is eventually identified with Tahiti. "His imagination had long been haunted by an island, all green and sunny, encircled by a sea more blue than is found in Northern latitudes" (Maugham 184), remarks Captain Nichols, who reports on Charles' passage from Paris to the South Seas via Marseilles and Australia.

Charles appears awkward in the circles of London society and the company of artists in Montmartre. He is a huge man with reddish hair, who seems a boorish fellow amid social repartee in an English drawing room. Charles is more at ease in Paris because he is totally immersed in his art and the inner life of spirit and imagination, which he longs to express. He is indifferent to the shabby room of a dingy hotel that he inhabits, indifferent to convention and to his own appearance. He grows a beard, accentuating the coarse, primitive aspect of his visage and the rude manners that surface in conversation with the English writer. The latter espies sensuality in this man who is devoted to the life of the spirit, a "curiously spiritual" sensuality (105). This paradoxical combination of qualities evokes comparisons with mythical figures in the narrator's mind: "He seemed to partake of those obscure forces of nature which the Greeks personified in shapes part human and part beast, the satyr and the faun. I thought of Marsyas, whom the god flayed because he had dared to rival him in song. Strickland seemed to bear in his heart strange harmonies and unadventured patterns" (*ibid.*). Charles would inevitably feel at home on a distant isle in the South Seas, spearfishing, bathing in streams, and painting undisturbed in his bungalow. He would "go native" with a vengeance.

Viewing the paintings Charles completes during his years in Paris, the narrator is bewildered, though he tries to understand the work in terms of the person he has befriended. He sees intense colors, belonging to a subjective spectrum, and distorted forms of reality, for instance, a still life of lopsided oranges on an irregular plate and portraits resembling caricatures, presumably the results of clumsy technique. But he finds the sensuousness of the images tantalizing, and he ascribes this effect to an expression of sexual instincts or emotions, substantiating his earlier remark that "art is a manifestation of emotion" (Maugham 2). The writer is also impressed by the power and eloquence of the visual images, guessing that Charles was attempting to convey something hidden in the phenomena he painted, "as though he found in the chaos of the universe a new pattern, and were attempting clumsily, with anguish of soul, to set it down" (165). He senses that Charles was striving for liberation from constraints that held him, aiming for some "inscrutable Nirvana" (167), expressing the state of his soul in his pilgrimage. He associates this Nirvana with the ideals of Truth or Freedom or Love—all but the Beauty which Dirk Stroeve perceives in Charles' art.

Once the territory of Charles' art is charted by others, the narrator can more accurately assess his initial impressions, especially his intuition of a new pattern in the paintings. The irregularity in form and composition, which he had taken for clumsy technique, Stroeve terms "bold simplification" (149); the intensity of color he had interpreted as an expression of emotion or a longing for Nirvana, Stroeve describes as "passionate sensuality which had in it something miraculous" (*ibid.*) The narrator can agree that the unique beauty of Charles' painting is achieved by an adjustment of outer forms of reality to inner vision, making for images tinged with the elusive and ineffable, perhaps glimpses of spirit or particles of light within matter. Charles' painting might recall the spirituality of El Greco, as well as the solidity and sensuality of portraits by Velasquez, painters who were among Charles' favorites. Nonetheless, this art reveals an individual vision, a new synthesis, adhering to no school of art or traditional concept of beauty; as Stroeve predicted, it would be a revolutionary milestone in modern art.

The beauty that Dirk Stroeve extols with regard to Charles' portrait of a woman in Paris, Captain René Brunot recapitulates in terms of Tahitian landscape, which was inherent in the artist's vision, thus perceptible in his paintings before he arrived in the island. (Tahiti was déjà vu for Charles.) Brunot sympathizes with Charles' pilgrimage on the basis of his own experience of creating a beautiful plantation where there was barren desert on an atoll in the nearby Paumotus; he sees the spiritual dimension in Charles' art as Truth on the basis of his own belief in God. He understands Charles' passion to create beauty as an assertion of individuality and talent analogous to his own achievement. Brunot visits Charles on one of his business trips to Papeete, to play a game of chess and see his latest work. He walks about eight kilometers from the main road to a bungalow in the fold of a mountain fenced in by trees—leafy bananas, cocoanuts, alligator pears, mangos—and suffused with the flaming scarlet blossoms of crotons and flamboyants. During Brunot's stayover, the exuberant colors of this luxuriant terrain come to rest, ceding to stillness and the scent of white flowers (*tiaré*). He remembers, "It was a night so beautiful that your soul seemed hardly able to bear the prison of the body. You felt that it was ready to be wafted away on the immaterial air" (Maugham 212). His description of the enchantment of the place corresponds with the stasis amid vitality felt in Charles' paintings and their effect of both disturbing and arresting the viewer.

Another Frenchman, Dr. Coutras, is the sole observer (besides Ata, Charles' wife) of the murals Charles painted in his bungalow during the last few years of his life. Coutras remembers the sensation of entering a tremendous primeval forest, intimating the beginning of the world in its mysterious composition, at once sensual and sublime. The supernatural images evoked spirit in natural phenomena, divinity and earthy clay in human forms, changing forever the way the doctor looked at cocoanuts, banyans, and human beings. Coutras concludes that the murals were the work of a man both subhuman and superhuman, beastly and divine, recalling the mythical monsters possessed of strange harmonies to which the writer had likened Charles.

A still life of fruits gifted to the doctor juxtaposed extravagant luster with opacity in its colors: swooning red tones, debauched purple, and somber blue merged with sparkling yellow and immaculate green in the arrangement. The still life was an aesthetic expression of vital and fatal instincts alien to Mrs. Coutras' sensibility, cultivated European that she was. At her request, it was moved from the drawing room to the consulting room to give the doctor's patients a taste of exoticism, perhaps the flavor of "a Polynesian garden of the Hesperides" (233). The enchanted fruit attested to a primitive force that the English writer had perceived in Charles early on ("a primitive force that existed before good or ill," 106), which Tahitians also saw in the painter whom they called "the Red One."

The various narrative accounts concur on the originality of Charles' representation of reality and its revelation of mysterious essences of phenomena according to his vision. Nevertheless, comments on the effects of Charles' painting—*tantalizing, disturbing, arresting, awe-inspiring*—are inconclusive, as it were intended to direct readers to a museum or an album of Paul Gauguin's art to see for themselves. The Heritage Press edition of Maugham's novel facilitates this search by offering reproductions of Gauguin's paintings as illustrations for the second part of the novel, concerning Charles' years in Tahiti (W. Somerset Maugham, *The Moon and Sixpence*. New York: The Heritage Press, 1919; 1941).

We find pictures of island natives, mostly women and children, standing and sitting, arrested in their movements, amid silhouettes of trees on rich brown and orange ground. "They seemed to possess something of the clay of which they were created" (Heritage Press 272). Elsewhere trees are in the foreground; their flaming blossoms and blue-green foliage encircle women bathing or picking fruit. Then a landscape composed of layers of reddish brown, amber, green, bronze, gold, and a sliver of violet sunset in irregular rectangular arrangement, with a few rounded, earth-colored trees in the center and miniature figures of women and children on the side, as if hidden in a puzzle. We may sense pervasive calm in the paintings but at the same time, implicit rhythm or movement in both the landscape and the natives' figures. Charles had said to the English writer that he painted what he saw in the light of eternity, for his main concern was "the everlasting present." An intuition of infinity or eternity simplifies and intensifies the shapes and colors of reality, attaining the effect of vibrant stasis, or static vibrancy.

The effect of stasis amid vitality is achieved by means of circular forms within rectangular planes, in conjunction with nuances of color in the compositions. The circle is a symbol of unity and perfection, representing heaven in contrast to earth, or the spiritual in contrast with the material. As an endless line, the circle symbolizes time and infinity. "The square, or rectangle, is a symbol of the earth in contrast to heaven, or the limited in contrast to the infinite" (*The Herder Dictionary of Symbols* 180). The square has signified the combined effects of the four elements, thus earthly matter or life (*ibid.*).

The paintings also contain spiraling forms in proliferation: undulating streams, branches of palm, exotic birds (like peacocks), the designs of women's dress and their figures. Spirals are associated with a complex of meanings: cyclical development, moon phases and their influence on water, fertility, the movement of involution and evolution in the cosmos as a whole, return and renewal (*Herder Dictionary* 179). All of these imply an everlasting present, a present that is eternal on account of perpetual change and renewal—especially palpable on a tropical island, where cyclical development might be measured by moon phases rather than seasons. Spiraling forms, sparkling with fresh color, are cheerful and pleasing to the eye for the vitality they suggest and the promise of change. They are familiar as decorative motifs on baskets, ceramics, textiles, architecture, murals, and body art since prehistoric time.

In Gauguin's painting titled "Tahiti is like a Lovely Woman" (Heritage Press 210) luminous spiral shapes emerge from solid masses of earth and mountain as from dark mystery. Exuberant tones of yellow, pink, orange, and chartreuse within curving lines and spirals on earth (spiraling because permeated by water) are bound by a limb of palm extending over a mountain and there connecting with an arc of sky. In the fold of a mountain at the center of the composition is a triangular cottage, indicating the painter's home. This painting features the juxtaposition of circular and rectangular forms (the limb of palm versus foreground with cottage) while it highlights the spiraling shapes that evoke vitality and luxuriance in the landscape. Might this be the landscape that was etched in Charles' mind before he arrived in Tahiti? His "home" before he actually inhabited the verdant valley depicted in the painting? The palm tree joins earth and sky, domains respectively symbolic of matter and spirit, suggesting the synthesis of sensuality and spirituality observed in Charles' painting since his apprenticeship in Paris. Its unique synthesis informs numerous phenomena Charles painted—still lifes, nudes, primeval forest, Tahitian natives—all manifesting vibrant stasis.

In Maugham's title *The Moon and Sixpence,* "moon" is a metaphor for Charles' painting; "sixpence" denotes the approximate value of each of his works during his lifetime. As a synaechdoche, a part for the whole, "moon" implies the influence of the long-mysterious cosmic body that is traditionally a measure of time and a measure of fertility associated with the feminine principle, which tends toward syntheses. "Moon" also suggests the uniqueness, in the sense of outlandishness or extravagance, of the syntheses Charles achieved, as voiced in Dr. Coutras' response to the murals in Charles' bungalow, at once sensual and sublime, or the still life that was both lustrous and opaque. Maugham's portrait presents Charles' vision of beauty as a reflection of his personality, which is extraordinary in its appearance and manners, as well as its pursuit of adventure from London to Paris to Australia and the South Seas. In view of the reproductions of Paul Gauguin's works in the Heritage Press edition of the novel, one might conjecture that the inner vision of an everlasting present, realized by the effect of vibrant stasis in the paintings, stems from the painter's particular sense of space and time and from his individual heartbeat, which accorded with the rhythm of nature on a tropical island, apt to be measured by moon phases. This rhythm favors continuity over change and space over time, so that the array of colors in reality assumes extraordinary intensity; the multifaceted forms, shapes, and contours of reality appear unusually distinct though interrelated, calm and composed.

Postscript

Given Maugham's representation of the influence of the painter's inner vision on the unique syntheses achieved in his art, one might note Paul Gauguin's renown as a representative of the Symbolist movement in painting. This reputation is based on an analogy between the painter's approach to his art, especially his reliance on inner vision and memory, with the late nineteenth-century Symbolist poets' dependence on inner creative power—mind, imagination, and memory—rather than reference to observed reality, as well as an analogy between the painter's inventiveness with color, form and composition in his art and the Symbolist writers' "language magic" (Charles Baudelaire's term).

On his path to the discovery of his own method and style, Gauguin is known to have emulated and worked with the Impressionist painters and naturalists. In 1875, he befriended Camille Pissarro, who advised him about technique as they worked side by side and encouraged his collecting of Impressionists' artwork. Gauguin contributed to the last four Impressionist exhibitions in Paris, 1880-1886. With the naturalist painter Émile Bernard, Gauguin shared an interest in Japanese prints and Paul Cézanne's simplifications of natural forms. Gauguin practiced and later perfected a style created by Bernard known as "cloisonism" (later "Synthetism"), characterized by the use of flat, often strongly delineated shapes, bright colors, and symbolic treatment of abstract ideas. His "Vision after the Sermon" (1888), featuring aspects of "cloisonism" but remarkable primarily for its juxtaposition of real and imaginary figures stemming from memory and imagination ("abstraction" in Gauguin's term) rather than imitation of reality, is a milestone in Gauguin's departure from both Impressionism and naturalism and the liberation of his painting from conventional restrictions (Ronald Alley, "Introduction" to *Gauguin,* 1964).

This milestone was preceded by Gauguin's sojourn to Pont-Aven in Brittany (1886) and his travel to Martinique (1887, with the painter Charles Laval), where he sought to experiment with techniques and develop his own style. In Brittany, which Gauguin liked for its rustic scenery and archaic customs, he painted peasants working in the fields or worshipping, so preserving a literal element in his art (Alley 13-14). On Martinique, Gauguin and Laval lived in "primitive" fashion, nourishing themselves with fruit and fish while they painted tropical trees and natives. Gauguin produced ever more simplified forms and bold, unusual colors on canvas. These travels anticipated his extended stay at Le Pouldu in Brittany (1889-1890) and his subsequent departure for Tahiti in 1891, where he settled in 1895.

While in Paris between travels in the 1890's, Gauguin enjoyed the acquaintance of Symbolist writers like Jean Moréas, Charles Morice, Stéphane Mallarmé, Paul Verlaine, and Octave Mirbeau, and was considered by them a representative of Symbolism in painting (Alley 15). He frequented the cafés where Symbolist writers gathered, as well as Mallarmé's "Tuesdays." On the occasion of his first departure for Tahiti, he was given a banquet by the writers at the Café Voltaire. Gauguin's relation with these writers was based on similar views on art and creative process, particularly their mutual agreement on the importance of the creative power of imagination for the attainment of beauty and realization of envisioned ideals; therefore, the necessity of inventiveness in the medium of expression. Take the crystalline imagery in Mallarmé's poetry, achieved by visual poetic properties of words or the flowing, musical verse of Paul Verlaine, evocative of nostalgic moods and gentle beauty by its sound effects. Similarly, Gauguin would cultivate his inner vision, along with the allure of the exotic terrain he found in Tahiti, to produce the effects of an extraordinary reality, characterized by a unique rhythm attuned to his own. His bold compositions, vibrant with color but serene in atmosphere, attest to originality in the medium of painting analogous to the Symbolist poets' achievements in verbal art.

Contrary to most of the Impressionist painters, Gauguin maintained a literary element in his art, whether a theme, such as Paradise and the Fall of Man, or merely a situation; however, like the Symbolists, he aimed to suggest rather than describe the topic at hand. Unlike the Neo-Impressionists (Seurat, Signac), he sought harmony instead of contrasts or complements between colors, and this deliberately, allowing for no accidents in the medium of expression. He often referred to colors in musical terms and justified the use of arbitrary colors, different from those in surrounding reality, by their emotive effects. With regard to the liberties he took with colors, Gauguin is quoted as saying,

> They are intended, absolutely! They are necessary and everything in my work is calculated, premeditated. It is music, if you like! I obtain by an arrangement of lines and colours, with the pretext of some sort of subject taken from life or from nature, symphonies, harmonies which represent nothing absolutely real in the vulgar sense of the word, which express directly no idea, but which provoke thoughts as music provokes thoughts, without the help of ideas or images, simply through the mysterious relationships which exist between our brains and these arrangements of lines and colours (Alley 25).

These words refer to the "strange harmonies and unadventured patterns" which Maugham's narrator perceives in Charles' personality (Maugham 105) while they also pertain to the synthesis of the fine arts of music and painting occasionally achieved by the Symbolist poets.

-CHAPTER 12-

M. Allen Cunningham, Lost Son: Change

> *"But to say—understand this now—*
> *oh to say these things*
> *in such a way*
> *that the* things *themselves would never*
> *have thought to exist so earnestly"*
> (Rainer M. Rilke, Ninth Duino Elegy, tr. Cunningham 335).

The desire expressed in these lines, written at the Castle in Muzot, Switzerland, *ca.* 1917, is anticipated in Rilke's childhood and in the Paris years, as represented in Cunningham's fictional biography. Little René Maria has avid interest in the objects surrounding him at home in Prague: gilt picture frames, glass figurines, dolls, porcelain plates, napkin rings. These objects are animate and vibrant to the child, like his father and his father's hands, which are also considered *things*. René is no less interested in words and their vibrant qualities. He memorizes lines by Friedrich Schiller, recites them rhythmically, and records them in his notebook. He rhymes his own words and plants them within as if tending a private verbal garden. "And words continue growing, rooting themselves inside him and stirring noiselessly like flowers. Soon there are fields of them in that dim terrain within" (Cunningham 41). Thus René can find refuge and solace in his inner world of mind and soul and his native gift for words when exposed to the austere, regimented routine of military school at age ten. "With his verses he speaks and speaks the mute world—world always feigning muteness, but he believes it is not mute, not mute, only pretending" (57). In the years to come he would recurrently confront and attempt to overcome this "pretension."

Rilke resumes his insightful observation of things as a young man in Paris with the name Rainer. He spends days looking at Auguste Rodin's sculptures, admiring the auras emanating from exquisite material forms; he familiarizes himself with the masterworks at the Louvre. He observes people in the streets—beggars, vendors, invalids—empathizing and giving of himself as he looks. He relates to animals at the zoo, flowers and trees in the Luxembourg Gardens. Rainer takes notes and writes poems about the things he has seen, yet his goal is persistently out of reach, elusive, and faraway. Sitting in a theater one evening, he yearns, "But to *look* at all this first: to see it and know it and one day, perhaps, to *say* it" (122). In his practice of looking, Rainer is a seeker of the invisible essences of things, and to his own mind, he is an eternal beginner in the creative endeavor of saying things, suggested, for example, by the November 19, 1902 entry in Rilke's Journal of Westerwede and Paris, "Oh, this longing to make a beginning" (cited in Cunningham 200).

For the most part, Cunningham's *Lost Son* represents Rainer on the path to his goal of saying things, in phases of in-gathering, at moments of inspiration and reflection preparatory for writing, and on the wings of creative process. The goal that is subliminally formulated in childhood is continually in the making, contingent on new experiences and relationships, changes of scene and circumstances in Rainer's life, but driven nonetheless by the certainty of his choice of path and his identity of poet. The latter involve Rainer's search for "wholeness" or "home" as a consequence of his incomplete childhood: a wholeness Rainer finds initially in the person of Lou Andreas-Salomé in Münich as well as his travels to Russia with her; a home that is tentatively established among fellow artists in Heinrich Vogeler's colony in

Worpswede and later with the sculptress Clara Westhoff in Westerwede, Germany. Rainer's quest for wholeness is increasingly identified with his yearning for solitude and at-homeness in the inner sphere of mind and soul, so that fluctuating circumstances and relationships are influential on his path in so far as they nourish his creative work and provide solitude for the inner cultivation of ideas and images. Rainer's advice to a young poet, written from Paris, is a dictum he realizes himself: "The creator must be a world unto himself and find everything in himself and in nature, to which he has connected himself" (letter to Franz Xaver Kappus of February 17, 1903, quoted in Cunningham 211). We see Rainer traveling from his station in Paris to Italy, Sweden, Denmark, and Capri in search of solitude in some garden cottage or beach hut, where he might dedicate himself totally to the work at hand.

Relationships are highlighted in *Lost Son* in proportion to the poet's humanity, which is considerable (indeed, a *raison d'être* for Cunningham's fictional biography), so that we may see their importance on the poet's path. Rainer enjoys camaraderie with the artists in Worpswede, particularly the lovely, resourceful sculptress Clara Westhoff, whom he marries, and their mutual friend Paula Modersohn-Becker. He forges a tenuous balance between marriage ties and dedication to creative endeavor, even as he considers marriage between artists an effort to protect each other's solitude ("mutual consent to aloneness . . . a holy promise to guard the solitude of the spouse," 210). When he opts for a family holiday at the seaside in Belgium, then suffers over his denial of Paula's request to join in the getaway from Paris, he is shown erring off his path and vacillating between commitments, poignantly human. Among other relationships, Rainer's liaisons with Lou Andreas-Salomé and August Rodin are prominent, for they enrich his outer path of experience while offering guidance for his poetry, especially the alternation of subjectivity and objectivity in its making. Rainer corresponds with Lou throughout the years, maintaining the friendship and seeking the encouragement he had so fortunately met with in Műnich. In the person of Auguste Rodin, whom Rainer serves as personal secretary for a time, the poet finds a mentor and model for a way of life, of continuous creative work.

Moreover, Rainer attracts patronesses: the writer Ellen Key, who arranges for his restful and productive sojourn in Sweden, and Princess Marie von Thurn und Taxis, who later provides him seclusion at Duino Castle on the Adriatic Sea. The earlier relationships and travels fill him with memories he can retrieve for sustenance long after their time, like his vision of "home" in Russia, visited with Lou, or the joyful Christmases celebrated at Westerwede with Clara and their daughter, Ruth.

Rainer is eager to absorb poetry and visual art from his cultural milieu, which offers models for verbal expression. The verses of Friedrich Schiller he'd recited as a child impressed upon him exquisite diction in his native German language. At the National Library in Paris he reads Gustave Flaubert, a master of precision and clarity in French; Paul Verlaine, Charles Baudelaire, and Stéphane Mallarmé—"Symbolist" poets, considered "language magicians" for their virtuosity with sound effects and metaphorical imagery. The sculptural works of Auguste Rodin teach Rainer to shape figures with the eyes in order to describe them dexterously with the pen, as with the touch of one's hands. Ideally, this sculptural style in verse would render the forms of things so accurately that they would become animate, expressive of soul or spirit. Such models influence Rainer's effort to see and speak of simple things and to speak clearly, comprehensibly, as Lou had advised upon reading his first collection of poems (*Dream-Crowned*, 1897). They also fuel his idealistic inclinations and the depth and feeling he brought to poetry from the start.

Simplicity is a challenge for Rainer, try as he might to directly address the animals and flowers at the *Jardin des Plantes* in Paris or a fountain in Rome. By transforming the flower or animal in his inner space of heart and soul, he achieves such roundedness in verbal expression that the things assume symbolic value and universal significance. He experiences and chooses to say complex things, such as the torso of Apollo at the Louvre and the statue of the Buddha at the end of the garden path in Rodin's villa at Meudon. On an excursion to Chartres with Rodin, Rainer is fascinated by a smiling angel with a sundial in Romanesque stone relief, kin to the cherubs he had observed in Italian Renaissance paintings. The angel mystifies him, striking deep into the recesses of his mind, as did the grandeur and power of a huge acacia he had once encountered in an Alpine forest.

Depth and heart are the primary requisites for Rainer's poetry, as suggested particularly by the generosity expressed in Paula Becker's portrait of the poet: "His eyes, as she has seen them, receive and receive, while his mouth, like a dark, low-slung nerve, wants to give back all that it has tasted and breathed. To return it all unalloyed, newly complete" Cunningham 418). To re-create all that he has received, the poet must hold things within, let them germinate in his mind and heart, and hearken to murmurs of his inner voice that initiate the saying or the writing. "Everything is germination and then bearing forth . . . . Patience is everything," he writes in another letter to Franz Xaver Kappus (23 April 1903, quoted in Cunningham 235). The process is slow and unpredictable. The figures are demanding of time, not least the magnificent tree that penetrates Rainer's mind at the instant of its encounter, then weighs on him indefinitely, "a bundle of murky phlegm in your brain . . . a ragged seed to overgrow the truer perceptions a seed to outshadow it all" (186). This seed would sprout in *The Book of Hours* as well as *The Sonnets to Orpheus* a few decades later. The figure of Malte Laurids Brigge, the poor young poet who mirrors Rainer's inner life, haunts him for years, expressing itself in murmurings at propitious moments of quiet and centeredness. On the other hand, the sight of a panther caroming in its cage at the Paris Zoo lends itself to description in the course of a few weeks: "His gaze, from the passing bars, / has grown so weary that it can hold nothing else. / To him there are a thousand bars / and beyond the thousand bars no world at all" ("The Panther," st. 1, from *New Poems I*, tr. Cunningham, 199). Rainer empathizes with the animal immediately, for the panther's plight strikes the chord of a deep-seated instinct for freedom within him, felt even in childhood when he would give his squirrel the longest leash possible, according to his mother's, Phia Rilke's, account in the novel.

Rainer tends toward idealism and mysticism in his attempts to penetrate appearances and gain insight into the kernels of animate beings, including his own person. He posits the validity of an invisible world of spirit or soul, as demonstrated most clearly by his extrasensory perceptions in Sweden during his exploration of the chapel and crypt at Borgeby-gård and his arrival at Ellen Key's estate at Jonsered (discussed in "Receptivity," Ch. 2); therefore, he maintains an invisible world of being within and without all the phenomena he observes. *Saying* for Rainer involves a rendering of the invisible in words—of something unique, inimitable, fragile—so that at its inception, the attempt at saying arouses fear lest his words miss their mark and betray a thing. As stated in the First Duino Elegy, "the beautiful is nothing but the beginning of terror, which we still unguardedly endure, / and we admire it so because it spurns us, stopping short of our destruction" (tr. Cunningham, 34). Accordingly, beauty is a fragile hope harbored in the effort to say something faithfully and truthfully, having sifted it in the mill of the inner world of heart and mind. With reference to Cunningham's image of the garden within Rainer, if the germ or seed of an idea or perception is nourished, endured, and given time and space to grow, it might blossom in tenable poetic form and reveal beauty.

The project of expressing invisible essences in visible, audible, tangible words requires verbal craft. Rainer describes things empirically and intuitively, drawing on specific pivotal diction, so that words might suggest more than they literally designate. He joins lines by "enjambment" to effect movement in the object represented, or to connect ideas in his interpretation of their mode of being. For instance, "Das Roseninnere" ("The Inner Rose"):

> Sie können sich selber kaum
> halten; viele liessen
> sich überfullen und fliessen
> über von Innenraum
> in die Tage, die immer
> voller und voller sich schliessen
> bis der ganze Sommer ein Zimmer
> wird, ein Zimmer in einem Traum
>
> (Rilke, *Gesammelte Gedichte* 378).

(tr.: "They can hardly contain themselves; many, full to the brim, overflow from their inner space into days, which appear ever fuller

as they close at sundown, and the whole summer becomes a room,
a room in a dream.")

He interweaves visual imagery with the sound effects of rhythm, rhyme, and alliteration. In such exquisite expression of its essential quality of being, as perceived by the poet, each thing signifies more than itself, inevitably becoming a symbolic entity. Rainer's apple, pear, and banana evoke all delicious fruits; his rose, the book of life in its inexhaustible fullness; his tree, the cosmic tree. In *The Notebooks of Malte Laurids Brigge,* the poet explains that "the *things* vibrate into each other, across and out into the air, and their coolness makes the shadows clear and the sun into a lucid, spiritual vision. Then there is no main thing . . . every *thing* is everywhere" (tr. Cunningham, 40), presenting a Rilkean version of S. T. Coleridge's "translucence of the Eternal in and through the Temporal, of the Special in the Individual, or of the General in the Especial."

Rainer's gift to the reader is then his perception and expression of the integrity of things, stemming from their participation in the wholeness of being, or the "great unity" of life and death. Beauty inheres in symbols of wholeness as well as the sonorous words that bring them forth. However, the effect on the reader that the poet might have intended, as indicated toward the close of *Lost Son,* is a transformation, or change, in our ordinary views and habitual mindsets. This effect follows from Rainer's struggle with the world's muteness or pretension of muteness: his earnest inquiry into and empathy with the things he encounters and his respect for all things in their particular states of being. Given the figures in the poems, metamorphosed in the poet's inner realm so as to be faithfully said, the reader might respond with an appropriate adjustment of his or her lenses.

The preludes to Rainer's creative process hold for ever longer periods of time; the Elegies come years apart, and with the onset of World War I, ten years apart. During this interval Rainer finds himself, paradoxically, on the battlefield until he is transferred to the Imperial War Archives in Vienna. One day at the Archives, in an outpouring of emotion and disillusionment with the war, addressed to himself as well as his colleague Wenzel, Rainer asks,

"What does any artist do if not open a path to change . . . to change, and maybe ennoblement . . . in people's hearts?" (Cunningham 452). The poetic aim voiced here, as if in afterthought, in a context removed from scenes of creative work, nevertheless correlates with the poet's intentions throughout his years of writing poetry. These involved experimentation with approaches to verbal expression but consistently maintained the project of balancing the work of eyes and heart in order to achieve an expression of essences beyond appearances. Simply stated, Rilke's style depended on in-seeing or insight. With reference to the creative work represented in *Lost Son* and the poet's letters quoted in the novel, Rilke's creative process was analogous to processes in nature, as suggested especially by natural metaphors for the poetic process, beginning with the image of a garden inside the child René. Long periods of in-gathering and preparation for writing bear comparison to tilling the soil. The selection of impressions or subject matter for poems is, figuratively, planting them in the "terrain within." The germination and growth of ideas and images within the poet's heart and mind is a slow process of nurturing that optimally brings an outpouring of words adequate to the initial image, idea, or germ of an idea. A poem is then analogous to a seed coming to fruition as a result of a complex process of growth and transformation, although the poem ramifies in the poet's individual microcosm and so reflects the poet's unique experiences and perceptions of the world and its phenomena. As Rilke stated, the poet must "find everything in himself and in nature, to which he has connected himself" (p. 191 above).

In the epilogue to *Lost Son*, titled "Rue Linné, Paris: Present Day," Cunningham recalls his visit to the Rainer M. Rilke Archive at the Hôtel Biron in Paris, where Rilke lived for several years, to read the poet's letters and handle memorabilia. He quotes a few lines from Rilke's poetry that impressed him as if they were directly spoken to him via the archival material:

"Da ist keine Stelle, / die dich nicht sieht. Du must dein Leben ändern."

("There is no piece of this that does not see you. You must change your life," from "Archaic Torso of Apollo," *New Poems II*, tr. Cunningham).

These forceful lines, attributed to Apollo, Greek god of the sun, music, and medicine, echo the message of the angels in Rilke's poetry, harbingers of transformation and new beginnings. Focusing as he does on the life and human character of the poet in this fictional biography, M. Allen Cunningham entrusts the angels to the invisible world of Rainer's mind and soul. He represents the poet in the throes of numerous life changes and new beginnings, so that, speaking of change, Rainer draws from his own experience and is the more eloquent and believable.

Conclusions

The aesthetic agenda are evidently formative elements, ideas, or ideals in artistic expression that influence, shape, or color the poems, paintings, or performances of the artists represented in the selected fiction. They attest to the unique ways in which artists adapt patterns and principles of nature according to their perceptions in childhood, their individual sensibilities, and desire for self-expression; in other words, according to their particular identifications of inner microcosm and outer macrocosm (or intuition of harmony between inner and outer, or relation between self and world). In the process of experimentation and practice in a chosen medium, the aesthetic perceptions manifest themselves as qualitative contents of visible or audible artwork, making for signature styles or presences in performance. These qualitative contents may appear to be concentrated or diffuse, to range between center and periphery of the artists' concerns, for they express artistic selves as well as the artists' perceptions of a range of subject matter chosen for their art work.

Charles' inner vision of a tropical isle, involving an intuition of vibrant stasis, which propels his pursuit of painting in Paris and eventually brings him to Tahiti, harmonizes with the subject matter of his painting, the land and natives of Tahiti, and so gains force as a formative element in his individual style. Similarly, Lily Briscoe's coordination of surface and depth in her painting reflects a pattern in her feminine mind and constitution that is progressively affirmed by her identification with Mrs. Ramsay and her surroundings on Skye, especially the waters of the blue bay. By contrast, Zack's identification with nature in sum, its variety of forms, colors, and shapes, as well as their changes throughout the seasons, reflects his own vital being in nature rather than other phenomena and depends on the body as medium for the expression of his moods and thoughts of the moment. As a result, his paintings, colorful geometrical figurations of his moods and meditations, are seemingly devoid of subject matter other than Zack's self and his vitality.

Ideas and ideals tend to be more easily perceptible as formative elements in literature and music. Cassandra's fairy tale vision of the castle, correlated with the castle's appearance in spring, shapes and laces the narration of her family's life in the English countryside amid the vicissitudes of daily routine. The ideal of integrity which Thea maintains from childhood to maturity, having experienced it sensually, spiritually, and mentally in the midst of nature at a turning point of her growth as a singer, is demonstrated by her singing for the idea in musical scores by numerous composers, as well as her faithfulness to herself as an adequate vessel for the various operatic roles she assumes. Rainer's poetic endeavor of saying things in such a way that they symbolize the great unity of material and immaterial realms hinges on the perception of death as transformation and bridge between the two spheres, as well as transformation in poetic process: rendering invisible essences visible and audible. Change is then inherent as idea in the various subject matter treated by the poet, and it is also perceptible as a formative element in his verbal style.

Stephen, in Joyce's *A Portrait of the Artist as a Young Man,* offers the most distinct and palpable concept of beauty among the aesthetic agenda: radiance. Shown to develop from perceptions of light in Stephen's childhood, this aesthetic is resuscitated by the epiphanies on the strand and discussed intellectually with reference to St. Thomas Aquinas' theory of beauty with his friend at the University, but in terms of artwork, manifested only in the process of writing a poem for Emma Clery. Although Stephen does not develop a style of his own in the course of Joyce's youthful portrait, he might be taken as a spokesman for the other artists, whose aesthetics also partake of wholeness and harmony and comprise spiritual and mental dimensions in addition to the physical. Stephen's epiphanies on the strand elucidate intuitions of spirit in nature (particularly *anima* and Daedalus in his experience), in other words, the imminentness of spirit in nature's realm, and so render identifications with facets of nature meaningful in human terms. The various intricacies of nature become intelligible concepts of beauty, as Stephen demonstrates.

In contrast to the twentieth-century art novels discussed in this study, in which the artists' relation to nature is contextualized in life stories alongside other issues and traits that are important in an artist's growth and career, the Romantic artist novel tended to exaggerate, or *romanticize,* this relation to nature to the extent of shrouding it in mystery or magic, thus influencing the reputation of artists as outsiders. In E.T.A. Hoffmann's *The Golden Pot* (1814), Archivarius Lindhorst's realm of colossal gold-bronze palm trees and bushes tinkling with silver bells is set in opposition to mainstream society lest its members be charmed and led astray by the artist-magus' dream world. The hero of Romain Rolland's *Jean-Christophe* (1899) is seemingly intoxicated by nature and aggrandized by his relation to nature as he perceives its splendor in terms of musical sound and desires to express its entirety in his musical compositions. In this novel, which provides ample realistic representation of social and cultural milieu (in Germany and France), Jean-Christophe's relation to nature, bound up with his genius and distinctive individuality, is pivotal in alienating him from society as well as reinforcing the nature-culture opposition lingering from the previous century. While the authors of Romantic novels were eloquent and psychologically astute in expressing the significance of the artists' relation to nature, their audiences were likely to appreciate their representations of artists vis à vis nature as wonderful, peculiarly Romantic literary phenomena instead of windows on artistic individuality.

The twentieth-century artist novel is more psychologically informative than its Romantic predecessors, and it is in turn informed by advances in the field of psychology. The genre "artist novel" ramified in the branches of autobiographical fiction and fictional biography, based either on an author's own life experience or research of the life and work of artists chosen for representation or portraiture. Moreover, the genre was empowered by innovative narrative techniques to express facets of psyche and creative process that resonate more directly with concepts in psychology than with magic and myth. Therefore, the artist novels considered in this study contribute source material to the field of psychology while they benefit by reference to psychological theory in the process of interpretation. We have discussed instances of day-dreaming and *anima* influence in the novels, kinship with nature in scenes of awakening to artistic vocation, assertions of self, and encounters with the transcendent realm (the collective unconscious in psychoanalytical terms) at moments of acute perception. We have explored accounts of childhood in several novels, which reveal artistic individuality in budding, potential form. The fictional renditions of artists' behaviors and mental adventures offer support for psychological concepts while they diversify these concepts and supply them with examples that would rarely be found in psychological research with patients or surveys of human subjects, particularly artists, in the community.

Mutual illumination between the artist novels, especially their expressions of individuality, and the discipline of psychology pertains most consistently and clearly to two areas of psychological research: advances in the study of the unconscious (beginning with the work of Sigmund Freud, Carl G. Jung, and Eric Neumann) and studies of the biological basis of imagination, which implicate unconscious influences as well as Romantic organicism.

Psychoanalytical psychology, particularly C. G. Jung's concept of the collective unconscious, or objective psyche, is basic to the discovery of archetypes, including *anima* and self; it also sheds light on kinship with nature and inspiration to be gotten from nature. Consequently, aesthetic agenda stemming from the artists' kinship with nature offer support for psychoanalytical theories of unconscious influences on creativity and related concepts in transpersonal psychology that indicate the relativity of the term "unconscious" (its interchange with "conscious"). For example, Pim van Lommel, a Dutch cardiologist, maintains a shared human consciousness, elicited by research on DNA, heredity, and consciousness, that is analogous to transpersonal aspects of consciousness, particularly Jung's concept of the collective unconscious. The "shared human consciousness is similar to the collective unconscious," he remarks;

> Alongside the ego, as waking consciousness, Jung recognizes the self . . . which encompasses both the conscious and unconscious components of personality. Individuality, therefore, is distinct from the embodied ego. The unconscious individual component of consciousness is in contact with other aspects of the collective human unconscious, of which the individual unconscious essentially forms a part. Each part is linked non-locally with the whole (van Lommel 2010, 297-98).

In striving to express themselves via relation to nature, the artists partake in the all-encompassing unity (for nature is traditionally the object symbolic of the whole, the beyond, or reality behind appearances) while rendering themselves distinct, individual parts of the whole. Their perceptions are then simultaneously universal and individual; as suggested by the psychological studies, they are individual to the extent that they express themselves as distinct parts of a whole and therefore partake in the whole. From the reader's or scholar's perspective, the similarities among the various artists portrayed in literature that make for comparison of individual traits and coherence amid diverse aesthetics would be astonishing without the possibility of reference to theories such as those of the collective unconscious or shared human consciousness. The scientific studies provide a basis for comparative studies in the humanities while the latter lend support to the scientific theories.

An understanding of artistic expression inspired by kinship with nature also benefits by and supports mid-twentieth-century studies of the biological basis of imagination, for example, R. W. Gerard's commentary:

> Form, structure, relationship, organism . . . part-whole systems, gestalt or closure is basic for the product of imagination and for its process . . . . Since the imagination only regroups sensory material, there is truly nothing new under the sun. Perception is really a harder problem, for red rays and green rays, even falling on separate eyes, do give the 'new' sensation of yellow; but imagination cannot conjure a hue for ultraviolet . . . . A new and

fertile pattern of thought may come from a conceptual re-slicing of the universe into fresh classes and the making of new combinations of them. A good insight is likely to recognize the universal in the particular and in the strange (Gerard 1946, 229-30).

For the artists represented in fiction, appreciation of nature is not only an impetus for self-expression but also a means of discovering and adapting patterns or principles of nature to their artwork. While these artists share traits and perspectives with other artists inspired by nature and with folk artists of today and previous eras motivated to express their aesthetic appreciation of nature, they excel in *perception*, which is the basic meaning of *aesthetics* (from the Gr. *aesthētikos*, "perceptive," and *aisthanesthai*, "to perceive, to feel"). As indicated by the artist novels, especially scenes featuring the artists' responsiveness to nature, engagement with nature increases perceptiveness as well as self-awareness and motivates the desire to express one's perceptions of self and world in the various media of art.

Beside the interrelation with psychology, my study elicits relevance to the emergent or re-emergent field of aesthetic appreciation of nature. With regard to various approaches to an appreciation of nature discussed in recent scholarly work, the artists represented in fiction exemplify, for the most part, an "engaged" aesthetic, not merely contemplation but "a sensory immersion in the natural world that reaches the still-uncommon experience of unity" (Berleant 1992, 170, cited in Parsons 2008, 85-6), recalling the harmony between inner microcosm and outer macrocosm experienced by Stephen on the strand, Thea in Panther Canyon, Rainer in Sweden, and Charles in Tahiti. Some features of the engaged aesthetic are the involvement of all senses, making for more visceral and enveloping contact with nature; a decrease in thought in one's aesthetic response to nature; and the ineffability of the experience of a state of engagement, its resistance to clear description or explanation (Parsons 2008, 87-89, with reference to Foster 1998). These features resonate with aspects of kinship with nature, particularly the influence of the unconscious, set forth by ecological psychology.

Other approaches to the aesthetic appreciation of nature, such as the formalistic, scientific, post-modern, and pluralistic, may be associated with various kinds of art informed or inspired by nature, or with other endeavors (environmental studies, conservation, to name a few). The formalistic approach, which refers to the perception of nature as a spectacle of shapes, lines, and colors, may be observed in arts and crafts that adapt geometrical patterns and natural motifs to the weaving of textiles and baskets, the molding and decoration of ceramics, and crafting of numerous objects for use or aesthetic appeal. Environmental art, which usually embellishes natural milieu and highlights the attractions of natural phenomena, may be informed by knowledge of natural science, thus a scientific approach to the appreciation of nature, as well as a formalistic one. Environmental art that manipulates natural objects and sites according to the artists' sensory, thoughtful, or affective responses to nature may reflect the post-modern, "anything goes" approach or the pluralistic, which embraces several approaches but delineates certain categories of appropriate responses to nature more clearly than the former. The pluralistic and post-modern perspectives might be linked with "back-to-nature" movements on the part of the folk, such as the hippie movement of the 1960's, which manifested expressions of personal significance of nature as well as cultural and traditional responses to nature in the form of May Day, Midsummer's Eve, and equinox celebrations. But the *raison d'être* of such popular activities in the twentieth century and the present might be a desire for engagement with nature, as it was for much of the folklore and folk art revival prior to and during the Romantic era in Europe (*ca.* 1790-1830).

The spectrum of approaches to an aesthetic appreciation of nature mirrors the spectrum of humanity, including artists as well as people in other walks of life with different perspectives, values, and concerns—different "beams" and "rays" in Virginia Woolf's words. To recapitulate the notion of multiplicity in unity, there are various ways to express one's individuality and participate in the whole. As suggested by the fictional portraits, the artist dwells on his or her "self" more than most and strives to express that self to utmost degree, which ideally pertains to universal experience while maintaining uniqueness or signature style. In the series of novels considered here, the human experience has more to do with beauty and related perceptions than social, economical, political, or scientific concerns, which provide subject matter for other novels and other genres of literature. Artistic expression represented in these novels conveys perceptions of nature as well as perceptions of world influenced by kinship with nature; therefore, the art work is apt to be a source of pleasure, insight, or inspiration for fellow human beings, bearing traces of its provenance and attaining very unselfish ends.

Bibliography

Primary Sources

Cather, Willa. *The Song of the Lark.* Ed. with an Introduction and Notes by Sherrill Harbison. New York: Penguin, 1999; first published by Houghton Mifflin, 1915.

Cunningham, M. Allen. *Lost Son.* Denver, Colorado: Unbridled Books, 2007.

Hoffmann, E. T. A. *The Nutcracker and The Golden Pot.* New York: Dover, 1993; first published in English translation in 1827.

Joyce, James. *A Portrait of the Artist as a Young Man.* New York: Viking, 1964; originally published by B. W. Huebsch in 1916.

Kafka, Franz. *The Metamorphosis.* Tr. and Ed. Stanley Corngold. New York: W. W. Norton, 1996.

Maugham, W. Somerset. *The Moon and Sixpence.* Illustrated by Frederic Dorr Steele and Paul Gauguin. New York: The Heritage Press, 1919; 1941.
_____. *The Moon and Sixpence.* Introduction by Philip Holden. New York: Barnes & Noble, 2007.

Mykolaitis, Vincas. *Altorių šešėly* ("In the Altars' Shadow"). Vilnius: Žaltvykslė, 2005. Abridged from Vincas Mykolaitis, *Altorių šešėly.* Vilnius: Alma littera, 2002.

Novalis (Georg Friedrich Philipp von Hardenberg, 1772-1801). *Henry of Ofterdingen.* Tr. Palmer Hilty. Prospect Heights, Illinois: Waveland Press, 1964.

Rilke, Rainer M. *The Notebooks of Malte Laurids Brigge.* Tr. M. D. Herter Norton. New York: W. W. Norton, 1949; first published in 1910.

_____. *Gesammelte Gedichte* ("Collected Poems"). Frankfurt am Main: Insel, 1962.

Rolland, Romain. *Jean-Christophe.* Tr. Gilbert Cannan. New York: Henry Holt, ser. 1, 1910; ser. 2, 1915.

Smith, Dodie. *I Capture the Castle.* New York: St. Martin's Griffin, 1998; first published in 1948.

_____. *Look Back with Love.* A Manchester Childhood. London: Heinemann, 1974.

Stevens, Wallace. *The Collected Poems of Wallace Stevens.* New York: Vintage Books, 1982; first published by Alfred A. Knopf, 1954.

Vasari, Giorgio. *Vasari's Lives of the Artists.* Tr. Mrs. Jonathan Foster. Ed. Marilyn Aronberg Lavin. New York: Dover, 2005.

Updike, John. *Seek My Face.* New York: Random House, 2002.

White, Patrick. *The Vivisector.* New York: Penguin, 1973; first published in 1970.

Wilbur, Richard. *New and Collected Poems.* New York: Harcourt Brace Jovanovich, 1988.

Woolf, Virginia. *To the Lighthouse.* Foreword by Eudora Welty. New York: Harcourt Brace Jovanovich, 1989; first published in 1927.

Wordsworth, William, and Samuel Taylor Coleridge. *Lyrical Ballads.* Ed. Harold Littledale. London: Humphrey Milford, 1920.

Secondary Sources

Alley, Ronald. *Gauguin.* London: Spring Books, 1961.

Arieti, Silvano. *Creativity,* the Magic Synthesis. New York: Basic Books, 1976.

Barker, Deborah. *Aesthetics and Gender in American Literature,* Portraits of the Woman Artist. London: Associated University Presses, 2000.

Beebe, Maurice. *Ivory Towers and Sacred Founts*: The Artist as Hero in Fiction from Goethe to Joyce. New York: New York University Press, 1964.

Blackmur, R. P. "The Artist as Hero: a Disconsolate Chimera." In *The Lion and the Honeycomb,* Essays in Solicitude and Critique. London: Methuen, 1956. 43-50.

Brooks, Van Wyck. "The Hero as Artist." In *Sketches in Criticism*. New York: E. P. Dutton, 1932. 93-98.

_____. "The Doctrine of Self-Expression." In *Sketches in Criticism*. New York: E. P. Dutton, 1932. 131-136.

Budd, Malcolm. *The Aesthetic Appreciation of Nature*. Oxford: Clarendon Press, 2002.

Campbell, Joseph. *The Inner Reaches of Outer Space*. Novato, California: New World Library, 1986, 2002.

Coleridge, S.T. *Biographia Literaria*. Vol. I. Ed. J. Shawcross. Oxford University Press, 1979; first published in 1817.

Corngold, Stanley. "Kafka's *The Metamorphosis*: Metamorphosis of the Metaphor." In Franz Kafka, *The Metamorphosis*. Tr. and Ed. Stanley Corngold. New York: W. W. Norton, 1996. 79-107.

Ellman, Richard. "Ten Passages from the Life of the Artist." In *Portraits of the Artist*, A Casebook on James Joyce's *A Portrait of the Artist as a Young Man*. Ed. William E. Morris and Clifford A. Nault, Jr. New York: The Odyssey Press, 1962.

Emerson, Ralph Waldo. *America the Beautiful,* in the Words of Ralph Waldo Emerson. Ed. Robert L. Polley. Waukesha, Wisconsin: Country Beautiful, 1970.

Fordham, Michael. *The Life of Childhood*. A Contribution to Analytical Psychology. London: Kegan Paul, Trench, Trubner, 1947; first published in 1944.

Freud, A Collection of Critical Essays. Ed. Perry Meisel. Englewood Cliffs, New Jersey: Prentice-Hall, 1981.

Freud, Sigmund. "The Relation of the Poet to Day-Dreaming." In Sigmund Freud, *On Creativity and the Unconscious*. Papers on the Psychology of Art, Literature, Love, Religion. Selected by Benjamin Nelson. New York: Harper and Row, 1958. 44-54.

_____. *Introductory Lectures on Psycho-Analysis*. Tr. and Ed. by James Strachey. Introduction by Peter Gay. New York: W. W. Norton, 1966.

Gerard, R. W. "The Biological Basis of Imagination." In *The Creative Process, a Symposium*. Ed. Brewster Ghiselin. New York: Penguin, 1952. First published in *The Scientific Monthly*, June 1946.

Gimbutas, Živilė. "The Nature of the Artist" (Ital. "*La Natura nell Artista*"). *Prometeo* 25:99 (September 2008).

Grove, Valerie. *Dear Dodie, The Life of Dodie Smith*. London: Chatto and Windus, 1996.

Hamerton, Philip Gilbert. "Artists in Fiction." In *Thoughts about Art*. Rev. Ed. Boston: Roberts Brothers, 1885. 101-124.

Hartman, Geoffrey. "Reflections on Romanticism in France." In *Romanticism—Vistas, Instances, Continuities*. Ed. by Geoffrey Hartman and David Thorburn. Ithaca and London: Cornell University Press, 1973. Reprinted from *Studies in Romanticism* Fall 1970.

Herder Lexicon. *The Herder Dictionary of Symbols*: Symbols from Art, Archaeology, Mythology, Literature, and Religion. Tr. Boris Matthews. London and New York: Continuum International Publishing Group, 1993.

Hillman, James. *Anima*. An Anatomy of a Personified Notion. With excerpts from the writings of C. G. Jung and original drawings by Mary Vernon. Dallas, Texas: Spring Publications, 1985.

_____. *The Soul's Code*. In Search of Character and Calling. New York: Random House, 1996; Warner Books, 1997.

Huf, Linda. *A Portrait of the Artist as a Young Woman*. The Writer as Heroine in American Literature. New York: Frederick Ungar, 1983, 1985.

Jung, Carl Gustav. *The Integration of Personality*. Tr. Stanley Dell. London: Routledge and Kegan Paul, 1940, 1950; first published by Farrar and Rinehart, 1939.

_____. *Psychology and Religion*. New Haven and London: Yale University Press, 1971; first published in 1938.

_____. *The Undiscovered Self*. Tr. R. F. C. Hull. New York: The New American Library, 1957, 1958.

_____. *Psyche & Symbol*. A Selection from the Writings of C. G. Jung. Ed. Violet S. De Laszlo. New York: Doubleday, 1958. ("The *Syzygy*:

Anima and Animus," "The Self," and "Christ, a Symbol of the Self" from "Aion: Contributions to the Symbolism of the Self," 1951.)

_____. "Ulysses: A Monologue." In *Hidden Patterns*, Studies in Psychoanalytical Literary Criticism. Ed. Leonard and Eleanor Manheim. New York: Macmillan, 1966; first published in 1932.

_____. "Psychology and Literature." In *The Spirit in Man, Art, and Literature*. Tr. R. F. C. Hull. Bollingen Series XX. New York: Pantheon Books, 1966.

Kagan, Jerome. *The Nature of the Child*. New York: Harper Collins, 1994.

Kris, Ernst. "On Inspiration." In *Psychoanalytic Explorations in Art*. New York: Schocken, 1952. 289-302.

Kris, Ernst and Otto Kurz. *Legend, Myth, and Magic in the Image of the Artist*. Preface by E. H. Gombrich. New Haven, Connecticut.: Yale University Press, 1979.

Lewis, Edith. *Willa Cather Living*. New York: Alfred A. Knopf, 1953.

Lommel, Pim van. *Consciousness Beyond Life*. New York: HarperOne, 2010.

Moore, Thomas. *Care of the Soul*. New York: Harper Collins, 1992.

Neumann, Eric. *Art and the Creative Unconscious*. Four Essays. Tr. Ralph Manheim. Bollingen Series LXI. Princeton, New Jersey: Princeton University Press, 1974; first published in 1959.

O'Hara, Frank. *Jackson Pollock*. The Great American Artist Series. New York: G. Braziller, 1959.

Parsons, Glenn. *Aesthetics and Nature*. Continuum Aesthetics Series. Ed. Derek Matravers. London and New York: Continuum International, 2008.

Rank, Otto. *Art and Artist*. Creative Urge and Personality Development. Tr. Charles Francis Atkinson. New York: Alfred A. Knopf, 1932.

Rockmore, Daniel. "A Style of Numbers Behind a Number of Styles." *The Chronicle of Higher Education*. 9 June 2007.

Romanticism—Vistas, Instances, Continuities. Eds. David Thorburn and Geoffrey Hartman. Ithaca, New York, and London: Cornell University Press, 1973.

Seward, Barbara. "The Artist and the Rose." In *Joyce's Portrait, Criticism and Critiques*. Ed. Thomas E. Connolly. New York: Appleton-Century-Crofts, 1962.

Smith, Dodie. *Look Back with Love*. A Manchester Childhood. London: Heinemann, 1974.

Shelley, Percy B. "A Defense of Poetry." In *Shelley's Critical Prose*. Ed. Bruce R. McElderry. Lincoln, Nebraska: University of Nebraska Press, 1967.

Stewart, Grace. *A New Mythos*. The Novel of the Artist as Heroine, 1877-1977. Montreal: Eden Press Women's Publications, 1981.

Swan, James A. *Nature as Teacher and Healer*. New York: Villard Books, 1992.

Wellek, René and Austin Warren. *Theory of Literature*. Third Edition. New York: Harcourt, Brace and World, 1956; first published in 1942.

Index

CPSIA information can be obtained at www.ICGtesting.com
Printed in the USA
BVOW080652300513

321967BV00002B/6/P